D0876984

Desiring Paradise

...a true story of succumbing to the dream

Karin W. Schlesinger

Copyright © 1999 Karin W. Schlesinger. All rights reserved

Printed in the United States of America

ISBN # 0-9673721-3-5

Cover Design by: SkyMax Design, Henniker, NH

Typesetting by: Dunja Hein Designs, Chester, NH

Copyediting by: John Ficociello, Billerica, MA

Conch Publications
P.O. Box 1559
St. John, United States Virgin Islands, 00831

email: kaybob@islands.vi

To Bob, with whom life is always an adventure.
And to our wonderful friends, without whom our
adventures would be less fun . . .

all dreams are possible.

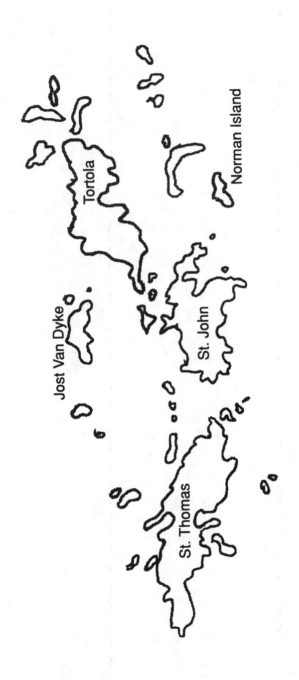

Acknowledgements

As with any book, this one would not be a reality if it weren't for a lot of special people. Jan, Mary, Joe, Gerry, Janine, Marcie, Bob, Mike, Jessie, Jay, Andre, Karen, John, Pat, Dan, Maureen, Barbara, Michelle, Marianne, Dorothy, Shelly, Charlie, Chris, Diane, Will, Liz, Pamela, Tim, Elanore, Ron, Marsha, David, Chuck, Katie, George, Issaih, Laura, Moe, Aaron, Sheila, Cindy, Jim, Suzanne, Rob, Beverly, Jo, Ted, Ed and Frank – you all made a difference.

A special thanks to Birdie who helped me keep the dream alive and kept me sane through it all.

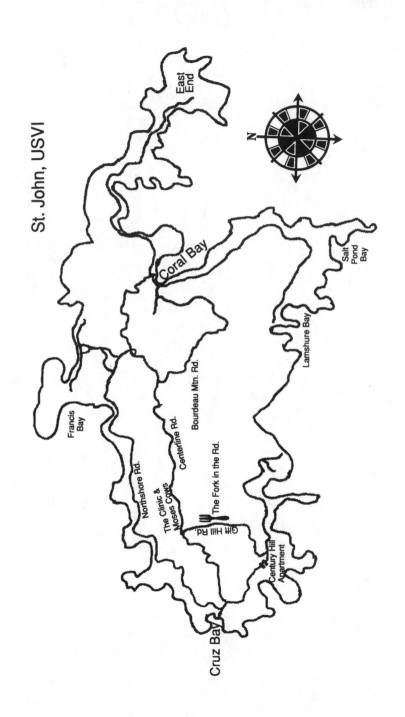

Chapter 1

Island Fantasy

We stayed at the Maho Bay Campground at Little Maho Bay on our first visit to St. John, which may have had something to do with it. Perhaps we swallowed some rare organism in the water or breathed in some bizarre pollen from a rare yet undiscovered island flower that grew nearby. Our island friends insist we must have.

It's a documented fact that in the first half of this century, Ms. Ethel W. McCully (1886-1983) was passing by this same area on a Tortola-bound sloop when, suddenly enthralled, she jumped ship and waded ashore at little Maho. Ms. McCully was already well past her prime, with white hair and a strong disposition, when she discovered her passion for living out her years here on St. John. She soon bought the land above the bay, built a house, and became an island legend, remaining here for the rest of her long life.

Over the years, Little Maho Bay seems to have had this same effect on so many who have glimpsed it for the very first time. For at least fifteen St. Johnians we know personally, just one trip to Maho had them going native.

But this is our story: Bob's and mine.

While it's true that Bob and I became enamored of the island during our first stay at Maho Bay, it was the huge plywood sign in the shape of a salad fork that we ran across on the island's Gift Hill Road that first intrigued us. There were no words on the sign, nor any restaurant near-by, just a narrow dirt road that led us to it that ambled away from the main road we'd driven down to explore that day. Bob was the first to understand what the sign meant—that we'd arrived at a fork in the road—as he gamely steered our rental onto the dusty side path in search of adventure.

That evening, I sat with my husband on the balcony at Pusser's in tiny Cruz Bay, tired but exhilarated from our island explorations. As we watched the sun setting over St. Thomas, past the palm tree-lined beach below, Bob and I sighed in unison, realizing for the first time that we could live here forever. Probably anyone who has ever viewed the sunsets from Pusser's (now Café Wahoo) balcony has had the same thought; for us, though, it marked the beginning of our dream.

On each subsequent vacation to St. John, the dream beckoned more deeply: at the beach, on the deck of a rented house, or driving slowly past goats blocking the roadway. We held each of our successive vaca-tions to a higher standard than the one before. Campground visits evolved into house rentals, each more extravagant than the last, and with each vacation we fell more in love with thoughts of our future here. And, yes, like Ms. Ethel McCully, we swam often at Maho Bay, and that helped draw us to the place. But we also continued to giggle as we trav-eled past the plywood fork.

* * *

Our future was finally decided, not by forks, but by rakes.

It was a typically cool fall day at our small New England home, and our yard was knee-deep in oak leaves. With twenty-three bags of raked leaves ready for the garbage man and more still to rake, our future looked dismal and boring. Resting on our patio swing in mid-afternoon,

Bob and I reminisced about how far we'd come since we'd first met. We were both exhausted, and both ready for a change in lifestyle.

Some good friends of ours had recently pulled up their middle-class stakes and moved to Juneau, Alaska, to start a new life. Bob was jealous, though with winter just around the corner, I thought they were crazy. Still, these folks were actually living an adventure—and they seemed so happy! Suddenly it seemed inspiring to consider a new life.

Our leaf-induced exhaustion put us in the mood to dream. I brought out pens and paper and suggested that we each rank the top ten spots in the world where we'd like to live. Once finished, we shared the results of our brainstorming slowly. As we worked our way up from our 10th place choices, it became obvious that Bob and I had been thinking worlds apart. For me, it was the Beaujolais region of France; for Bob, the wilds of Nepal made sense. The chuckling and incessant giggling at each other's concepts of Paradise slowed us down: Bob's "Mount Everest" suggestion begged me to guess, "so you'll be moving there with your next wife?", while the thought of moving to a desert brought tears of laughter to the eyes of my whitewater-kayaking husband. By the time we got to the top of our respective lists, I had already resigned myself to living in our little cape-style New England home forever.

Then my husband announced his number one image of Paradise.

"St. John in the US Virgin Islands," he announced.

I was struck silent. Most of the locations on Bob's list seemed like a joke to me, but not this one: Bob's face had become devoid of all expression. St. John had no snow-covered mountains or fresh water for kayaking, or even much for drinking, but he was serious. I shuttered my eyes then as I revealed my number one selection. "St. John, USVI," I said out loud. Only silence followed. But as I lifted my eyes to check on Bob's reaction, I saw the corners of his mouth start to turn up, until they broke into the widest grin I had ever seen on his face! And though I didn't know it at the time, I'm told my own smile was equally huge.

In celebration, we grabbed our rakes, faced each other, extended the tines, and gave each other a monumental "high five."

Our world had changed forever. Excitedly, we started discussing specifics. When should we go? How long would it take? How soon could we leave? It seemed natural that we would "just do it," since that was our nature. But sensing middle age just around the corner, we had the baggage of our lives to consider....

Bob and I sat there on the swing talking for hours, even as darkness and the thin New England cold descended around us. Everything about a move to St. John seemed right. It *would* be Paradise. We envisioned ourselves with weekends at the beach, with no leaves to rake or snow to shovel, and the endless possibilities of starting a new life from scratch.

Okay, we decided: ten years from now. Ten years.

That soon? we thought.

We were obviously not risk-takers.

* * *

To some extent, the *facts* started deciding *us*: Bob and I had worked hard to own our home; we had friends and family nearby, and we were somewhat happily employed at the time. Starting over completely was a scary proposition. And how could we earn a living on a remote island? For those who are in a position to carry all their life's possessions in a backpack and take each day as it comes, a move to Paradise might be simple. But we had complications in our lives, and deep Yankee roots. Sure, we were enchanted with our fantasies about Paradise, but could we commit ourselves to such a dramatic change in every aspect of our life together?

How could we decide? As for me, I shared our plan with my best friends every chance I got, while Bob, in his typically quiet fashion, said nothing outside our home. At first my friends figured I was just kidding, so their reaction was to challenge the seriousness of our plans in a way that only close friends can dare to do.

"What happens if you change your mind, Karin?" they asked.

"It doesn't matter," I said, as my heart began to beat wildly at the thought. "That won't happen."

"What happens if Bob changes his mind?" they asked.

"He won't," I said, guessing about Bob's feelings, and with a lot more confidence than I felt about my own.

I could see they weren't convinced though, and their concerns admittedly struck close to home.

I'd been married once before. My ex-husband was a wonderful man who'd relocated for the sake of a career move I felt I had to make. He had been miserable in his newly adopted home, though I took too long to notice and we drifted apart, desiring different things in life. Still, I was confident that I'd learned much from the past. And moving to St. John someday was something Bob and I both desired.

So with our fantasy defined, Bob and I began to develop a framework for a ten-year plan--a plan that would change many times before we finally moved. We daydreamed out loud almost daily, about how we might earn a living on St. John, about starting a business (which seemed the most logical route to self-sufficiency), about the selling of holographic keepsakes of the islands, about helping people develop Internet web pages or running a kayak guide service.

But we also knew that most businesses, small businesses *anywhere*, go under quickly due to a lack of capital, and like most folks starting out on their own, we had very little available cash at our disposal. It would take years for us to save enough money to launch any business successfully, and I couldn't really picture either of us being happy just selling palm frond hats to tourists on a beach. There had to be a surer, more concrete way to make a living.

Admittedly, we had minimal debt: the standard two cars, a home mortgage, and debt accrued for an occasional large purchase, but nothing else. Seldom had we even considered budgeting, but we did live within our means. There was no credit card debt; we'd worked for years eliminating that. Yes, we bought what we wanted when we wanted it and were always finding new toys and gadgets, but in truth, our needs were simple.

Unlike many married couples, Bob and I never fought over money. We kept two separate checking and savings accounts and each wrote a check for half of every bill that came in. It worked for us. Bob paid for the stamps, mailed the checks, and snookered me on the phone bill every month. We were content. But to escalate our rate of savings and track our expenses, we would first have to combine our accounts. Joint savings and checking accounts: what a concept! After seven years of marriage, it was time.

Other changes followed. Research had always been important to us for any major household purchase, and Bob and I approached the fantasy of living in Paradise as a very major purchase. A spiral notebook was designated for writing out our thoughts and ideas on every topic that pertained to the move. Every week we'd come up with a new idea for developing a business, but nothing seemed to excite us both with the same enthusiasm. And while we both had skills useful in high-tech industries, neither of us had any small-business skills or hobbies that we believed could be turned into a viable business on a small island. So we continued to fantasize.

We stopped buying new gadgets we saw advertised. More often than not, our old toys sufficed. This dramatically increased our savings from disposable income, and it happened at a surprising rate. According to our notebook, the sudden increase in our joint savings made me wonder if we needed ten years until this move could happen. Combine this increased savings with the rush of excitement I got each time I looked at a picture of Paradise, and you can imagine how my impatience grew.

Occasionally Bob would dig out mementos from St. John and I would buy magazines with articles about the Virgin Islands. My husband was the type of person who saved every piece of paper or receipt he'd ever received. When the weather got bad or he needed a little lift, Bob would pull out a huge file with every St. John brochure and flyer imaginable, along with hundreds of photos culled from previous vacations. Late in the evenings, I would get on my computer and search the Internet for information on any subject that could help us along with our plans. These activities kept warm Caribbean thoughts in our household throughout the cold New England winter.

* * *

Years before, I'd brought back a unique souvenir from St. John which was now buried somewhere in our basement. It was an old USVI license plate that had been recycled and hand-painted by some local trying to make a few tourist dollars. I rediscovered it in a large box of junk long-forgotten and got Bob to attach the plate to the front of my car, as a vanity plate that proclaimed to the world our new dream. People noticed it and commented on it wherever I drove. I considered the plate a great idea, and a great addition to my car's décor.

But sometimes the best ideas in thought aren't always the best in action. A short time after attaching the plate to the car, we encountered a traffic cop while we were on our way to visit Bob's mom in upstate New York. As the policeman motioned our car to the side of the road, I could see Bob trying to read his mind. "He's going to give us a ticket for that license plate, I'll bet. Expired official license plates are illegal as vanity plates, but you wouldn't listen to me," Bob said under his breath. I was sure Bob was right and prepared for the worst as the policeman moseyed on across the intersection with a smile on his face.

"Did you drive all the way here from there?" he said, motioning at my vanity plate. "It must have been a long drive," he emphasized with his pen.

This guy is serious, I thought to myself. Maybe he figured there was an ocean bridge from St. John to Florida. In any case, we realized he'd just stopped us to voice his wonder.

"Uh, yes. It certainly is a long way. But we love upstate New York," I smiled, totally without any trace of sarcasm. Just then the cop turned his head to check out another vehicle and we silently slid away, hoping he wouldn't notice the Massachusetts plate on the back of my car.

"Lucky," Bob muttered.

"Yeah!" I said smugly. After all, we were already on our way to Paradise, weren't we? Suddenly I felt happier and younger than I had in years. According to Bob, it was our singular focus on the future that had us acting like newlyweds all over again.

Whatever the reason, our lives had gained a new sense of vigor.

* * *

The only constant, they say, is change, and very soon for us a jolt of reality suddenly had us reconsidering the whole idea of a move.

My father became very sick. It happened in Florida at the end of my parents' first cruise ship vacation. While in port in Florida at some point, he started feeling ill and stopped their rental car in front of a police station to get directions to a hospital. Apparently he collapsed inside the door of the police station, and within moments he was being routed to a hospital by ambulance.

My mom stayed behind at the station to answer the authorities' questions and was then directed to the hospital where my father had been taken...or so she was told. Five hours and three hospitals later, she finally found her husband. As it happened, my dad remained in intensive care for more than six weeks.

While this was the worst of it, Dad's illness had other downsides to it. A major boat show was in town, and the only room Mom could find for the first few days was at a hotel far from the hospital. So Mom—who hadn't spent more than a few days apart from my father in forty-nine years—found herself alone in Miami without any sort of local support system. Ironically, Miami Beach was where my parents had fallen in love and married so long ago, but the area bore little resemblance to that little friendly town of long ago. Things were confusing at best, and in some ways terrifying, for someone so unprepared for this interruption in her life, and especially for someone so suddenly alone and a thousand miles from home.

After a while, though, the boat show left town, and Mom took up residence in the closest motel to the hospital, but this was not a safe neighborhood. Meanwhile, my two brothers and I took turns flying down to Miami to be with them both and to make sure Mom was safe, though nothing we said or did could convince her to move to a nicer location, even though it might be just a few minutes further away from the hospital. It was a very trying situation for all.

I spent almost every other week that winter in Miami, attempting to keep my job by working when I could with my trusty notebook computer. It was telecommuting at its worst. I felt guilty as I worried about how fast I was spending money, since every penny took us that much farther from Paradise. And despite long work hours and regular conference calls with my staff, I was risking my job with an unsympathetic boss. But family was more important than anything, right? So Miami came first.

Besides, the crisis taught me a lot. I learned a new respect for my mother, with her iron disposition and tremendous inner strength. And though my relationship with my father had always been strong, this crisis further strengthened that bond. I also got to know my two brothers on a different level and learned to value their individuality. Finally, around Easter, my father went back home, and life for everyone slowly settled back to normal.

During this time of crisis, Bob and I reconsidered our plans more than once with the realization that if we lived on St. John, our families would be more than two thousand miles away. We wouldn't really be close enough to help with any crisis, and with aging parents, that certainly mattered to me. Yes, Miami was closer geographically to the Virgin Islands than to New England. But any future crisis would most likely occur up North.

Despite the Miami ordeal, once spring arrived in earnest the urge to move became stronger. We shortened our timeframe for the move from ten years to five and nixed the plan to open our own business. Five years was enough time to learn skills that would be useful on the islands and still save enough money to last us at least one year. In fact, five years seemed like a long time away.

So a first-year budget for Paradise was drafted-and it was depressing! Even by hedging our bets at finding quick jobs, living for a year without any income was daunting.

We started doing crazy things to maximize our savings. We made purchases using only paper money, never loose change. Then every evening, Bob and I would sort the coins we'd accumulated that day and put that money away. It's amazing how fast our extra coins added up to significant savings using this approach. We saved over three thousand dollars in a short time. Bob saved our soda and beer cans for recycling and reimbursement. This worked well until we stopped buying soda and found cheaper ways to satisfy our need for sweets. With every paycheck we tried to save more than the paycheck before. And we did. Our friends tell us now that we always seemed to have money on the brain back then, and they are probably right.

* * *

Every spring Bob and I welcomed the new season by trekking to Vermont for the first camping trip of the year. For Bob, the West River kayaking weekend was a religious experience. I called this annual trek my "be a good wife" weekend. The state-owned campground opened preseason solely to accommodate hundreds of whitewater enthusiasts from all over who were eager to emerge from their winter hibernation. Camping in the cold, unpredictable weather surrounded by slowly melting pockets of ice and snow just added to the adventure.

The first evening this year brought handfuls of people wandering into our campsite, drawn to us by the roaring campfire, the sounds of laughter, and the smell of our extravagant gourmet efforts over open fire. Everyone stonewalled the inevitable-retiring to their cold bedding—by staying up late and toasting their bodies at our fire. Finally, everyone gave in and left us to our sleep.

The kayakers, including Bob, woke early the next morning. Bundled in their drysuits and helmets, they resembled aliens as they roamed the campground, telling tall tales and lingering over their coffee. As usual, this stalling ritual lasted late into the morning as the kayakers screwed up enough courage to face the frigid water and prove to everyone that spring had arrived.

I wasn't around to witness the morning ritual this time, however. A cold drizzle had welcomed me as I tentatively unzipped the tent that morning. Had it been just two degrees colder outside, it would have been sleet that fell instead of rain. Everyone was still asleep as I stuck my head out into the cold, so I quietly called out to a neighboring tent, where my good friend Birdie had spent the night.

Birdie came with us to the campground every year, though she had absolutely no interest in kayaking and hated camping in cold, wet weather. It was the all-day adventures she and I had away from the campground that kept her coming back. In fact, we were gone before most kayakers were awake, especially that first morning. While everyone thought Birdie and I were anxious to explore, it was the thought of the car heater that got us motivated enough to get up and move out before anyone else. As our toes warmed in the car, our smiles widened, and finally we headed out for our annual adventure.

Birdie and I never allowed a map to dictate our hearts or travels as we whimsically explored the back roads of Vermont. A quilting barn, homemade fudge from a roadside vendor, new roads to explore, and lots of laughter: These made the day pass swiftly. This year I tried out ideas on her for eking out a living in Paradise, though my girlfriend teased that I would never move, never give up the West River weekends.

That evening we cooked an extravagant, candlelit dinner while listening to tales from kayakers who never even ventured beyond the campground. As the night passed, I never mentioned out loud the lack of fresh water kayaking in Paradise.

***

This most recent West River weekend hadn't changed our resolve. Bob and I still visited bookstores every month to purchase new books on any subject imaginable that might inspire us or help us realize our dream. I'd put together a virtual small library on early retirement, living simply, searching for jobs, getting home-based businesses started, and, of course, living in the Caribbean. Each book provided fresh ideas and wisdoms we would need. Bob and I are both avid readers, and used to buy books frequently; but now, for pure reading enjoyment, we limited ourselves to borrowing books from the local library. Our purchases would be limited to books that would actually help expedite our move.

By summer, Bob and I were unknowingly shrinking the timeframe for moving again. Only a couple of months earlier, we had narrowed our timeframe to five years. Now when we told others of our plans, we'd often respond with a confident "three to five years," or even tell people "at least three years out" without thinking.

In any case, our timeframe was still far enough out in the future so that our friends considered it a fantasy; they rarely took us seriously when we talked about the move. Their belief in the seriousness of our timeframe was in no way increased by the caveat we usually added when asked about the move. "If we don't move," we'd tell them, "at least we'll have more money saved than we ever thought possible." This hesitation eventually started to sound like our stuttering mantra.

But one spring day, as I started to recite it, the "if" got stuck in my throat. Why, I asked myself, could we never bring ourselves to say "when" instead of "if"? I resolved to find out why. So out came the notebook, and into the night I contemplated the numbers and the timeline, determined to pinpoint the elusive "when" exactly.

Numbers don't lie; being the daughter of a successful accountant in a small city, I'd learned *that* simple truth long ago. So we had some numbers facts to deal with. First, Bob and I had both agreed that our retirement money could not be compromised. And our planned move to Paradise also held to the determination not to move until we'd stashed away enough to be able to live above the poverty line when we retired some twenty-five years away. We also needed enough money to live on for a year in case, when we moved, there were no jobs, and we needed the money for the move itself. My father's voice sounded over and over in my head that night: "stay conservative and the numbers won't lie." Ignoring Bob's pleas for me to come to bed, I continued working the numbers. And working. And working.

I woke Bob up at three in the morning to tell him the amazing news, that I'd solved the dilemma of "when". "That's nice, dear," he spoke out of the fog. "Come to bed," was his final, sleepy response.

Suspecting a conversation was futile at this point, I tried to take his advice. Over my shoulder, I heard a muted, "Can't we, Karin? One more vacation first?" But when I turned to respond, I realized my husband was talking in his sleep.

"We'll need to, and soon," I murmured into his ear before I turned away and let sleep come.

* * *

We vacationed again on St. John that fall. A full year had passed since we'd begun planning our permanent move, and our ten-year plan had turned into a firm three-year plan, but we were keeping it a secret. We were already a third of the way to Paradise; it was a heady thought. Despite our efforts to keep things mum, a few days later our secret was out.

I remember distinctly that moment frozen in time. It was late afternoon at our rental villa in Rendezvous Bay, about three-quarters of the way through our stay on the island. Five of us were cooling off in and around our private pool. Bob and I had spent the afternoon with a real estate agent researching for the future. Our relatives, meanwhile, had explored the back roads and beaches of St. John. The house shaded the setting sun and the gentle trade winds were perfect. My brother Joe was making rum punches for everyone with exotic juices he'd bought at an open-air stand in town while reggae music from a poolside radio gave him rhythm. It was a time for reflecting and philosophizing.

In a moment of weakness, I blurted out our secret. "We're definitely moving here within the next two years," I announced, eyeing Bob as he closed his eyes to the shocked faces around him. I then floated gently to the center of the pool.

"Really?" Joe said, and stopped his stirring with a frown. "I thought that was years from now," his wife chimed in.

"We won't be living like this, that's for sure," I added quickly. "Yeah, we'll be too poor," Bob added. By all outward signs, Bob looked as though he were asleep; only his voice hinted that he was awake and aware.

"Will it matter?" my sister-in-law asked. To her it would have mattered. Joe and Janine preferred the securities of the material world. I knew my heart and could have easily answered, but I didn't. The seconds stretched long against the reggae beat.

"No," floated out Bob's answer. "No way" I sighed, happy that Bob had verbalized it first.

"You two are really going to do it?" Bob's sister Dee asked, excited and supportive. While she owned a small but hectic business in Manhattan, Dee had told us earlier in the day that she could actually see herself waiting tables if she could live in this wonderful place.

"That soon?" Joe asked doubtfully, the drink preparations now forgotten. I was pretty sure he thought our plans were just a passing whim—one that we'd tire of in a few months. To be fair to them, we all knew my childhood had been littered with half-finished projects I'd always started with enthusiasm but got bored with when a project took too much effort to complete.

"Will you buy a house?" Janine jumped in. Her beautiful New Hampshire home and gardens were also her hobby. Bob, quietly floating towards me in the pool, moved nary a muscle, and I knew he was waiting for my answer.

"Probably not; I doubt we could afford it right away," I admitted. Our day spent researching real estate had burst that little bubble of hope, unless we put off our plans to move for many more years. I knew it, and Bob knew it, but we hadn't yet discussed the outcome. His eyes still closed, my husband instinctively grasped my hand as he announced, "It doesn't matter." We were still keeping a realistic grip on our plans, and both of us knew that living on St. John would be much different and our spending would have to be much more modest than that of a vacation getaway.

"Lots of hurricane-damaged places—those may be affordable," Janine persisted, trying to be helpful.

"Not even," said Bob, remembering the extraordinarily priced shacks we'd visited that day.

"Won't you be bored after a while?" Joe asked, as he began passing out the beverages.

"Not a prayer," I said with conviction. Surprisingly I heard my husband add, "I'll miss having a pool though."

Before I could react, Dee jumped back into the conversation. She still wanted the dream— if not for herself, then for her brother. "But you don't have a pool now, except on vacation," she reminded Bob.

A mumbled "true" was Bob's only reply.

"Does it matter?" she asked.

I knew the answer before Bob's quick though well considered "No" hit the air, but I also understood that my husband could float forever in this vacation pool and die happy.

"So you're really going to do it." Joe finally said, starting to accept our reality.

"Within two years!" we told him.

You could see Dee was already planning her next vacation.

"Yes!" I raised my glass.

"Yes!" My husband raised his.

"Why?" Joe's wife Janine said, needing to understand.

"Because it feels right," I said while clinking my glass to my darling husband's.

"Yeah!" Bob agreed as he proposed a toast to Paradise.

Chapter *2*

Commitment to Paradise

A couple of months before that vacation, Hurricane Marilyn had devastated the islands. Power had been restored to the villa we'd rented only two days prior to our arrival. It was an eye-opening bit of knowledge for us. On the surface, much of St. John was back on its feet, but there were very few tourists—fewer than we'd ever seen before. Many restaurants were closed or offered only limited menus. On St. Thomas, the devastation was visible everywhere.

The Federal Emergency Management Agency was still providing on-site assistance and assessment. Their donated "FEMA Blue" tarps were visible everywhere on St. Thomas, covering or replacing roofs destroyed by the storm. Few buildings had gone unscathed. Back on St. John, though, these FEMA-blue landmarks were few and far between. Still, we saw one house that had slid right down a mountain with the people inside; luckily, the people survived. Bob pointed out another home, one we'd previously admired, high on a distant ridge where now a familiar speck of blue gleamed in the sun. As we drove closer and approached from a different angle, the home seemed fine. Rounding the last switchback to the house, though, the source of the blue became evident. A tarp with "FEMA" written on it had been cut up and turned into awnings on one side of the home. Past another curve, we spied our favorite fork in the road. It even boasted a new coat of paint. Despite the ravages of the storm, all was steadily returning to normal, St. Johnian style, and I was heartened.

One local St. Johnian summed up for us his opinions on the differences between the islands: "On St. Thomas they wait for the insurance folks to come through and then they'll do repairs, but here on St. John we tend to pitch in and help each other first." As an afterthought he added, "then we pray for the insurance money to make us whole."

Whether that was true or not, this approach to community life on St. John was comforting. It made some sense—St. John is a relatively rural island, unlike the more urban St. Thomas. The local St. John *Tradewinds* newspaper was filled with stories about people helping people and the quick progress they were making in returning life to normal; life here was very upbeat, considering the devastation that had occurred two months before.

During the vacation, Bob and I consciously attempted to expose the flaws in our Paradise. I saw cockroaches larger than I thought possible. We drank water that locals qualified as "good," but which we couldn't stand to taste. Millions of no-see-ums—those little sand fleas that seem to prefer fresh tourists to other types of dinner—dined nightly on my legs. I scraped my knees falling on uneven pavement, and Bob lost his prescription glasses. Joe got two flat tires in just one day of touring the island in a rental vehicle. We waited for ferries, waited in long lines at businesses, and were occasionally treated rudely by the supposedly pleasant locals. I never did find a good cup of coffee.

We met some people who were negative about life in general and experienced the frustration of trying to buy a simple spiral notebook anywhere on the island. I turned off the shower while lathering up but ran out of water regardless. Bob found seas of ants crowded next to the tiniest dropped crumbs, and I saw a large rat—not easily confused with a mongoose—at the regularly overflowing garbage drop-off. But none of these "inconveniences" seemed to discourage us from our plans.

* * *

Our minds made up, my husband decided our next step was to buy a copy of the local telephone book. The purchase was quite an introduction to the daily rhythms of on-island living. We learned that formal politeness is expected for even the most minor personal interactions, that patience is a mandatory skill set for daily survival, and that persistence is important to accomplishing ones goals. But even our learning of these important customs was an adventure in itself.

Our learning went something like this: Bob and I went to *Connections*, a place where everything on-island seemed to center. Inside this tiny business stood a wall where jobs and apartment ads were posted, private phone booths were for rent, and faxes and telegrams could be sent or received. A large clock on one wall was labeled "Grand Central" and showed the local time, and a row of clocks lining the opposite wall accurately displayed times for Tokyo, Paris, London and so on.

Bob pointed out one clock in the row titled "Coral Bay," which was the tiny settlement on the other side of the island. This clock had no hands.

"Pretty accurate," I smiled. Coral Bay was the most laid back and quiet place I'd ever been.

The nice ladies at *Connections* let us know that phone books could only be picked up at the VI Telephone Company office, which was located in a small trailer parked down the street. At the office, Bob and I waited patiently for our turn. When it came, Bob asked if we could buy a phonebook. Without hesitation, the person we were talking to sent us to a corner of the room with a disgruntled "Wait!" Three people behind us were then serviced while we tried to determine what we'd said to cause such unhappiness.

Then I noticed that everyone else began their conversation by saying "Good Day," then waiting for a similar response and a query as to what their business was. Ahah! I whispered my discovery to Bob.

When we were finally waved back to the reception desk, Bob tried out my technique. This time his greeting– "Good day!" –was met with a broad smile and permission to buy a phone book, and for a very reasonable price!

But they could not accept cash or a personal check, and we were told to come back with a money order. We went back to *Connections* with our best manners in hand, and this time a smiling face redirected us to pick up our money order at the U.S. Post Office. There we stood in line for what seemed like an eternity before our turn came. Bob and I made the most of that time chatting with others in line and learning the fine art of patience. Those who were the most serene were the "professionals"-those who earned their living standing in line for other people or for businesses and making a tidy profit for the pain. Nevertheless, we had to pass twice through the line before we were done, as we hadn't filled out the prerequisite form in advance.

With our money order finally in hand, Bob and I went back to Vitelco, only to find that the telephone book would be mailed to us in a week.

Ah, patience. I sing thine ode.

Six weeks later, the phone book arrived in our Massachusetts mailbox. Meanwhile, we had filled another notebook with insights gleaned from our travels.

* * *

During our time there, I talked with seemingly everyone on St. John about daily island life. I made a special effort to speak to working-class folks, especially those who didn't seem to be in jobs that would make them rich. When we moved to this Paradise, we would likely be a part of that crowd. Waitresses and store clerks and artists and construction workers all contributed their thoughts to our effort. While some encouraged and others discouraged our dreams, I began to get a solid understanding of the problems we'd face once we moved here.

The people's stories were amazing. They confirmed that anyone could make it here if they really wanted to: single mothers with children, and even whole families. Most people were happy, but not all. I was amazed at the number of people who'd gotten divorced once they'd been here for a while; the main reason most gave was that their spouse didn't share their particular vision of Paradise. Alcohol abuse was also an issue; this made sense in a place where rum is cheaper than Kool-Aid.

Bob and I returned home from that Thanksgiving vacation with a new resolve. And before that resolve waned, the local USVI phone book arrived, along with our new subscription to the St. John biweekly newspaper. These investments proved invaluable over the following year. Every two weeks, whenever the *Tradewinds* newspaper was due in our mailbox, I tried to beat Bob home to ensure I got a chance to read it first. That newspaper had become the single greatest tangible link to our future, and Bob tended to hoard.

In addition to these links to St. John, businesses occasionally advertised on Internet sites; once I found these sites, I then researched them for more information. I kept these sessions to myself, feeling that others might think I'd gone a little overboard in looking for the smallest St. John news tidbits. But that winter I discovered that while I was quietly researching the Internet at night, Bob had been doing the same thing in the early morning hours. It became a game of sorts to find a new Web site that contained previously unknown (but useful) information that Bob and I could share with each other.

Projects at our home in New England now began to plague us. Like most homeowners, we'd put off so many projects to the future, and now we had a home fix-up and improvement list five pages long. It was important to get the house into saleable shape; after all, the sale of our current home was critical to funding our dream!

Our neighbors still didn't believe our plans, and one went so far as to suggest that our home improvement projects were even part of an unconscious nesting instinct on our part. They couldn't accept that we were really ready for a migration.

Finally, the floors were refinished, built-in cabinets were added in the upstairs bedrooms, and walls everywhere got a fresh coat of paint. But the list of needed home improvements grew faster than the list of completed projects. And so for the first time in months, Bob and I started reading newspaper inserts looking for sales on tools and building materials and decorative items that might go well with our home's new look. Just a few inexpensive purchases and some creativity were all that we felt were needed to give each room its own special appeal.

After the clutter of the ages had been removed, that is. It took a full basement sale and two yard sales to make it all work, but the results were pleasing. As an extravagance, Bob bought an inexpensive ceiling fan and had it installed in what passed for the master bedroom.

The room, with it's unevenly slanted walls, got a coat of bright, glossy white against the advice of almost everyone. With the hardwood floor newly refinished and a couple of inexpensive palm plants tucked into corners, the room all of a sudden had a distinctively Caribbean feel. When I added an old Bentwood rocker and removed all the personal clutter, it was impressive. Instantly, it became our favorite room.

* * *

The Holiday season had always been a big deal in our home. We still bought mounds of presents for each other, but the tone of the gifts had changed. We bought each other gifts we knew each of us had been privately wanting but had been living without. An expensive bottle of Scotch and luxury food items made their way into wrapping paper. We jointly ordered a subscription to *The VI Daily News*, the daily newspaper from St. Thomas. Gifts that were practical and yet still fun were the best. My favorite was a mosquito net that added just the right effect to our Caribbean-style bedroom—and which might actually be useful on St. John. Little did we know.

Our Thanksgiving St. John vacation had convinced us to reconsider our timing for the move. According to our current timetable, we'd be moving at the beginning of tourist season less than two years out. We knew what that meant, since we'd just visited during that time of year, and it just wasn't practical. Housing would be hard to find and everything would be selling or renting at a premium price. With the influx of tourists and our lack of local knowledge, it would be difficult to distinguish us from the crowd, since tourists are often smitten with the island on their visits and decide on impulse to stay. But too often they are unprepared for daily life and go back to the mainland after a few months. Potential landlords and employers are always wary of transplants from the mainland, especially during the winter tourist season. We were determined to be and seem long-term residents who would overcome the odds, so it was more logical to move months later, once the winter tourist season was over.

We'd been saving to cover our expenses for the first year without any income anyway, so the lack of jobs off-season was only of minor concern to us. Fewer people meant more time to settle into the rhythm of the island. Once we had housing, Bob and I could search for jobs, and with luck we'd find them before tourist season started. This approach was rational and it was logical to us. But it wasn't palatable to either of us. That cold February, the thought of adding six months to our schedule prior to the move was depressing. And the idea of moving six months earlier than planned seemed impossible, barring a miracle. I was anxious to get to Paradise, but doubted we could reach our financial goals in a little over a year just to accommodate our desire to avoid being thought of as tourists. For now, a convenient blizzard both sapped our energies and redirected our focus, and we put off our decisions for a few days that eventually turned into months.

We determined that we should have started our subscriptions to the island newspapers much sooner. The wealth of research information in these papers was amazing. Ads for groceries, cable TV, household goods and restaurants helped me define a realistic monthly budget. Even my friend Birdie, who browsed through *The VI Daily News* one

Wednesday (I'd told her this was "food" day for the paper, complete with supermarket ads, etc.) wryly commented that she should do her food shopping on St. Thomas instead of central New Hampshire; the prices appeared cheaper, at least for some items. But her perspective was a little flawed, since the non-sale items are generally a good bit higher than they are in the States. Still, it made our food budget seem more promising.

Bob and I became frugal in every way. In the Northeast I had almost always used coupons at the local supermarket anyway. We tried with every frugal bone in our bodies to buy only what we needed, and to buy only what was on sale. Bob had begun washing our cars at home rather than at the car wash. We pumped our own gas. I even remembered some family folk lore about my grandmother cleaning and reusing old foil wrap and plastic and saving discarded string for some useful future. In fact, she seldom threw anything out without giving it five lives first.

At last, I'd become my grandmother.

For Bob's birthday, I bought a topographical map set of the Virgin Islands and a solar battery recharger. I'd received summer clothing and a Caribbean cookbook for my own birthday. All other indiscriminate shopping had stopped. Our former twice-weekly restaurant forays became history, and our lives grew simplified.

I even started trying to figure out when my life had become so cluttered with "things." Had I ever really been that young college girl who traveled through Europe for a month with just one small duffel bag?

The truth is, Bob and I'd been pack rats for years. I'm convinced Bob was born that way. Our pantry had always been full (Bob insisted on having not one, but three backup bottles of laundry detergent—"just in case". Add to this the extra canned goods, garden supplies, garage paraphernalia, and every other household item one can imagine, and it was evident we had a real long way to go before we could start to consider ourselves "free spirits." In fact, it took us a long time to wean ourselves—even temporarily—from these habits. While depleting these extraordinary supplies, our "necessity" shopping slowed down, while our savings account balance soared.

Our pack rat tendencies were not limited to household supplies, either. I found I had clothes that I'd never worn and probably never would. So I attacked my clothes and linen closets with a vengeance; the resulting rag pile better resembled a small mountain. And while Bob's collection of screen-printed clothing from kayaking events was considered off limits, a drawer full of unopened new underwear spoke volumes about Bob's hoarding instinct. My threat to throw an entire drawer of the stuff onto the rag pile caused most items to become unpacked and be put promptly into use. Meanwhile, I sneaked his old underwear into the rag mountain. Nothing in our lives was to be immune from consideration for the rag mountain, in fact. Our paring down of material possessions was to be merciless.

But Bob now found himself in a terrible quandary. During our purge of material goods, he suddenly found he had too many "toys" and that some would have to go. Since he'd find little whitewater in the Caribbean, he figured the right thing to do was to sell his backup whitewater kayak and put the money aside for a possible sea kayak somewhere down the road. Parting with his battered beginners kayak was an emotional process, however, even though Bob hadn't used it in years. The day Bob sold it (to a good home) was a defining moment: Bob's resulting depression lasted only a day—which brought a big sigh of relief from me. And despite the fact that he still owned a newer kayak, no friend ever again questioned his commitment to Paradise.

We painted the house that spring, deciding on a pleasant blue that we felt was more pleasing than the drab green we'd been living with for years. The trim would be a darker blue, and with the inevitable white trim on the window sills and doors, our New England house would be more reminiscent of the colorful homes on St. John, with their multi-colored trims.

And was it ever! The color we selected for the main color dried a brighter color than we'd expected. After a couple of days, Bob and I got used to it, and we decided we'd keep the color. It had grown on us, and our house now felt like a little Caribbean island right in the middle of New England. When the project was nearly complete, I spied a neighbor across our back yard working in his garden.

"So what do you think of our new paint job?" I hailed over the dividing stone wall.

"Pat," John called to his wife over his shoulder. "Get out my sunglasses. Get out all the sunglasses! I can't see who's calling me through all that BLUE over there!" he chuckled.

"It's not THAT blue," I threw back at him, but I knew he was right. John just chuckled louder. From that day on, our old New England homestead was known as "the Blue Place." Though it may have been a little too Caribbean for New England, it certainly fit its owners' mood that spring.

So now, with my USVI vanity plate on my car which sat in front of our Big Blue house, our intention to move was now as clear to the whole world as our house was.

* * *

Time for Spring cleaning also meant time for a comprehensive review of our financial status. So I pulled out the notebooks and the mounds of backup data and got down to work.

As I looked over our figures, imagine my surprise when I discovered that we were saving at a rate equaling over 53 percent of our net income! Two years earlier Bob and I had been saving at a combined rate of less than 5 percent! And neither my husband nor I had recently been denying ourselves any item we truly wanted or needed.

I did the numbers three times looking for errors. We were closer to our goal than we'd known. It had paid to be conservative for once.

At the back of my mind, I kept coming back to the thought of moving to St. John six months earlier than planned. Could it be done? Bob had abdicated the budgetary planning to me. He was sure I could figure it out, though I was sure I couldn't. An unexpected phone call from Juneau, Alaska, helped me make my decision. Our friends who had moved there had just passed another long, dark winter in their version of Paradise. But their enthusiasm for their adopted home was still infectious. They'd never been within a thousand miles of St. John, but they shared our passion. Their parting words of advice were inspiring.

"If it's right, it will work out, no matter what. Just pick a date and maybe next year at this time you'll be in your own Paradise."

These words stuck with me as I reworked the budgets and played with the timetable. By evening, I quietly suggested a revised timeline to Bob. "Sooner."

He was excited, to say the very least. Totally out of character, he called numerous friends that night to share the news.

"I've been reworking the numbers and I've picked a new date to move . . . " he started every conversation. I was so pleased by his excitement that I forgot to be annoyed by his taking credit for all the budgeting and figuring.

Paradise would be our home four short seasons from now. We were moving to Paradise in less than the three years we'd agreed on earlier, and *lots* earlier than the ten years we'd vowed during our backyard pact long ago.

There was no turning back now. Lots of people knew about our updated schedule for the move, and so we were solidly—*and socially!*— committed now.

Island Facts

St. John is located three miles east of St. Thomas in the USVI. The island consists of 20 square miles of mostly mountainous terrain. Less than 9 miles across from west to east, it's only about 4 miles wide from north to south. Almost 2/3 of the island falls under the jurisdiction of the VI National Park, providing visitors and residents with plentiful opportunities to commune with nature. The island population is less than 5,000 people. There is no traffic-light, no trash pick-up service, no high school and no airport on-island. Ferries run regularly to St. Thomas, "the Big City" to most St. Johnians (JOE-nians).

Chapter 3

Out With The Old

So with our commitment firmly in hand, we faced our next-somewhat sad-task: selling our home...and soon. If it were possible, we would have taken our whole neighborhood with us when we moved; it was that good a neighborhood. I would especially miss watching all the local children growing up without me.

Spring and early summer were the best times to show off the beauty of our property, since we had an abundance of flowers, plants, and landscaping we'd worked hard at; besides, we had no idea if we'd sell quickly once we put the house on the market. We knew our tight financial planning could not support the burden of a mortgage when we moved to Paradise. We even expected to sell our current house at a loss, due to a downswing in the local housing market; but if we were lucky, the loss would be minimal. And waiting for prices to improve would be too risky.

From our vantage point, the house was ready to be sold. Most of the home improvements had been completed, and things looked darned good. The late spring flower bulbs had blossomed and the yard was filled with the color and sweet smells that promised a long, beautiful summer. Neighborhood kids occasionally trekked through our yard with their bikes, or just stopped by to visit for a while. We were enjoying living here more than at any time in our past. Nostalgia was everywhere.

Then reality set in. A new state law required that our septic system be replaced before we could sell our home. Bob took on this arduous task, managing all of the contractors and agencies it entailed.

Then it was my job to find a realtor. I'd met a wonderful one a year earlier when she stopped by on an old bicycle at one of our yard sales. Warm and charming, she'd displayed good taste too, buying a small braided rug I now miss dearly. With a smile, she'd given me her business card and said, "call me if you're ever looking for an agent." It was an invitation with no pressure or expectations attached.

Miraculously, I still had her card. A phone call was all it took-she vividly remembered my yard sale and our home. We held our breaths waiting for her visit and her verdict.

So now we proclaimed the house "ready," despite the septic work yet to be done.

* * *

Our realtor arrived and suggested a price. I gulped, but I agreed with her.

The price seemed generous, but was probably realistic compared to similar properties selling in our area. Though we would still be selling at a loss, we wouldn't be losing nearly as much as we'd thought we would. The real estate agent was amazed at the work we'd done and smiled in agreement with the improvements Bob had decided weren't necessary. She actually liked the bright blue color of our home. We'd found our broker.

With a good deal of frankness, she warned us that with summer right around the corner, it was unlikely the property would sell before fall.

We were prepared for that, and, secretly, even glad. It meant enough time to get the new septic system installed, and even time to rake the leaves one last time. It wasn't that I was getting cold feet, just that Big Blue in summer was magical.

The next day I began planting my last vegetable garden and my last flower garden in New England. The flowers were especially important to me, since for over five years I'd dabbled in various floral crafts. By now I'd become fairly well skilled and would enjoy the endeavor. There'd be time to grow, dry, and sell floral bouquets for one last season.

* * *

Two weeks later the property was on the market. Imagine our surprise when the property went under contract in less than one week. The price was right, apparently; we got lucky. The family that bought our home had been ready to buy once before, when a final home inspection turned out negative. Their humble goals were a large yard, a big master bedroom, and a place their only son would love.

Bingo! Our neighbors "interviewed" these folks (let's just say they were very inquisitive), to both realtors' horror, on the second walk-through of the property. But everything fell into place. The little boy made fast friends with the entire neighborhood that afternoon, and when the adults started sharing soft drinks and beer, the sale was a done deal in everyone's minds. Bob and I sat on the swing, stunned.

From that day on, our summer was frantic. The law required that the new septic system be installed and completed before the sale could go through. The home closing would be at the end of August-months before we'd expected. There were still huge amounts of accumulated "junk" we owned that it wouldn't be practical to haul to a short-term apartment rental. And what about the garden crops? And us? Where would we go? Our friends and family were united (and with good cause, perhaps) in their belief that Bob and I were crazy.

* * *

Advice from the naysayers had its impact on us. Though we'd already settled on St. John as our ultimate Paradise, we felt perhaps our research had been rather incomplete. While we'd spent time on nearby St. Thomas during each of our St. John vacations, we'd never visited St. Croix, called by some the Quiet Virgin. St. Croix is almost fifty miles south of St. John, and while tourist literature described St. Thomas as urban and St. John as rural, it described St. Croix as suburban.

We'd already ruled out St. Thomas in our minds. While it was a wonderful place, there were too many people there to suit us. We had good cause to think that way; while our Massachusetts home was only a short thirty-minute ride to downtown Boston, we visited there only a couple of times a year, so obviously we weren't into the urban environment. Besides, we might need the serenity of St. John if we had to commute to St. Thomas for jobs .

But St. Croix was another story. Housing on St. Croix was much more reasonably priced than on St. John. Finally, we felt we had to make a visit to St. Croix before finalizing our St. John plans.

As it happened, Bob had met a couple on the Internet who'd moved from New England to St. Croix a few months earlier. George and Lisa were convinced that St. Croix was the better Paradise, even though neither had ever visited St. John; but St. Croix was good enough for them, so we hedged our bet on St. John a little and made a quick, unscheduled trip to visit their island.

We easily found an inexpensive hotel in downtown Christianstaad. Leaving the oversight of our septic system replacement to our friend Dan, we headed south while our cats went on their own vacation to Birdie's house. By the time we'd arrived at our hotel on St. Croix, we had three separate messages waiting for us. Two were for job possibilities that Internet friends had come up with, and the third was an invitation for dinner and drinks from George and Lisa.

The next night at dinner, George and Lisa were generous in sharing their experiences in moving and in describing how their lives had changed on the island. Before they arrived, they'd rented a condo, sight unseen, which seemed unthinkable to us. Within a few months both were working in new job fields, but still using old skill sets. They candidly answered our many questions without a second thought. They told us how to get our cars over on a barge from the mainland, how to register an automobile, and how to cook local vegetables.

Truly, St. Croix was a wonderful island. It was much larger than St. John and had miles of gently sloping farmland along with the steep mountain roads that are also a St. John hallmark. There were real shopping centers here, as there were on St. Thomas, but everything was more spread out. Everywhere, we saw glimpses of St. Croix's proud history in its restored buildings and museums and other landmarks. The people we met were all warm and friendly and there was a camaraderie here that was quickly comfortable.

But our visit to St. Croix did not all go smoothly. Within twenty-four hours our rental car was broken into, though the would-be thief would be disappointed there were no valuables in the car. We found later that the rental agent had forgotten to warn us not to lock the doors, since this encouraged would-be thieves. But Bob and I didn't discuss the incident until a long time after it happened, since we were both trying to give St. Croix fair consideration and didn't want to influence each other's decision.

This trip combined typical vacation activities with more practical ones. We went swimming and snorkeling, though the inevitable comparisons with beaches on St. John left St. Croix wanting. Bob and I visited a Social Security office to get new cards, as our new friends said we'd need original cards for a variety of purposes once we moved. We met with potential employers and found concrete job opportunities on St. Croix within three days. I spent time in the grocery stores verifying prices, and we discussed our thoughts about living on St. Croix with many people we met. Unlike people on St. John, everyone here was encouraging.

But St. Croix appeared to be still struggling with the aftereffects of Hurricane Hugo many years before. More recent hurricanes had stalled recovery, and it seemed to me that many had lost their confidence along with their homes. Still, it was an island of great potential. Real estate was surprisingly inexpensive. If St. Croix could begin to believe in itself again, any investment by its natives would bring large returns.

Meanwhile, our vacation coincided with the Summer Olympics being held in Atlanta, and between our other activities we'd return every night to our room and watch the Olympic events unfold. As we watched, neither Bob nor I talked much about our individual opinions and observations about the island. I think we were each a little afraid of what the other person thought. During commercials, we each took out our separate notebooks and summarized what we'd learned that day.

With only three days left to go before our visit ended, we finally felt it was time to bring matters to a head. During an extraordinarily long Olympics commercial, I broached the subject.

"So what do you think?" I finally asked.

"Well, we could easily live here," Bob said, which didn't really answer my question at all. I had hoped this soft approach would get Bob to open up.

"It does seem like we'd fit in and have jobs pretty quick," I agreed.

After a short pause Bob added, "And we'd have a support group already in place to help us get settled." I knew he was referring to George and Lisa, who'd dined with us again the night before.

"But is this what you really want?" I pushed.

His next words were almost whispered. "It's not St. John."

That was certainly an understatement. I'd tried hard not to compare the two islands during this trip, but it was an impossible task. I nodded in agreement as he continued.

"Our money would last longer, and everything is less expensive than St. John." Ah, this was getting to the crux of the matter, wasn't it? And Bob was right. We could move to St. Croix immediately and be on budget with the money we'd already saved.

"True," I said with more perkiness in my voice than I felt. I was hoping this wasn't Bob's way of telling me his decision had changed to St. Croix, so I held my breath for what came next.

"But, it's not what we've been saving for," he finally commented.

I quickly agreed. "We've been preparing to be poor," I said. "This would be so much easier," I added, hoping I wasn't actually convincing him to move to St. Croix.

"You're right," Bob answered back. "But being poor is fine if we're in Paradise." When I heard these words, my hopes soared.

"This isn't Paradise," I said. I had to be blunt. It's what I felt.

"Not mine, anyway," Bob said, as the Olympic music began to signal the return to the show.

"Maybe we should 'Go For The Gold'," I said with sudden inspiration.

"St. John is definitely the Gold," Bob answered, still lost in his own thoughts. I doubt he even heard my reply when I agreed. After a few moments of silence, my husband turned to me and smiled. "Then let's go for the Gold," he concluded.

And I wonder even to this day whether what happened next was just coincidence or fate? At that very moment, the Olympic fanfare blared again in earnest, signaling another commercial break. In unison we began humming the Olympic theme—"Nah - Nah, nah-Nah-Nah-Nah-Nah..."—and so sealed our fate.

* * *

Memories of our last days on St. Croix are fond ones. Sensitive to our new St. Croix friends' feelings, we decided to wait and tell them of our decision by e-mail once we got home. If nothing else, we'd still be neighbors of sorts, and maybe we could visit them for Carnival and they could do the same on St. John.

Rejuvenated from our trip, Bob and I came home to a frenzy of packing and cleaning. The closing date on the house had gotten moved up a week to mid-August now, and we had nowhere yet to move. We still had three yard sales ahead of us, and the gardens were growing slower than normal; it looked like the new owners would get most of the harvest. While we were away, the town Health Inspector had decided that the only place the new septic system could go was under the old concrete patio directly behind our house. The buyers insisted that the patio be replaced as close to its original condition as possible. And before the closing. Of course.

To say we survived those last couple of months at our little homestead "with a little help from our friends" would be a gross understatement. Neighbors and friends from miles away all offered their assistance and their wisdom, on even small matters. Offers to store household possessions, help with yard work, board our cats on occasion, and even to clean and bring in the harvest were made. Neighborhood parties on the weekends lightened our load and brought us all together, but would also eventually make parting more difficult.

I was charged with selling off most of our belongings; Bob was in charge of whining about what we were selling. But even he eventually had to agree with my philosophy on what to keep.

Long ago I'd taken a class on Creative Thinking, where I'd learned that a chair is only a chair if and when you use it as a chair. It could also be a table or a cage or even firewood, depending on how you use it. This was the wisdom we applied in deciding which items we should keep. We couldn't take everything—the moving budget wouldn't allow it—so moving any multi-use items would be ideal, since we expected to be living in a smaller place and we'd learned most long-term rentals on St. John came furnished. Some of the things we kept would be considered bizarre by the uninitiated.

Selling most of our furniture now made sense, though we'd need to keep some pieces until our move to Paradise, since we'd be living in an apartment locally for at least eight months. Nevertheless, we opted to sell most things and live if we had to with a portable camp table and lawn chairs in our temporary kitchen. To us, this was a sure sign of our strong commitment to the future.

Our two cats would not be able to go outdoors when we moved to a temporary apartment; it was too risky. I'm sure they sensed this; in preparation for confinement, one insisted on spending as much time outdoors as possible that summer, and the other was always perched near a window.

The yard sales grew progressively more eccentric as we worked frantically to eliminate our excesses. We'd had two yard sales the previous year, but the old schedule was nothing like this. I was absolutely amazed at the interest in our goods displayed by the professional buyers. Although I should have been immune by this point, I was continually stunned by some of the items people would pay money for at yard sales. Some items that went first and fastest I had even purchased at such sales over the years, confirming my good taste in the eclectic. But we also sold weird stuff easily, like used wine corks, little bottles of hotel shampoo, and old pieces of macramé.

Our property included three quarters of an acre of manicured lawn and gardens that required constant work. Selling our home in summer meant keeping the lawn and shrubs in pristine condition during a period when we had even less time than normal to address this time-consuming task. Bob became a weekend warrior in keeping weeds at bay. His tasks were made more difficult by the septic system installation going on in the middle of it all. Mountains of dirt and strewn rocks combined with a dug-up patio to provide constant havoc.

The crew our friend Dan had hired to help remove the pieces that made up our patio did a commendable job. Every slab of concrete was identified and numbered as to its exact location to ensure proper refitting later. This was especially necessary since the patio was made up of poured concrete slabs of differing sizes and shapes, all pieced together in an exacting way to form the curved edges that eased the eyes as they moved toward the green lawn and gardens beyond. Keeping dirt and dust out of the house during this ordeal was a big challenge. We'd never owned an air conditioner, and the fans we used in summer months to keep the kitchen area cool now pulled in great quantities of dust.

* * *

My Massachusetts job required occasional trips out of town, so that summer spousal trust would play a big part in many decisions. The task of finding temporary living quarters, for instance, fell solely on Bob's capable shoulders. It would not be easy, with two cats in tow and an unbending vow between us not to sign a one-year lease. Bob also owned the myriad of other moving tasks, like sending out mail forwarding forms and scheduling utility shutdowns and phone number transfers. Bob was a junk mail junkie, though, and mail was important, so I could only hope for the best—or expect the worst.

We packed those things we were taking with us with little regard for the move next year. Eight months would give us plenty of time to finetune the list of which items we were taking with us. The rest would be donated to charity or thrown out. Friends had already spoken for a couple of items, like our beds and a bookcase. We'd given one bed away with the caveat that we'd use it when we revisited New England. It was also a creative way to be charitable to a good friend who had a lot of pride but not much money.

On warm summer evenings, I visited the gardens, picking the blooms for pressing and drying along with the occasional vegetable for dinner. Tending the gardens had always been a kind of therapy, mellowing me out after a stressful day at work. Whenever a flower came into full bud in the drying garden, I'd briskly snap the bud off the stem and toss it hard into my harvest basket; Bob called it my "sadistic" garden, and I must admit that my mind sometimes conjured up the faces of those who didn't believe we would make it to St. John as I plucked these buds.

Since we would be gone before the full harvest was in, every little flower mattered. Each evening I would poke wires through flower buds and dry these in our cellar, which was either completely crowded or completely empty, depending on the time elapsed since the last yard sale. The dehumidifier was on constantly in hopes of speeding the drying process while the buds slowly bloomed on wired stems. That last month, Birdie would descend on us on a weekly basis, graciously taking the dried bouquets to her home to keep until the fall crafts fair season.

* * *

Suddenly, it was over. We'd slept our last night in sleeping bags in the master bedroom, with potted palm trees for company on the hard floor. The new owners had liked the room so much that they'd even bought the plants. We were moving out in the morning, although the closing wasn't until the following week. My work and travel schedule was volatile, so we had gotten all to agree to have the closing without us.

That last morning, my husband and I sat on our patio swing looking out at the back yard. The gardens were just reaching their prime and a cat was lounging comfortably overhead, soaking up the warm morning sun as Bob sat, lost in thought.

"This is it," I said. But the only response was silence.

"We're really doing it," I tried again, with much the same result.

Maybe sentimentality would get Bob to open up, I thought. "I'm going to miss everybody," I suggested. But even this had no effect. So I sat and brooded.

"Everything will change," I meant to think. But I must have said this out loud, because to my surprise, my husband answered my thought.

"Life is change. Change is good." That was all he said as he continued to gaze on our former home. It was the Tao of Bob.

"Let's go find our temporary abode," I said, hoping Bob was right.

Chapter 4

Living In Hell

To be up front about it, I have to admit we didn't handle the move from our house to our apartment very well. Later, however, the quick move from the apartment to a condo went much smoother. It's a sad saga, but with a happy ending...

I'd never been to the new apartment before. We got there around noon that Sunday, following the trucks our friends had volunteered to carry the bulk of our possessions. Our cats had been farmed out to Birdie for a couple of weeks to simplify our move. With only the promise of free food, our mover friends gave us near-professional assistance. Before we knew it, we were moved.

Millions of you reading this have lived in an almost identical apartment, I'm sure. It was a corner two-bedroom unit on the bottom floor of a huge three-story building complex. There was a swimming pool we'd maybe use twice before we moved again, and parking all around the building. I'd lived in a similar place over twenty years ago. Even my husband had lived in its twin before he knew me.

It appeared that Bob had played it safe when it came to apartment hunting. The complex belonged to a large property management company in the region. Our building was directly across the parking lot from the rental office, with its model apartments for prospective renters. Because we were on the ground floor, most items were simply brought in through the sliding glass doors separating the living room from the small, concrete-enclosed patio.

We had moved more things than we needed, we discovered, including some potted tomato plants and flowers still in bud, just to cheer up the place. As a big picture frame was placed against a wall on top of a stack of boxes, Birdie saw and killed an errant bug. She made a little joke about the bug being a new neighbor, and I gave the comment little thought. Instead, I was busy directing the small army of men carrying boxes to and fro, and I was tired and in no mood for frivolous observations. Besides, Bob had inspected the apartment during a lunch break from work the previous week, and the rental paperwork we'd been given said the apartment was in "move-in" condition. By two o'clock we *were* moved in, just twenty minutes away from our old home.

Birdie stayed a little longer than the others to help me settle in while I sent Bob off for a couple of hours with his buddies. She used my new dishwasher, then filled an open cabinet with clean dishes. By sunset, Birdie was gone and Bob had returned, leaving my husband and myself to our new apartment. As we had often done at our house, I heated some water to make us each a cup of tea.

When I opened the cabinet where the cleaned dishes were kept, I let out a screech.

"Roaches!" I screamed.

There were cockroaches scurrying everywhere. There were even roaches climbing into the newly cleaned cups. I ran into the small living room.

"Show me," Bob said in disbelief as he followed me back to the kitchen. But his disbelief didn't last long. "There's some in the sink now," he screeched as he opened a drawer and found more rushing for cover against the sudden light.

I was thoroughly disgusted. I HATED cockroaches.

Yes, I knew there were many in Paradise. And yes, I know there are *really big ones* down there. But, I still hated them and I didn't expect to have to deal with them until we had moved to the Caribbean. Besides, living in New England, we were hardly prepared for an infestation.

Bob did his best to calm me down and make light of the situation. He called the property management office while I sat out on the patio, feeling much safer there. The person who answered the phone told Bob nothing could be done until the office reopened the next day. We were stuck there for the night.

Bob turned on lights all over the apartment to keep any other cockroaches in hiding. He coaxed me inside after a few hours and convinced me there were no bugs in the bedroom. Meanwhile he'd moved some essentials back into our cars to hedge his bet. Maybe, I thought, I had overreacted, but I was tired and stressed out. Exterminators would come in the morning and the cockroaches would be history. I refused to go into the kitchen or even the bathroom that night, but I did go to bed, though sleep was a long time coming. Despite our misgivings, we both went to work the next day.

When we came home, we found that no exterminators had come. A note on our doorway from the exterminating company said the premises were to be fumigated the next day, Tuesday. Having found more live cockroaches that very morning in the living room and the bathroom, I was paranoid. Fumbling, I opened the door only a crack, reached into the apartment, and turned on a light. I prayed this would eventually make the little pests run and scatter and I wouldn't have to see them. Then I went out to the apartment building steps to wait for Bob. When he arrived, we sat and we deliberated.

Bob came up with a creative solution for an interim living solution. We'd sleep at our old home in sleeping bags he'd packed in the car the previous night. The house was still ours for a few days. Thank goodness for our camping vacations, because we were both prepared to "rough it." We vacated the premises. In fact, we decided to give the new apartment an extra day or two after fumigation before setting foot back in. This would provide extra time to do final cleaning at the old house—a task our weary souls still faced.

It was a plan, but it didn't work. I got out of work early that Friday and rushed to the new apartment to get it aired out a little before the sun set. Taped to the door was the exterminator's note verifying that the work had been done. I opened the door and the smell from the fumigation process was very strong. I pulled the protective plastic covering off of the bed mattress and opened the screened windows. The clean linens I'd brought with me were spread on the bed. Then I went out to my car to get pillows and blankets. When I returned from the parking lot and entered the bedroom, I thought I'd lose my mind.

There was a large, very live cockroach crawling across the bed sheet I'd just placed down minutes ago. Another was on the wall in front of me. I flew out of the room. There was another scurrying across the living room wall and another one running to safety between the couch cushion and it's frame. I didn't scream this time. I was too grossed out even for that. By the time I'd gathered my senses, I'd already taken the phone out to the patio.

I called the property management office. Their answering service told me they were closed but I insisted on talking to SOMEBODY immediately. I finally got to someone in security who told me there was nothing he could do until the office opened the next morning. No amount of hysteria would change this. He promised they would fumigate again the next morning.

Bob was out of town until Sunday. He was blissfully kayaking at the annual Merrimack Valley Paddler's Pig Roast Weekend and couldn't be reached. I called Birdie and asked if I could join my cats in bunking at her place.

Being such a dear friend, Birdie told me to come immediately. I hadn't been coherent enough to explain what had happened—just that Bob was out of town and I needed a place to sleep. She knew something bad had happened, but she didn't push. By the time I traveled the thirty minutes to her home, Birdie had a bottle of wine and some snacks ready and the couch made up as a bed.

It was to be home for two nights.

* * *

The drive back to the complex that Sunday morning gave me time to focus on the previous week. On a hunch, I went to the apartment first. Walking in, I saw no sure sign this latest fumigation had taken place, but I did see lots of cockroaches-mostly dead, but some very much alive. It was like they'd completely taken over the apartment. There were literally thousands. In hindsight, I wish I had taken a photograph. I ran halfway across the parking lot to the management office before I realized I was still gripping a cordless telephone from the apartment. By this point, I was angry-very angry! The receptionist tried to placate me.

"Yes, I know who you are. We've never had roaches before in this complex, so we've been awfully concerned... I know I would be a little flipped out too if it happened to me... I understand why you want to talk with someone... I'm sure there's just a few stragglers...it takes a few days for them all to die when we fumigate."

I didn't believe her; there were too many cockroaches everywhere for this to be a freak situation. She was just too calm for my peace of mind. I wanted a solution and I wanted it now. We'd already stayed away a week and were paying for an apartment we couldn't even live in.

I demanded a temporary place to live—one that was cockroach free—and demanded to see someone in charge. I was told to sit and wait. A polo-shirted man bearing the management company logo over his heart came in and tried to minimize the situation. He suggested that in a day or two they would be able to come up with an alternative apartment. It would be on a second floor—not great for our cats, but it was ours for the asking.

After sleeping on a floor for a number of days, then a couch, and hardly sleeping at all—wrapt in fear—the night before, I was in no mood for compromises. My agitated state and blunt response must have had an impact: again I was told to wait, and within minutes the man returned saying there was a furnished one-bedroom apartment on the third floor of our own building available.

Once Bob returned, we went to our infested apartment together to get some items. At a minimum, we needed clean clothes for the next workday. I'd left a couple of lights on, which helped. We rushed through the apartment, grabbing what we needed, and tried not to notice a couple of scurrying shapes. Quickly, we rushed upstairs and out to the small deck outside the temporary quarters, where we literally dropped the things we'd collected.

Later on, in the late afternoon sun, Bob picked up each item one by one, giving each a thorough look and a good shake before bringing it inside. There were no cockroaches on these few items. The procedure was repeated twice, though the last load stayed outside on the deck overnight. We were dead tired.

The next day, our jobs kept us away and the day went too slowly. By the time I'd gotten to the apartment complex, Bob had cleared out the deck and was bringing up a new load of goods from the infested apartment. As he walked outside, I saw a very dead cockroach between the deck slats. Though I knew it had probably come up with some of our possessions from the day before, I rushed into the kitchen and quickly pulled open drawers and cabinets. No cockroaches. In every room I repeated this action just to be sure.

There was nothing. I was relieved. We could beat this thing, I thought.

With renewed vigor, we emptied the contents of boxes Bob had retrieved onto the deck and searched for little critters. Bob had bought many canisters of roach repellent during his lunch break, and we used them freely. Unfortunately, most of our precious possessions were still downstairs getting more infested with every day that passed.

We lived moment by moment for the next couple of days. Neither of us wanted to live in this complex any more, and we needed to find somewhere else to live fast. We looked through the listings of apartment rentals, and circled any that looked even remotely hopeful. Phone calls nixed quite a few places. On Saturday we spent the day looking at apartments and filling out applications. No one could commit an answer until Monday, when our applications would be reviewed.

In the Saturday paper, there appeared some new ads. One was for a condo on the opposite side of town, which sounded perfect. I tried not to get my hopes up as I circled other places for a Sunday hunt. Bob had already reached his limit; guilt over his original apartment selection combined with the hard work and little sleep from the previous two weeks had caught up with him. So we agreed: I would look for a new place the next day, while he would take the day off and go kayaking for maybe the last time. This worked for both of us.

That Sunday I looked at three more apartments and got lost looking for a fourth. The second was the condo on the other side of town that sounded too perfect to be true. As I drove there, I saw that it was located just off a highway entrance, but that it was far enough away so the only sounds were those of the birds in nearby trees.

Nestled in a quiet residential area of single family homes, the complex had much appeal. The condo unit itself was one in a long row that was separated from the others by a long, shrub-lined driveway that led down from the road above. It was townhouse-styled, with a one-car garage underneath, two bedrooms, and one and a half baths. Almost as large as the home we'd just sold, it was in immaculate condition.

The condo was over our budget, but not by too much. And the owner seemed to understand our need for urgency in the move. I'd filled out the requisite application and the owner seemed warm and friendly and reminded me of a kindly, yet firm, grandmother. Bob and I had to sign a one-year lease, though our plan to was to move to St. John in ten months. Still, it was the best living situation I'd seen and the place was clean. There was no way a cockroach had ever found it's way into this condo. I said a silent little prayer and gave this woman our work phone numbers. Then I went to my next appointment, just in case the condo didn't pan out.

Luckily, the following day the condo owner called with the sweet words that answered my prayers. We rushed over after work so she could meet Bob and show him how the central vacuum system worked, as we'd never owned one before. The increase in monthly rent quickly faded from our minds. Before the day was over, we were ready to move in.

Chapter 5

Living In Limbo

Within a day we'd moved in. Our mover friends had come to our rescue again. I wished I could have given them a medal or something. It meant that much. The condo was like a breath of fresh air after the cockroach-infested apartment-from-hell. It was months before I could laugh about that situation. After some off-handed comment, Birdie was threatened with lifetime banishment if she even mentioned the word "cockroach" in my presence again during the next six months.

Our friends moved us quickly, since the bed, living room couch and armchair had to be left behind; the cockroaches had had too much time to make new homes in our old furniture, and we were worried about health issues if we fumigated further. We'd planned to leave that furniture behind anyway when we moved to Paradise. So we faced reality bravely.

Even discounting the furniture and other items we'd lost to the cockroaches, we should have eliminated more things before we moved. The condo had more space than the apartment had, but we later found we needed that space to sort, pack and stage items for shipping. In the beginning it seemed like wasted rent money for empty space, but it certainly seemed to be paying for itself now.

Our new plan was that everything that had been in the apartment would be put in the new garage. Even so, before anything went inside, a few canisters of roach spray would be used to fumigate every crack and seam. Once things were moved in, the entire garage was sprayed again. I was determined that not even one cockroach would survive the trip to the new condo.

For the next days and nights in our new lodgings, Bob and I slept in our trusty sleeping bags, while a blanket in the corner warmed the cats. These were the only items we had ready for the master bedroom. Two lawn chairs served as furniture for the living room; the rest of the place was empty. Occasional forays were made down to the garage for items we just couldn't wait for. Our workdays seemed very long and our nocturnal activities were few and rare. The garage was filled to the brim with our remaining furniture, our "toys," and boxes of every size and shape.

Whenever we had to open the garage door, we sealed it with roach spray before closing. We rescued a lamp at some point for the bedroom; a short time later we grabbed a pot for the kitchen. A week after the move, we began spending all of our free time rescuing and cleaning items one by one. Judging by the number of things that ended up in the dumpster, I'm convinced we threw out more than we brought inside.

Bob spent much of his free time getting our mail situation straightened out. Moving twice in one month made the task frustrating and confusing, and Bob grumbled but kept at it. Meanwhile, my back was getting sorer each day: After two weeks of sleeping bags, I put my foot down; I wanted somewhere comfortable to sleep. And we needed some furniture in the living room, even if it was for only eight months. Eventually, Bob gave in, found a furniture outlet store, and purchased an inexpensive sleeper-couch. It made a big difference. At least we were able to sleep somewhere other than the floor.

And again our friends came to our rescue. Our friend Dan loaned us a kitchen table with four matching chairs. He'd always had an extra key to our living space (for both his and our convenience), and the new condo was no exception: The "new" kitchen set was a wonderful surprise, already in the dining area and set up when I arrived home one day. We were now living in relative comfort, with both a "furnished" living/bed room and dining room. I began trying to convince Bob to splurge a little further on a new mattress and box spring, but I knew that would be an uphill battle.

* * *

In the confusion of the past few weeks Bob and I had begun the very bad habit of constantly eating fast food and other take-out meals. We were getting fat. It was time to find kitchen items and begin cooking again. Cooking meant "home" to me, and once I started to cook on a regular basis, both Bob and I began to relax within this phase of our transition. This was also why our kitchen got redecorated before any other room. "To add a few homey comforts and minimize the condo's sparseness" was the excuse I used to justify earmarking a small weekly amount of money from my budgeted cash for this effort.

Looking back, it was worth it. Once I'd begun redecorating, I'd decided that the kitchen should be decorated in an "island" motif, using some items we'd bought during past vacations and using color to make it all work. The table Dan loaned us was made of oak butcher block accompanied by four cane-seated chairs. Above the table hung a colonial-looking chandelier, which I covered with cheap plastic ivy plants; next to it we hung a little mobile of parrots we'd bought for a couple of dollars years ago on St. Thomas. The ivy theme got carried throughout the dining and kitchen areas. I later added a wooden parrot in a swing hanging above the sink, which Birdie and I picked up at a craft fair that fall. Island-style warmth radiated throughout.

I didn't limit this island motif to the condo. My USVI license plate had fallen off my car at a car wash soon after our move, so I decided to post it on my office wall as a conversation piece. By this time the poor thing was rather beat up, but that only made it even more endearing. It was a constant reminder to me of our plans as well as serving as a response to the naysayers who were my closest office co-workers. What selling our home couldn't accomplish, the battered license plate did. Co-workers finally began to believe that Bob and I were serious about Paradise.

While they wondered about Paradise, Bob and I were still unpacking an endless pile of boxes. Ten months until our planned move felt like a very long time. And while I hated the idea of paying rent money for the extra months on the lease, I'd been brought up to accept responsibility and never skip town. Bob—always the wise one—told me to put it out of my mind and act like a St. Johnian: "Go with the flow," he'd say, and I did. But only because the crafts fair season had already begun and took my mind off things.

Despite our short summer at the old homestead, I'd managed to harvest a respectable amount of flowers. Birdie and I had been "doing" crafts fairs for years, mostly for quality girl time alone and to enjoy some nice fall days outdoors. We never made any real money to speak of, but we had many fun times together. This year the schedule Birdie and I had agreed on was short—we'd only take part in three craft fairs—but still we weren't prepared. Birdie was "retiring" from the crafts tour at the end of the season. It just wouldn't be fun to pursue, she insisted, if we couldn't do it together.

By the end of the last fair, we still had some items left; these would become Christmas presents and personal souvenirs to take to Paradise.

* * *

Our mail and newspaper subscriptions caught up with us at the condo after a few short weeks of confusion. On days when we didn't receive *The VI Daily News* or when our copy of *Tradewinds* was overdue, both my husband and I felt let down. We'd come to depend on these links to our future. Sometimes two or three papers arrived in one day; sometimes none; the weekly mail cycle ebbed and flowed. When we received a Friday's paper before we had received that Thursday's, it reminded us both that St. John would not be perfect. And while the news was always a few days old, it hardly mattered. Bob and I ate it up.

By this time, most of our friends and family had finally adjusted to the idea of our moving to Paradise sometime soon. Since we'd sold the house, there was no denying that we were really going. Advice and opinions flowed freely. My mother-in-law was very worried about our move. She kept us informed of every TV show and news clip she saw showing crime in the islands, hoping to discourage us. While her efforts more often amused us, we also took them seriously.

Once she sent us a long article about someone who had made the move to St. John but didn't last and moved back. We read it with great interest. The writer's disillusionment didn't faze Bob or I, as we could easily tell the writer wasn't well prepared for island life: He wasn't adaptable to life outside of a city, or one without lots of conveniences. If anything, the article was reaffirming.

In the article, there was a two-column insert titled "If You're Planning To Go" that had recommendations for what type of research to do first. But we'd already bought and read the books and had subscribed to the newspaper, hadn't we? Surely, we were ready for the realities of the big move!

On the other hand, my own parents' approach was a little different than Bob's mother's. I could tell that my mother thought our plan a pipe dream; it wasn't something, after all, that we were really going to do. Despite our having sold our house.

When we'd talk, she would express great interest in our plans for the move. She'd listen and talk. Then she'd inevitably laugh and let us know we were crazy and end our conversation with "Well, honey, you should go for it if you want it." It was that final spring leading into our move before she was convinced we were really going.

My father, on the other hand, attempted to assess our success potential in a more circumspect manner. He regularly asked Bob if he was as excited about moving as I was. I'm sure my dad was thinking about my first marriage and the move with my first husband—a move that portented disaster. When asked about his excitement, Bob always answered my father in the affirmative. But Bob's so quiet by nature, few things he says ever come out sounding enthusiastic. So my father set about expecting the worst—or the best (for them), depending how you looked at it.

* * *

That Halloween, few children knocked on our door in the new condo. I found myself anxious for the night to be over so I could pack away the Halloween box, making it the very first of the boxes we would send to our home in Paradise. But I missed the children from our old neighborhood; we'd always been such lovely friends, and I wondered what they were wearing for Halloween this year. We'd never spent Halloween on St. John and didn't even know if it was a holiday that we'd be celebrating again.

After some real creativity on our part, the garage was finally empty enough to get a car in there. Bob had suggested organizing any remaining gear—camping, ski, snow, etc.—into sections along the walls, and to hold them with nails. At least that stuff was off the ground and out of the way. It was also easy to retrieve, even with a car parked in the garage.

The same day we got the car into the garage, Birdie called. She was throwing out all her craft supplies and gave me the option of taking whatever I wanted. At the time, I was already up to my eyeballs in trying to clean out the garage; now she wanted me to make decisions about accepting things I couldn't see (and couldn't take the time to figure out whether I needed). It was my own fault, though; I told her I'd take whatever she was throwing out.

I knew it was a mistake immediately, and the next day the garage looked like we'd never cleaned it out at all. Birdie's crafts stuff turned out to include lots of items I'd never seen before. Now I could only hope the garage would be empty by Christmas.

But some craft items, we knew, would be useful in Paradise. Bob and I both wanted to explore more deeply into our artistic abilities once in St. John. That meant bringing raw materials and other supplies with us, since research had told me it's difficult to acquire cheap supplies on the island. But with no clue as to the arts or crafts we wanted to try our hand at, I could only guess at the right things to bring. Of course there are always wholesale catalogs available to order from, but you can only buy a few items in enough quantity to make them reasonably afford-able. And some items would be difficult to find at all.

And crafts were something that might help us better make ends meet. My husband often beat me to the mailbox those last days in New England, and once in a while he'd forget to pass the USVI papers on to me, so I wasn't always fully aware of island events. but eventually I learned about the first recently held "St. John Saturday." This event would become a regular monthly Cruz Bay event, and would include craft booths with local talent, giving me my first on-island goal: to make handcrafts of good value to sell in my own booth. For the rest of our tenure at the condo, when pictures of the monthly event arrived in *Tradewinds*, I studied them in great detail.

* * *

Our last New England Thanksgiving was spent with our immediate families, and by then our lives (in transition) had almost returned to normal. However, in mid-December, word of an incident in Paradise soured our mood. We'd just gotten the latest *Tradewinds* newspaper and read it through as usual, noting the issue had a certain negative tone throughout. One article, about panhandlers, was prominent, and it made St. John sound more like what we'd seen on St. Croix. Another article, about two people who'd moved from Vermont a month earlier and who were attacked and robbed, disturbed us; it struck too close to home. And even though the facts in the article didn't quite add up, these stories were depressing. Combined with our having as yet no idea of how to earn a living once we got there, suddenly Paradise wasn't looking as great as the Paradise we'd imagined all along.

After a day had passed, however, I'd reread the article about the Vermont couple three times, and while my perspective on the occurrence of island crime had changed somewhat, thoughts of the incident lingered. That night I had drinks with some girls from work and I mentioned the article about the new St. Johnians from Vermont. Being attacked and robbed is a serious thing, I said.

Soon, I was relating all the details outlined in the article to my friends. Once mugged and unconscious, I told them, the couple was purported to have been transported by the robbers, then dumped in the middle of the road next to their house. My friends laughed; muggers don't provide taxi service, they pointed out. And the transplants had lost all the money they had to their name-four hundred dollars-and a pair of sunglasses worth one hundred and eighty dollars; but this didn't add up to any of us, even to me. How could someone with so little money have such expensive sunglasses, especially when they had so little money to their name? And how could they be so dumb as to carry all the money they had in the world with them while out drinking? These people even admitted they were very drunk when they were robbed and didn't remember much about the night's events. They also didn't report the crime until six o'clock *the next evening*!

By that point, I was laughing with my girlfriends at the unlikely tale, and the laughter somehow eased my mind. Even if the story was true, Bob and I would never be so stupid.

All the way home, my thoughts were of the fantasy lives Bob and I would be living in a few short months.

That night I got home late and Bob was in a down mood. He said he had made little headway on the Internet to prepare for the move. No contacts, no schedule for transporting the car, no job leads. Then he said that after thinking it through, he thought we should only take to Paradise what we could fit in our cars and store the rest, "just in case."

This didn't sound like someone who was looking forward to moving.

"Don't you want to move anymore?"

"Well it looks like crime is real bad," Bob snapped. His words stopped me cold.

"I'm not staying here," I said, waving my arms to describe the condo. "Where would we go?"

There was a long silence.

Then Bob said "Arizona. Except maybe it gets too hot in the summer. Maybe Alaska."

I had nothing quick to say. My first thought was that his mother's comments and newspaper clippings had gotten the better of him. Then the *Tradewinds* article that I'd made fun of only hours before with my friends popped back into my consciousness.

"It's the latest issue of the newspaper, isn't it?" I asked.

"Well, the panhandling is really bad," he blurted. But I still couldn't believe this was the real issue. We'd been through too much in the last few months for this to be the stone that tripped us.

I pointed out that panhandling had never been a problem when we visited St. John before. He reminded me we'd been approached in the park on our last visit. Bob was right, but I hadn't thought it had bothered him. I'd really even forgotten the incident. Not that it was a fond memory, but I'd lived in New York City for a while and perhaps I had become immune. But there had to be more.

"Wasn't the article about the two people who'd recently moved from New England crazy? That could have been us," he said in a rush.

I laughed and he blinked.

I had him reread the article with me, and shared my newfound perspective as we read. Besides, I told him once we'd finished, the incidents as reported weren't much if you compared them to those in our own area. *And this was a bi-weekly newspaper,* I pointed out; most of these crimes wouldn't have even *made* our daily paper.

I saw Bob visibly relax, admitting, "I guess it's just a little trouble in Paradise."

It was obvious that with less than six months to go, we'd both begun feeling a little insecure. We needed more positive reinforcement.

As it happened, there was no further mention of the incident in *The VI Daily News,* nor was any mention ever made of it again in later *Tradewinds* editions. Weeks passed, and the incident faded from our memories. But another minor setback in our lives would work to bring about a new icon in our lives—one that would rejuvenate us, rekindle our spirits and focus us towards Paradise.

* * *

At this point, we found another hurdle we had to jump: The mileage gauge on my car had long ago passed the one-hundred-thousand-mile mark, and the car's age was showing. A few weeks before, we had replaced the car's dead battery, and now we also needed new tires to get us through the coming New England winter. Then one night I was driving home from work in the dreary dark and, ten miles into my thirty-seven mile commute on a busy highway, my driver-side power window decided it was time to die. In its death throws, the window suddenly powered up without human intervention and then literally dropped dead into an open position. Normally, this would have been disconcerting enough by itself. But it was also a record-breaking cold, rainy day, and no amount of coaxing would raise that window.

A hasty visit to a Ford dealership proved my worst fear had come true. It would cost a minimum of three hundred and fifty dollars to get to the source of the problem and fix it. And if there were more wrong than a dead door motor, the cost would go up from there. At home, I layered plastic against the frame and hoped for a sunny week.

The next day was indeed sunny, and I was tormented by the decision on whether to fix my car or trade it in for something more appropriate to island life. But these things have a way of working out by themselves sometimes, to wit: As I entered through the passenger side and crawled over the center console the next day, I'd no sooner shut the door behind me when I heard the sickening sound of another suddenly powered-up motor and a draft at the back of my neck. That ended it. The passenger window had followed the driver's side's lead and dropped open for the last time. The automobile had decided its own fate.

Fortunately, a replacement vehicle was already in the budget for the move to St. John, since my little Ford Probe would never have survived the steep hills or the dirt roads, even in prime condition. A four-wheel drive vehicle would be much more appropriate to island life. Bob's four-wheel drive Subaru station wagon was too low to the ground for most of St. John's terrain, but it would be useful for shopping expeditions on St. Thomas. I'd hoped the Probe would survive the winter, but the cost to repair it just wasn't going to be worth it.

Unfortunately, there are not a lot of small convertible SUVs like Samurais or GEO Trackers for sale in New England in November. But, surprisingly, within a day, I had a new car anyway. It was a fuchsia-colored GEO Tracker convertible with a black top and new snow tires and mechanics that were relatively easy for amateurs to maintain. The car dealer who sold us our new toy informed us that the very pregnant previous owner loved the vehicle, but with twins on the way, she was concerned about the convertible roof and safety for her babies in the back seat. The truth of its history didn't matter; the vehicle was perfect for our move.

It was hard not to smile and see our future in that pink car. Even Bob got a silly grin on his face whenever he looked at it. Thank goodness the vehicle had a strong heater too. Though the Tracker was not meant to be driven in high winds on busy highways for long distances, in the winter to come it would survive—and so would we.

* * *

Freshly cut pine trees had always held a special meaning to me at Christmas time. Every year Bob made a big project of getting together gloves and rope and saws and other trivia and dressing for his annual traipse into the woods, mumbling all the while about "what a good husband" he was. This year was no exception. The first tree we saw, Bob wanted to cut, but I was having no part of making things that easy for him; instead, I made him hang in there until we passed the third one. Even so, it seemed to me a major concession on my part.

Bob was going through the motions of holiday chores, but his heart didn't seem to be in it. He went holiday shopping with me, but he just didn't have any real holiday spirit. This year he even left most of the gift buying and wrapping to me, and all the decorating too. He chipped in with some ribbon work and labeling a few times when I pushed him to it, but everything was just a chore to him this year.

I don't know why exactly, but I gave in to the urge to be overly generous to charity this year; maybe I knew it was unlikely we'd be able to afford it again for a while. My husband's holiday is Hanukkah, but he normally looked forward to getting Christmas gifts as a consolation for putting up with me during the holidays. To his credit, Bob didn't complain once at the bounty of items that I bought to give to charity. Then again, I'd always looked forward to our arguments over my generosity. His lack of interest in receiving gifts himself was even more disconcerting. So much for tradition.

In fact, many of our Christmas traditions fell by the wayside this year. It was a sad and extremely nostalgic time, despite the gayness of the season. In our visits with family, our pending move never came up. I think everyone was feeling the same nostalgia. For the past ten years, Birdie and Dan came to wherever we lived for a little sleepover party just before Christmas. We always ate too much, made silly toasts, and teased each other like twelve-year-olds—as only well adjusted adults could. Gifts were exchanged with lots of laughter and love while wacky photographs recorded the whole sordid event. Our best friends fought over who would get the guest bed or the couch for the night, and we all woke to a long, drawn-out breakfast before moving on with our lives.

This year, however, our role and our friends' were reversed: The sleepover event was held for the first and only time at Birdie's festive condo, and we were treated like royalty. Dan's dinner made the last ten we'd cooked seem like mere appetizers. For once, Bob and I were mere guests, and for the first time since I'd known her, Birdie had a real Christmas tree, loaded with ornaments I'd given her over the years. Before dessert was served, Bob got caught up in the holiday spirit and began—to everyone's amazement—humming Christmas carols. Our traditional evening of friendship was followed by an even lazier than normal morning breakfast and departure. Everyone got teary-eyed when Bob and I left.

Some people didn't know what to buy us for the holidays, so they gave us lots of toys for our cats. These two got so many presents, we decided to let them play only with a few; the rest were packed away so they'd have a whole new set of toys in Paradise. Even so, Bob received some wonderful gifts, including water floats and a blender. Bob gave me palm-tree-shaped wooden ornaments that he'd secretly bought on St. Croix that summer. I guess he'd actually had the holiday spirit all along.

That New Years Eve was quietly spent with old neighbors reminiscing about the past and sharing dreams about the future. It had been a fine holiday season...our last in New England. Too soon, it was over.

St. John Trivia

All the beaches on St. John are considered public property by law, from the low tide line to either the line of vegetation or fifty feet inland, whichever is the shorter distance. However, public access by land is not mandated, which keeps some beaches secret from most tourists. Others are hidden by lush foliage and steep hillsides.

There are thirty-nine accessible beaches on St. John, but most tourists visit only the beaches at Trunk Bay, Cinnamon Bay or Hawksnest Bay on the north shore, which are easily reached by open-air taxis.

Chapter 6

Plotting and Planning
and Picking and Packing

That New Year brought us a renewed sense of commitment and a simple resolution. Bob and I both vowed to get to Paradise in June while still retaining our sanity. It was not a resolution made in jest. While it seemed we'd just finished unpacking, it was time to pack again, and we started feeling the pressures build. But we'd become experts at this task. Because every item in the garage had been unpacked that fall to make them cockroach-free (even those we'd hoped not to see again until St. John), the garage had only been empty enough for a car for a few weeks. Now it would be our staging area. Our sanity was already in doubt.

But on a relatively warm Saturday afternoon in January, we finally regained some of our equilibrium. The temperature had reached a balmy sixty degrees thanks to the perfect timing of that quirk of nature known locally as the January Thaw. Bob and I donned loose-fitting fleece jackets and took our trusty lawn chairs outside to the small deck attached to the condo. Bob tempted fate with his shorts, while I remained snug in a pair of old sweatpants. Within minutes we were both content, soaking up the winter sun. It was a perfect time to phi-losophize and share ideas.

We contemplated the months ahead of us. And before we decided what and how to repack, we had to decide how we would move our pos-sessions. Bob told me this plotting and planning was like preparing for a long canoe expedition. He'd just finished reading a travel essay about a couple that'd canoed across Canada for a solid year. "Preparation was the key to their survival," he said. "These folks prepared for the long trip by having major stores of supplies waiting for them at the canoe put-in site, and then supplies timed to be air-dropped to remote vil-lages they would pass on the way. They would get the supplies they needed when they needed them and not a moment before." I caught his excitement as he continued.

"When they started their expedition, they brought just what they would need to get to the first drop-off point. Everything they brought was a necessity and had multiple uses-just like we're doing."

Our own trip would be different, yet we could use some of the same concepts. He'd obviously given our own expedition a great deal of thought. Bob rarely talked so much in a single day, so I prodded him on. His monologue continued, full of ideas on the logistics of our move.

"Our automobiles have to be driven to Florida. As for the rest of our things, options range from hiring an expensive global shipping compa-ny to move us, to hauling our goods ourselves to Florida—the closest point on the continent to the USVI. This last option means hiring a con-solidator for shipment to St. Thomas, then hiring a truck to barge it all to St. John. Or, we could mail everything to ourselves via the US Post Office."

This last option tickled my fancy as I tried to stifle a giggle.

"Mailing your life's possessions is considered a practical way to move by most St. Johnians," Bob insisted. No kidding? Maybe it was the warm sun in the middle of the winter, but this idea started making lots of sense to me. Besides, I knew the idea fit well with Bob's concept of this move as a "life expedition," and seemed doable now, since we wouldn't be taking much furniture.

Using the motto "If It Can't Be Mailed, It Can't Be Needed" we shook hands in the waning sunlight and sealed our agreement: Our plan now was to somehow mail our life to Paradise.

Also part of our new plan: One person would need to go ahead of the other to secure lodging and a mailing address. That pioneer would take some things, with the rest of our goods to follow. The other person would wrap up our life in New England and ship boxes full of immediate needs. Friends and neighbors would later ship any remaining boxes over time—at our expense, of course. There was no mention of who would go first and who would come later. I think we both envisioned ourselves as that first pioneer.

Since we'd be relying on the US Post Office as our lifeline, getting a Post Office box as quickly as possible was crucial. But we'd been told there was a two-hundred-person waiting list (which turned out to be true) for St. John Post Office mail boxes. And while we'd filled out the request form for our own box months ago, we were still way down on the list. So why didn't we just ship everything ahead of time in care of General Delivery to the on-island Post Office? Because, while our sanity was in question, we were not entirely crazy.

Nevertheless, we planned to have most boxes timed to arrive exactly when we needed them and not a moment before. If we could figure out the Post Office timing, it could work. Christmas boxes wouldn't be needed in July, but we'd be homesick for maple syrup by August. Our emphasis on timing meant depending on friends and old neighbors to help us out, but we were confident they could be counted on. Even those who were still in denial over our plans would probably help out. We hadn't quite ironed out the specifics, but our plan made sense.

The next day, the remaining skeleton of our Christmas tree came down, and we began the work we'd be doing every week for the next twenty weeks: packing. And as we started packing, sanity became an increasingly elusive goal. I used cloth decorations and garlands to line the sides of those first Christmas cartons. A couple of kitty toys were included as a holiday surprise for the cats, and videos on skiing and winter kayaking were thrown in for Bob. I included anything else I could think of that we would only use during the holiday season. This whole timing approach was kind of fun...at least at the beginning.

As I packed, I was again whittling down the number of belongings we'd take. It was very hard to throw anything out—even ornaments that had ended up ratty looking after years of abuse. Though I threw out more than I packed, an old habit had me shopping at after-Christmas sales for new mini-lights, wrapping paper, and tags. At these prices, they were worth the price to buy, pack, and ship them. We also had a cheap plastic Christmas tree stand we'd bought to replace the great iron one that one of us had inadvertently sold at our last yard sale. I insisted it was a multi-use item that would be of great value on the island (though I had no idea what else it could be used for). Bob just shook his head and grudgingly let it be packed.

The plan for moving our vehicles to Paradise—both "the beauty" (my Tracker) and "the beast" (Bob's Subaru)—came naturally: Our new St. Croix friends had freely discussed with us the pros and cons of buying vehicles locally versus barging them over from the mainland, so we pretty much knew what we had to do from the outset. Each of us would drive an automobile to Florida, where we'd put our cars on barges and then fly to St. Thomas, with our autos arriving—hopefully—a few days later. Both vehicles would be going with us: mine because the Tracker was bought specifically for life in Paradise, and Bob's Subaru because it was paid for and could carry lots of things. Our vehicles were assets to our expedition, and the price to ship them was relatively small.

We'd been cautioned to find a barge that would travel directly from the mainland to St. Thomas without stopping first in Puerto Rico. This would minimize the likelihood of our vehicles arriving missing a headlight or battery or other key component. A good friend in San Juan confirmed this. "It's sad, but sometimes I think ripping people off is a national pastime here," he said. I didn't know if I actually believed this or whether he might just be a little paranoid, but soon this was a moot point: Bob found a shipping company that would barge the cars directly to St. Thomas. They promised it would take only three to four days for the vehicles to make their ocean trip.

The cats, on the other hand, would be another problem. We couldn't leave them behind; they were like our children. Besides, both had adapted quickly to their three-story, luxuriously carpeted condo after their long "vacation" with Birdie up north. Both our outdoor adventurer and our indoor-bred princess had been kept indoors for the duration, and their months together were starting to wear thin; our outdoor adventurer also showed signs of cabin fever.

They needed to get out, yet we didn't want to risk having them get lost in our new environment, so we attempted a compromise: One Saturday my husband came home with gifts for our feline pets: a blue walking harness for our adventurer and a more petite and feminine pink harness for the princess. Both cats were offended. And while the adventurer eventually resigned himself to the harness with great indignation, it was short-lived: No matter how often we tried to get him to adapt, after a short few minutes outdoors he demanded his freedom. So we permanently curtailed his outdoors liberty.

Our feline princess, on the other hand, wanted nothing to do with the outdoors. But she'd be living partially outdoors on St. John, so we wanted her to get used to it. After weeks spent trying to lure her out of hiding just to get her to accept the harness, she was ready to take the outdoors plunge, we thought. Her Royal Highness had a great fear, however, of large, open spaces, and whenever we took her outside, she'd drop onto her belly and crawl fast in beeline fashion back to the outside door. Previously, she'd never lasted more than ten seconds (even with petting to soothe her) before she'd drop to her belly and claw her way to "safety" no matter what the weather or location. And the harness made no difference. Within two seconds of being placed on the ground, that cat was out of her harness and doing the belly crawl...fast!

We finally decided that perhaps it wasn't worth the effort. Our princess would never go off and get lost like our outdoor adventurer would (likely within days on-island). We just hoped the little gal would be happy living in a place where outdoors and indoors were often separated only by some imagined line.

I thought the cats could be flown down as cargo from New England on an airplane, but that wouldn't work. According to the airlines, the timing of flights and connections meant the cats couldn't arrive when Customs was still open in Miami or San Juan. Someone would have to meet their flight at the connecting location, keep the cats overnight, and return them to Customs the next day before they could continue their journey to St. Thomas. Then one of us would have to pick them up at the airport there, and ferry them to St. John. But there had to be a better way.

* * *

At some point, I created an inventory on my computer of all the things we were packing. For the lack of a better name, I titled this list the "Paradise Expedition." Bob, meanwhile, was inspired enough now about our trip to tack the topographical maps of St. John and St. Thomas onto our living room wall. He also put up a road map of St. John for further reference. We would study the maps often, and they would remind us to focus on the move every time we passed through the room.

Checking reference points on the maps, we were able to locate neighborhood names we read about in the newspapers. We learned a lot about St. John by doing that. First, we learned about the high crime areas. We wouldn't want to live there. Then we discovered the most desirable living areas, which we determined from the most expensive real estate ads. We'd want to live close by.

Almost immediately, we found a serious flaw in this approach. We discovered these neighborhoods—high crime and most desirable— were one and the same. High property values meant temptation to some. So we decided to revise our plan and look for long-term rentals in neighborhoods that were rarely mentioned in the news. Our friends laughed, but as we later discovered, it worked.

* * *

In line with our packing scheme, each box was identified by the month we'd targeted that box for arrival on St. John, along with a separate box identifier. Boxes 11-1 and 11-2 would arrive by November, if all went perfectly. If it worked, the unpacking and storage process at the other end of the world would be simple, if drawn out. Packed boxes were multiplying along every wall in the condo. I tried not to think about how long it would take to unpack at the other end of our move. Bob reread his many books on expedition travel, looking for clues on what and how to pack, and often gave me advice that contradicted the packing technique I'd just completed. Sometimes I had to stifle the urge to kill him when he insisted that these books be taken with us, as they'd be "invaluable for the rest of our lives."

Because things sometimes do get lost in the mail, we decided not to send all the linens in a single box, although packing that way would have been simpler. But consolidating into one box would certainly seem to tempt fate. I even started having visions of my checking the post office every day until I couldn't take sleeping any longer without my linens, then finally breaking down and buying all new linens on St. John for some astronomical price. The box would, of course, arrive the next day. And so, the linens went into three separate boxes.

Bob's research dictated that every box should be tightly packed so that jarring would cause no movement. As long as a box was well padded and was packed so that nothing could move, nothing would break. Towels, pillows, and rolls of toilet paper and paper towels were used, along with the more traditional bubble wrap and peanut-shaped packing materials, for cushioning. An unbelievable number of small items filled every nook and cranny of each box we packed. Scissors, flashlights, Band-Aids, pens, notepads and a myriad of other items we had multiples of were split up and shipped as filler items.

I discovered that scissors could be stuffed inside the cardboard that held wrapping paper, and that the insides of a coffeepot could handle lots of extra things. But we also learned from our mistakes. Sometimes we packed a few luxury items—maple syrup packed in four different boxes, and brownie and chili mixes—to make our adjustment to local fare a little easier. Of course, we overdid it. Somewhere along the way, I had forgotten that the world now lives in a global economy. And when I couldn't lift a box after spending two hours packing it tightly, I discovered an important factor in packing: Box weight was an issue.

The television was packed without my help. Bob didn't want to hear my grief about bringing it along. We were now officially out of control.

The "Paradise Expedition" list had meanwhile evolved from a simple inventory to a complete shipping manual. A Table of Contents listed a summary of the contents of each box. Each box had its own page in the manual, with a detailed inventory and the rough box weight as measured by our trusty bathroom scale. (The Post Office even proved that our scale was accurate, right to the pound. The scale, however, we left behind.) The "Paradise Expedition" concluded with an index showing each item cross-referenced. Now I could see that the boxes on pages 3, 9, and 30 all had pool toys, while the boxes on pages 5, 14, and 26 contained aspirin. Lots of aspirin.

While we weren't moving for another five months, nevertheless I felt the time was right to inform my employer formally of my intentions. It would take time to hire or promote a replacement, and, besides, I had a small staff who deserved to be told. So I verbally resigned my position as of the end of May. It was a big step. But management was supportive, though more surprised than they should have been, since I'd been telling them for two years of my plan to move to Paradise—and, when asked, of our progress. Some of these folks would end up mailing us boxes.

At work a few weeks later, I had a meeting that included my vice president. It was to be both prophetic and fortunate for us all.

I hadn't had an opportunity to speak to this man since the conference call when I'd announced my last day. At the beginning of the meeting, he shook my hand in greeting.

"Thanks for deciding to stay," he joked.

"And thank you for having the foresight and willingness to let me telecommute from my new home," I quipped without thinking.

We both blinked, and then smiled, as the seeds of possibility grew in both our heads at the same time. Perhaps the job advice Bob and I had consistently received from USVI locals during our vacations wouldn't be needed. We'd been told to plan on each person having three jobs: One for the healthcare benefits, one to pay some bills, and one to have some fun while making some money. The trick we were told is to link various skills and hobbies together to eke out a reasonable living. It was hard to imagine. I hadn't been able to picture just one thing Bob or I could each do for a living, much less six. Telecommuting would be perfect!

After a few weeks of expedition planning, we were really getting into the rhythm of the move. Though we were waist-high in boxes and seemingly always busy packing, putting the maps up had made a psychological difference. Most boxes were packed in the living room, with the wall maps quietly coaching. Yes, I talked to them when things got tough. My cats gave me strange looks. I often packed holiday gifts in their unopened wrappers: water floats, baking utensils, towels, and so on. Our new blender was nearly the last item we packed, since we'd started experimenting with exotic drink preparations to perk us up, especially during dreary winter weekends. In six weeks we'd packed twenty-seven boxes, marked them with the intended delivery month, and inventoried and stored them in the garage. Double this number, however, remained to be pack. Packing was getting out of hand.

It took real creativity to get some of the more "difficult" items packed: an old ski bag took care of a kayak paddle, 6 tiki lamps, some table legs, and a large roll of unprimed artist's canvas. (According to Bob, this last item had traveled with us through ten years of our relationship—from apartment, to house, to roaches, to condo—and I swore I'd never seen it before.) Bob's favorite paddle wasn't worth my effort to complain, and keeping the tiki lamps was a matter of principle for both of us. One of us would take the ski bag to Florida, check it as luggage for the plane trip to St. Thomas, and pray that the airport taxi drivers on-island wouldn't think we were loco.

That February we celebrated our wedding anniversary in Stowe, Vermont, in the same suite where we'd honeymooned nine years earlier. For months we debated whether we should spend the seemingly extravagant amount of money it cost for this little vacation, but in the end we decided life was too short and we deserved to enjoy it, at least once in a while.

This wonderful inn was owned and operated by a transplanted British couple who believed strongly in personalized service and who paid close attention to the little details that made fond vacation memories. As a result of our numerous past visits, our names were forever enshrined on a small brass plaque in their adjoining pub. We wanted to say good-bye.

It was a delightful and nostalgic time. Doubtful we'd be back anytime soon, we took full advantage of our few days there. We stretched our family budget a little for cross country skiing, skating, shopping, and even a movie at the local theatre. Every afternoon we enjoyed "tea," with delicate pastries in front of a roaring fire. Bob loved his daily bubble bath in our private Jacuzzi, with a half-pint of imported draft ale by his side. I loved the Laura Ashley bedroom with all its frills and colors. Our yearly visits to the Cranford Suite were a luxury we'd be leaving behind, so we cherished these last moments more dearly than we ever had before.

* * *

Upon our return home the day after Valentine's Day, Bob and I finally had it out over who would get to be the first pioneer to Paradise. Of course, forging the trail ahead had always been Bob's aspiration. In fact, the first time I met my husband-to-be was at a health club, where he told me his name was "Ranger Bob." For the next six months, that was the only name I knew him by as he strutted through the club trying to gain the confidence to ask me out on a date. Since then, my life had become one big, uncharted adventure.

Despite—or perhaps because of—the cockroach incident, Bob insisted on a chance to redeem himself by proving that his home-hunting capabilities were real. His willingness to handle necessary but mundane tasks like setting up bank accounts, getting utilities hooked up, and fighting for a post office box, was indisputable. So we decided Bob would be our "pioneer" for the move. Bob won, and I lost. But that was okay. Bob would drive his box-filled car to Florida alone and document the trip. My travel a few weeks later would be a simple matter of following his path.

With two cats fighting for their freedom all the way.

In a Geo Tracker convertible.

Oh, yes indeed—I lost. But a single phone call I made the next day put me in much better spirits.

"Hello, I'd like to book a one-way ticket for my husband to leave the country. Can you help me?" I queried the airline representative on the phone.

"Lady, I've waited my whole career for someone to say that!" chuckled the agent.

And to think, I'd only been waiting a few years. Never mind that I felt compelled to explain I'd be following my husband a few weeks later; it made for great office cooler chitchat that day.

* * *

Bob now had firm travel plans to Paradise, with ninety days to spare before the great expedition began.

It seemed right to begin the countdown. I marked a calendar up with all of Bob's key dates: when he would give notice at work, when he would leave town, when he would need to have the car at the dock in

Florida, when he would take his final flight. And yes, it was scary not having a home ready for him in St. John, but I was beginning to have faith that it would all fall into place. For him.

Of course, none of my dates were really firm yet.

I couldn't believe how nice the folks at work were being. Their support made me work extra hard to make sure the move didn't interfere with their workload or my own. One clue that this strategy was paying off came in a form I wasn't expecting. An industry-wide convention was being held in Las Vegas in May. This week-long event was always lots of hard work, but lots of fun too. While my staff needed to attend, I anticipated that I would be absent this year. Over eighty thousand people would be there, and hotel rooms and airline tickets had to be secured early, so I sent in the company-required approval forms for my staff, but left myself off the list.

My boss noticed. To my surprise, he stopped me in the hall one day and insisted that "of course" I'd be going. I felt humbled and yet proud—and promised myself I'd do a good job. It would give me a last chance to say good-bye to many cross-country business acquaintances, while being productive for my organization right up to the end. The month of May would be very eventful.

Unfortunately, Bob didn't have the same workplace support. His company was young and known to escort people immediately out the door upon their resignation. This made it much more risky for Bob to discuss our pending move, get feedback, and make plans to leave his job gracefully. He would simply give a two-week notice and hope for the best when the time came. Only a few close work-mates knew of his plans. Meanwhile, Bob was searching *The VI Daily News* for job opportunities.

As luck would have it, a casual discussion at my workplace developed into a potential job opportunity for Bob. I had just met a business associate who was a sales representative for another company, and he told me his territory included the Caribbean and Latin America. When I told him that Bob and I were moving to St. John, he surprised me by telling me one of his distributors was Bestech, the only small computer business on St. John. I shared with him that Bob had visited their office on our last vacation, and was preparing to write to them in search of a job.

This man then shocked me with firsthand news that, indeed, the Bestech owner had been considering hiring some additional help. While he wasn't quite ready to do so, the owner had plans to hire someone in the next few months. He and the owner had been discussing the difficulty in finding good help in the area only two weeks earlier during a business trip to St. John. It was perfect. To add to it all, this wonderful man then proceeded to go one step further on his own by putting in a good word for Bob with Bestech. It was an unasked-for kindness we would never forget.

Afraid to hope, Bob quickly sent off his letter of inquiry to St. John. From that moment on, he was focused and determined to land a job in Paradise before he arrived. He consulted with newspapers, the Internet, and even the library on a regular basis. And on an even more practical note, if one of us could find a job on the island similar to our present job before we moved, then the move might qualify as a tax deduction. My retired-accountant father would be proud of us.

On a related topic: Our financial position was a constant concern at this time. I wavered from moment to moment between feeling okay with our budget and being scared that it wasn't enough. We'd collected both depressing and inspirational books on the subject. When I got paranoid, I'd pull out the book titled *How to Live Without a Salary* and remind myself that we were doing our best to cover all the bases. If anything, according to the book, we were overly concerned.

So far, I'd had to increase our estimate for our first year's living expenses three separate times. The surprising thing was that we'd been able to escalate our savings to compensate, despite our occasional extravagances. As time went on, we managed to improve on our savings almost every month. And we were both hoping to have a steady income once on-island, despite the book's comments that we could find ways to survive without them. But we were determined to be prepared for anything.

One more packing consideration was the price of shipping versus the value of items to be shipped. This guessing game added an extra challenge to our packing strategy. St. John is a small island with limited shopping for everyday items, and we'd never even tried to buy household items or small appliances in the US Virgin Islands. There are major department stores on St. Thomas, and we expected to pay more for non-sale items than we did in New England. But how much more was a pure guess on our part. Some items we packed and shipped, we later found, were a big mistake. For instance, even now we have four huge boxes of miscellaneous computer parts growing more and more obsolete every day.

Bob had his own approach to choosing what to pack. "Metal will rust. Plastic is also lighter to pack." This piece of husbandly wisdom came long after I'd already packed, sealed, and indexed the metal mixing bowls and utensils. But it did give me an idea: There would be a need to store things long-term on St. John, wouldn't there? And cardboard boxes were a favorite breeding ground for cockroaches, weren't they? And besides, they weren't waterproof (which could be a problem in the hurricane-prone Caribbean), were they? So, if we could ship items in plastic boxes now, we could reuse them as storage bins later, couldn't we? I checked with the Post Office and discovered they had no restriction against plastic containers, provided they weren't breakable. My husband can be so smart at times, it's remarkable.

As time for the move grew closer, even those friends who'd thought all along that we were crazy or wouldn't go offered to help us in our move, and we graciously accepted their change of heart as being in the natural order of things. Of course, it also mattered to us that we needed about thirty people to ship us two or three boxes each over the next few months.

As it was, logistics would be tricky, as some willing people couldn't store boxes for long. Others could store boxes, but had back problems, so they couldn't help out with any box of significant weight. Some could store items for only a month or two. It was like trying to fit together a thousand-piece puzzle. Small people would get small boxes; other, stronger ones would get the heavier boxes. Weird friends got weird boxes. We found that matching people to boxes while considering weights and delivery dates took real skill. If only there were a job on St. John for this kind of thing, Bob and I would be all set.

Out of the first sixteen people we asked to store or mail boxes (or both), only one person said "no." In fact, most people were willing to handle more than we asked them to, though we tried hard not to take advantage of their generous offers. After they'd made a couple of trips to the Post Office, I was sure they'd regret their unselfishness.

Two people had already approached us to schedule their vacations with us—one in October and one during the Christmas holiday. I hoped many would come to visit; it would be nice. But it would have been nicer if we had even a clue as to where we'd be living or whether we'd be working. Still, our "visitors" planning already made it sound like we were local residents, and the fantasy brought us warm feelings.

Two days after the outside temperature had hit an unseasonable seventy degrees and Bob and I had basked in the balcony sun, a major snowstorm hit the region, with over two feet of snow falling by dawn. Bob's company announced on the radio early in the morning that his workplace was closed for the day. Since my company rarely closed its doors, I'd hoped to work remote and avoid the thirty-seven mile commute through the snow, but I couldn't get through to my office on my computer. Bummer. Moments later, Bob called me excitedly from the living room. A miracle had occurred: My workplace, too, had decided to close shop due to the storm. I thought Bob must have been mistaken, but then the radio interrupted its broadcast for a news flash from the state governor. He was declaring a state of emergency, was calling up the National Guard to assist in clearing the roads, and urged everyone to stay home and keep off the roads for the day. There would definitely be no work for either of us that day.

Then we lost power.

Even so, we thought, we had no driveway to shovel and we had no work commitments, so losing power seemed a minor inconvenience. Besides, it gave us a chance to practice and play with our hurricane preparedness skills. We located the candles and the flashlights and the propane stove. Since it was daylight, we didn't need most of these things yet, but Bob made a huge breakfast for us on our temporary stove just for fun, and there we plotted out our day of freedom.

We vowed to do no packing or anything else resembling responsible adult activities. It was nearly the end of winter, and we were being given a magical gift of some irresponsible time together. By late morning, the storm itself had passed and the sun was shining brightly. It was a day for childish laughter and the sort of winter fun I never thought I'd experience again. Out came the cross-country skis and the last of the hot chocolate. A little cruise through the neighborhood on skis, snow angels in the parking lot, and photographs of the snow-laden trees to keep the memory alive, and I was fulfilled.

Soon a few snowballs were exchanged. My aim was just not as good as my husband's. I ducked behind my Geo Tracker. It was parked outside, my having again lost the nightly race home to be the first vehicle into the garage. Behind this sturdy fortress, I could avoid most of my husband's rapid-fire snowballs. Under attack like this, I was laughing so hard I finally ended up with tears in my eyes, even as I continued to throw snowy projectiles as fast as I could make them.

Suddenly, there was a lull in the action. I peeked over the hood of the car, only to find Bob ready with a snowball in each fist. But he was laughing so hard, his aim was off, and, Slam!, they both landed squarely on the hood of the car as I ducked around the front.

I swear that, in my euphoric state, the headlights on my Tracker winked and the front grill widened into a grin for just a split second! Of course, my vision *was* blurred, but even so, I know what I saw. Stunned by my vision of things, I called a truce.

It was a magical time, and the last snow day we'd probably experience as "nor'easters" ever. Life was good.

St. John Trivia

Long term rental properties on St. John always seem to be in high demand. In those rare instances where choices are available, the following are common questions locals ask before making their decision:

- *How badly will it rain inside the apartment when there's a rain shower outside?*
- *Will I need a 4-wheel drive vehicle to get to the apartment, and will I need a new transmission and brakes within 60 days?*
- *If it's in Cruz Bay, just how loud is the decibel level at 11pm on a Friday night? (Carnival time doesn't count)*
- *Is there a view of ANYTHING?*
- *Are there rooms bigger than the size of a bathtub?*
- *Is it screened in, or open and inviting to outside critters?*
- *How hot (sunny) and claustrophobic (like a cavern) will it be?*
- *How many goats, donkeys, roosters, pigs and dogs wander past the front door in a 24 hour period?*
- *How often does it run out of water, or if in Cruz Bay – just how grungy does the water come out of the faucet?*
- *How much personal property damage will result from a minimum-level hurricane, or worse, a mere tropical storm?*
- *Is the rent < 50% of my yearly income?*

Chapter 7

The Countdown

My husband's expedition timeline was posted in the kitchen for all to see, and his excitement over his pending travel through Americana grew daily, until it became almost unbearable for both of us. I couldn't help being a bit jealous; after all, I would only be the "cleanup" person, staying behind to settle things up and mop up behind us. And though it would only be for six weeks, those six weeks loomed in my mind like a lifetime.

Elsewhere, our on-paper savings were down a bit—the whole stock market was down-and the timing was bad for liquidating some investments for our first year's expenses. But Bob was supportive of my decisions, leaving the finances up to me. I was on the fourth notebook of reworking the numbers and felt the burden of responsibility for making things work financially, but I couldn't complain. After all, Bob trusted me, and that mattered.

Surveying our goods and finances one night, I lamented: "Why couldn't we be the type of people who need nothing more than a change of clothes and a toothbrush to keep us happy?" Sixty-five boxes of goods and books had already been catalogued, assigned to our "designated mailers," and cross-referenced in the "Paradise Expedition" manual. Ten more boxes were in process. Our condo was an obstacle course. We had to start delivering boxes to friends for storage, just to make space to walk.

Meanwhile, Bob found a classified ad in *The VI Daily News* for a job that mirrored his resume perfectly, and he responded in writing within an hour of reading the details. It was much more promising than most of the responses to "feelers" he'd been sending out. Though Bestech—known as "the computer guys" on St. John—was still a possibility (Bob had been exchanging letters and phone calls with Chuck, the manager there), nothing concrete had developed. I guessed this kind of initiative was what it would take to find jobs in Paradise.

I had also stalled in my job search, even when I saw job ads appropriate for my skills. Of course, my company had been hinting about having me continue working in some capacity—as a contractor, perhaps, or even as a part-time employee—into the foreseeable future. It wasn't something I should have been counting on, however, but I was.

As if moving weren't enough, minor medical problems began plaguing us. In March, I had a dental emergency while traveling on business: Halfway between Boston and San Antonio, Texas, I began to have serious tooth pain. I knew the signs too well; I needed a root canal. When we landed in Texas, my first phone call was to my dentist, who'd spent years rectifying the damage caused by poor childhood dental work. During the course of multiple bridges, capped teeth and multiple root canals, we'd developed a strong working—and financial—relationship between us. Living fifty miles away now back in New England hadn't changed my opinion of him. He was the best.

My call to his office brought my dentist chuckling to the phone and immediately asking, "Are you in the Virgin Islands?" Actually, he sounded a little disappointed that we hadn't moved yet, but not surprised I was traveling on business, since he'd become used to the occasional travel emergency from his favorite patient. Without hesitation, he phoned in a prescription to a nationwide drugstore chain, and by the time my business meeting started in the morning, I was full of antibiotics and hope.

My business took me onward that day to California. But despite the pills, my pain was getting worse each hour, and a very important business dinner with a vendor was scheduled for that evening. The restaurant was a five-star Epicurean delight, but even a sip of tepid water had me crying out in pain. Luckily for me, my dinner partner was late, so I shyly confided my problem to the hovering waiter, Explaining that chewing was not a viable option that night, but that I was hungry, he agreed to see what the chef could do to adapt the menu for me.

When my business associate arrived, he raised a quick eyebrow when I told him I'd pre-ordered my meal, but he apparently decided to keep his thoughts to himself. As we ate, every spoonful of pureed potatoes and squash and poached salmon (he must have thought I was on The California Baby's Diet) brought tears of pain, but business negotiations went on as planned. Needless to say—and as my associate found out gradually—I was difficult to please that night.

Sleep wasn't a consideration in my hotel room hours later. Finally, I couldn't take the pain anymore. The medication was not working. An urgent message to my dentist's answering service brought a quickly returned phone call, a confirmed diagnosis and a new prescription at a nearby pharmacy. He assured me I'd feel better by morning, and asked me to call him with an update the next afternoon. When I called the next day, my dentist said he'd located a colleague in California who was willing to see me first thing the next morning but my pain was now bearable, and I told him I was determined to fly home on schedule at daybreak. He insisted I call him when I landed in Boston, and before the weekend was over, so was the crisis: another business-related root canal completed.

Bob wasn't faring too well either. Two days after my crisis ended, Bob's podiatrist confirmed he had tendonitis between the first and second toes of his right foot. *Another week, another medical problem,* we were starting to think. His injury was the result of pushing too hard against the foot pegs in his kayak; this latest diagnosis brought Bob six weeks of physical therapy. (Of course, this didn't deter Bob from continuing his trips into the rapids: Determined to stop this recurring injury, Bob got a friend to replace the foot pegs in the kayak with a foam bulkhead created just for his boat...the boat that would *stay behind in New England!*

The weather sometimes seemed dead square against us too. My husband attempted to fly to Rochester, New York, to visit his mother. Unlike me, however, he rarely traveled by airplanet. But this was to be his good-bye visit and he wanted to go—and alone.

While the weather was fine when Bob left the condo, by the time he reached the airport it had changed dramatically, and his flight got canceled due to weather, as did the next flight. Moreover, all the other flights for the weekend were overbooked. Bob persevered at the airport, waiting on standby for later flights, but after eight hours at the Boston airport, he finally realized the situation was hopeless. Without a back-up plan, and with time running out, it would be difficult to reschedule this trip that seemed so important to Bob. It wasn't until Mothers Day that my husband managed to squeeze in a short but worthwhile visit to his mom.

And so we learned. From then on, we drew up contingency plans for every detail of our move. In fact, we even coordinated our calendars for the next sixty days, and added some "reserve" days just to handle any possible future catastrophes.

* * *

Trying to ward off any future medical problems, we both scheduled full physical exams and preventative health visits to slow down the inevitable health problems, even though our schedules were becoming overloaded.

Actually, a death in the family brought home to us our own mortality and our need to attend to priorities. While my aunt had been ailing for a long time, death, as always, came unexpectedly. Our family had never been an especially close one, and it always seemed to take a major life's event to bring us all together.

Assisting as a pallbearer, my husband at some point discovered that many of our more distant relatives didn't know we were planning to move. With our parents only slightly younger than my aunt had been, some of these relatives disapproved of our plans. It was an uncomfortable situation. But Bob and I knew that the timing would only be right when we decided it was right. And we had to make our future. Right now.

* * *

April came and went, and with it went our federal tax returns and lots of cash to pay for our investment sins. Next year, our taxes would be paid to the VI Internal Revenue Bureau. This was a little scary for us, since all the newspapers from the USVI confirmed a fact that we had only believed to be idle rumor: that many people hadn't received their refund checks yet for prior tax years. For up to three years earlier, in fact. So it was strongly advised that VI residents endeavor to owe taxes at the end of the year. Which in itself was not a pleasant alternative.

One night in late April, I had dinner with a friend and she marveled that we could make this big change in our lives without any hesitation. Hesitation, I thought? My urge to push out the actual move date sometimes seemed irresistible. Bob was scheduled to leave town in a month, but we didn't have a place to live in Paradise, any firm job prospects, or even a decent support system on St. John to take the edge off our worry. We were also handing out our personal possessions to people by the box load without any guarantee we would ever see those possessions again—and we didn't even have an address where they'd be mailed! *"Hesitation?"* I thought. Hell, I was nothing *but* a hesitation at this point.

But with time running out, we needed to move into high gear, despite these fears. About fifteen of our boxes had already been delivered to people who would later mail them to us. I promised to deliver instructions and money for shipping costs once we figured all that out. There were still empty boxes in every room in the condo waiting to be packed, and items I didn't even know we owned started appearing like magic next to those boxes. For instance, my *darling* husband suddenly had just "found" over fifty T-shirts he couldn't live without. (In fact, he had hidden them until the last moment, in hopes I wouldn't throw them away.) Having secretly packed craft items I might never use, I grudgingly gave in to the T-shirts and just counted the days until Bob left town.

The Spring West River Weekend was upon us again. This time it would be the end of a tradition for us, and we were nostalgic about the event. I enjoyed telling everyone at work that I was heading to "Jamaica" for a long weekend here at the end of a cold, dark winter. "And we don't even have to drive through Peru to get there. Peru, Vermont, that is...that's ten miles north of Jamaica, you know," I babbled. I *really* needed a long weekend away.

Meanwhile, our friend Dan was newly in love and brought his girlfriend camping with us for the first time. I wasn't too sure of her at first (after all, he *was* "our" Dan), but I knew she was a "keeper" when she shared with us one night her long-held secret desire to visit St. John someday. It was also a secret dream of Dan's.

But first they had to survive the weekend. As usual, the campground was littered with mounds of snow and pools of ice—some over eight inches thick—where the constant freezing and thawing had left its mark. The days warmed up, but the nights were still downright cold.

While the kayakers did their thing, the rest of us took day trips around the countryside. Birdie, as usual, had joined us and looked forward to at least one quality Girl's Day Out. That morning, as we warmed our toes in the car and headed out of the campground, we decided to play "the driving game" one last time, just to make exploring the back roads of Vermont a little more challenging.

That weekend we decided we could only travel in a straight line or take left turns. Right turns were not permitted. Even a "straight right," such as a right-side fork in the road when the steering wheel needn't turn, was unacceptable. Our goal was to avoid repeating any road and to return to the campsite no earlier than sunset. No maps were allowed.

By playing this version of the driving game, we covered almost every dirt road in south/central Vermont that day, talking about the past and of the future the whole way. We decided that Birdie would be traveling with me all the way to St. John as both a companion and an assistant (to help with the cats). She had lots of ideas on how we might while away the long days driving to Florida. Some made me laugh and some made me cringe, but all made me sure we'd have an adventuresome trip together. Almost before we knew how much time we'd been at this, it was late afternoon, and we were only three left turns and thirty miles away from the campground.

Birdie and I usually prepared the bulk of the traditional Saturday evening feast. But this time, another campsite friend smoked a turkey and other guests prepared all the fixings for a Thanksgiving-like feast. Someone had brought a portable boom box and continuously played a tape of bird sounds throughout the evening. Not knowing the sounds were on tape, one kayaker kept calling off the names of the birds and expressed amazement that these birds were awake and chirping so late into the night. No one told him what was really going on or that he got all the birds' names wrong. We didn't want to ruin his fun. Or our own.

The next morning, Bob's knees were killing him from climbing over the dam the day before to get his kayak to the put-in site; he wouldn't be kayaking that day. But that seemed the least of his aggravations. Within our group, the King of Omelets was preparing our traditional Sunday breakfast while friends kept stopping by the campsite offering to buy Bob's whitewater kayak (he wouldn't be using it in the islands). Each offer seemed to depress Bob more than the last, but Bob wasn't budging: He was determined to store his favorite kayak somewhere in New England until he could come back and paddle during some future vacation.

Before the day was out, we'd given away excess camping gear to everyone who stopped by. Bob took hundreds of photos that day instead of kayaking. It was the end of an era. Back home that week, each delivery of boxes to friends also meant a social visit filled with nostalgia and dreams for the future. Often we shared a beer or snack and stayed far too long. We were saying our pre-farewells to everyone one by one. Sleep was elusive.

In early May, my Las Vegas convention meant a week away from packing, and for the first time in four years, Bob didn't come along. Because he'd be giving notice at work the week before the event, he didn't ask his company to send him. All week at the convention, as I met with business associates, I attempted to establish continuity for my staff, who would carry on after I was gone. I had little time for sleep, and called home only twice. Unsolved expedition details haunted my husband, and I realized being removed from the scene of the ongoing crime carried with it some real advantages.

Bob, too, was focused on work, but in a very different way. Ever since Bob learned that his company's policy was to escort people to the front door when they quit, he'd hoped that this would indeed happen to him so he could have two extra weeks of free time before his move. No such luck. Bob gave his notice, but because he was responsible for maintaining the company's phones, voice-mail, PCs, networks, and so on, the company approached the situation sanely, and Bob's hopes of extra free time were dashed. So while I was in Las Vegas, he was working long hours.

Actually, his work mates thought he was a lucky guy to be so needed and to be still heading off to Paradise. They even threw him a going-away party. Meanwhile, Bob was still pursuing job opportunities, and while under consideration for a couple of jobs, nothing was firm.

Nevertheless, the final phase of expedition planning was upon us. I started a list of items Bob would need to purchase on St. Thomas once he had a place for us to live. Heavy items like frying pans and fragile ones like everyday drinking glasses could be bought on St. Thomas for prices comparable to mainland prices—when on sale.

Avoiding distractions while maintaining a good work attitude took effort, but continued to pay off for me. Talks continued about keeping me as an employee. Meanwhile, a telephone company was running a series of TV commercials focusing on telecommuters—people work from the beach while performing typical high-tech white-collar jobs. It seemed that everyone we knew had seen these commercials and assumed they depicted my future lifestyle. The commercials certainly did depict a glamorous life-style, but I suspected the reality of this sort of arrangement might differ significantly from the commercial. Even working part-time for my company, I envisioned regular long business trips, first by car, then by ferry, then by a taxi van—all just to get to the airport and the start of any business trip. I also worried that these commercials might negatively impact my company's decision about my future.

I often found myself holding my breath, given the uncertainty we faced. Almost every moment was stressful. It didn't help when people ran up to me at work asking if I was ready to move, or if I were counting down the days; that just made me more nervous. Having a place to live, a job, a local bank account, insurance, or even a clue would make life easier. Our faith in the future would have impressed a nineteen-year-old, but few others.

Bob's thoughts were not on these matters, however; he was consumed with his trip to Florida, the process of delivering his car to the barge and boxes to the shipping company, and every petty detail in between. Contrary to the feelings that I'd previously had about losing out to Bob on the "pioneer" issue, I was beginning to realize there was a big advantage in traveling a month later than Bob. Most importantly, Bob's experiences would simplify my own trip, especially since traveling with the cats meant lots more stress for everyone in the car.

Our next step was to secure an Internet address with a local service provider in the USVI as of June 1st. This was a major accomplishment, as communicating with others via e-mail would surely cut down on our phone bill costs, even with the added monthly ISP costs. Bob planned to take his computer to Florida and then mail it to St. John so it would be at the Post Office when he arrived on island. Constant communication would be ours! We started giving out our address to technically inclined friends immediately, which eased our own minds about being able to reach them quickly, if nothing else.

Just days before he was scheduled to leave, we prepacked Bob's car with boxes earmarked for the trip. Our friends laughed at this, saying we'd taken planning to the ridiculous. It was a good thing we did, though, since we found that the car couldn't handle the number of boxes we'd thought it would. Bob had also packed all his clothes into a big canvas bag planned as one piece of his airline luggage allowance. But even with his arms strengthened by years of kayaking, he couldn't lift the bag more than a few inches off the ground. The whole luggage plan needed rethinking.

My own pre-moving checklist was growing. I added to the list: close our bank accounts and utilities, have our mail forwarded, pay the bills, throw out what we weren't shipping, get the cats vaccinated and health certificates that reflected that. Now all I had to do was prep for my own trip to Florida with the cats, survive my last days of work, say my last good-byes, and figure out whatever we'd forgotten to do. It seemed like this move would never end.

* * *

As our schedule closed in around us, I found a St. John's bulletin board on the Internet and left a message to the world saying we were moving and desperate and asking for opinions and advice. Amazingly, within twenty-four hours we heard from someone in Arizona, of all places, who had lived on St. John off and on most of his life. He had great advice for us—and even a lead on an apartment and other tips. While the apartment didn't pan out, his insights on a St. John long-term rental agency did. For us, this e-mail marked the point when our luck started to change consistently for the better.

Within days we'd sent off a check to the rental agency with our deposit for a two-bedroom apartment (no longer did we consider it crazy to rent sight unseen). The only downside was that we couldn't secure a lease: While our search had uncovered one viable apartment, the owner wanted the option of moving in himself for the months of December and January. Still, it was workable. He was willing to let us rent the apartment on a month-to-month basis, which would buy us time to find another place for the long term, without concern about an initial place to live. We felt pretty confident about finding an alternative abode by then.

Bob decided not to wait to start our own business in the USVI. Instead, we chose the name Paradise Expeditions, to give the business "substance." It was a prudent decision. Apparently, as a business we would get a post office box much quicker than a residential customer would. So what if our business was undefined?

As I said, our luck was changing. "The Computer Guys" on St. John contacted Bob and told him they would put him to work immediately upon his arrival. Now he was psyched, though how it would all work out he didn't know and was afraid to ask. But it was employment of some sort and that's all that mattered. My employer confirmed I'd be working at least part time for my company, in "some" capacity. I kept my fingers crossed that I could do so as an employee rather than a contractor, but I didn't push the issue: As yet, my company did not have telecommuters that I knew of (except in field sales positions), and I hoped they would let me be an experiment for future work trends. Bob and I were excited that our dreams were becoming reality, and we really didn't care what form that reality took.

Now plans would call for Bob to drive directly to Florida without delay, eight to ten hours per day, with a day to rest once the car and its contents were safely on the barge to the USVI. The extra day would cover any possible travel emergencies along the way.

Despite our satisfaction with our automobile shipping arrangements, we found out our shipping company was located in an unsafe area in southern Florida, according to two local taxi companies. Neither would agree to pick Bob up from the shipping office to drive him to a car rental office. Finally, Bob found a car rental company that would meet him at the barge office and drive him to their rental office to do paperwork and get temporary wheels.

Though our major concerns were suddenly being addressed in a better way than we'd hoped, we were both, I think, expecting the inevitable disaster. What if one of the cars had a major catastrophe on its way south? What if one of our pets got sick or lost? What if we lost our luggage or cash? As our plans took shape before our eyes, our imaginations compensated for our good luck with unknown disasters lurking in the future. And though our friends were convinced by this time that we were huge risk takers...if only they knew! Caution was quickly becoming our middle name.

Bob made sure he had multiple notarized copies of our car titles; we'd been told we'd need them to get our cars onto the island, get insurance and get them registered. And we needed those plates: That old, faded USVI license plate on my office wall had kept me focused and motivated in moments of doubt for the past two years. It was a symbol of our dream. The new plates would be a symbol of our dream *realized*. At my own going away party held by my office, I bequeathed that license plate as a good-luck charm to someone who had his own dream.

My friends gave me a small gift-wrapped conch shell I'd brought them as a souvenir from St. John years ago, so I could return it and have "Good Jumbies"—the island version of "good karma." They also chipped in and bought me a beautiful gold bracelet made up of golden seashells linked together, as a sort of retirement gift. I felt overwhelmed by their generosity. And when my boss sprung the news at the party that I wasn't really leaving, that I was going to telecommute and all, some wise-aleck asked out loud, "So what do we have to give you so you'll really go?"

That last night before Bob left town should have been a quiet time together. Instead, long into the night we packed and repacked his car, trying to maximize the number of heavy and odd-shaped boxes and goods that he could take. Boxes that couldn't be mailed due to postal restrictions had to either go in one of our cars or stay behind. Tensions and frustrations ran high that night. Fifteen phone call interruptions from those wanting to say a last good-bye didn't help. We fought over petty matters that were forgotten before the arguments waned. Bob's exacting approach to the final packing was unreasonable and I could do nothing right that night. Even the cats avoided us. It was one last night of hell before Paradise.

St. John Trivia

The highest point on St. John is Bordeaux Mountain, with a peak that's 1277 feet above sea level. Folks living in the Bordeaux area generally report temperature readings that are 5 - 8 degrees lower than those reported in Cruz Bay. In contrast, the salt pond between Salt Pond Bay and Trunk Bay is one foot below sea level while the trench in the ocean between St. John and St. Croix is more than 12,000 feet deep.

In 1998 a rare event occurred on St. John . . . a hailstorm. Despite the calm sunny day, the hail fell for fifteen minutes on the Ram's Head Trail. Tourists, returning from Ram's Head Point, the southernmost point on St. John, were caught in the sudden barrage. It hails on St. John about once every hundred years.

Chapter 8

The Paradise Expedition

Very early the next morning Bob left on his one-way trek to Florida. It was anticlimactic for me. I felt left behind, and looked forward to Bob's promised nightly phone calls to bring me news of his progress. Six more weeks in New England stretched endlessly in front of me. My office workload was heavy, but my mind and my heart were on the road to Florida. I should have taken the day off. It was the last day before the Memorial Day weekend and the thought of spending it cleaning and packing while Bob had real life adventures was depressing. A couch, a bed and other furniture had to be given away to new homes. The checklist of moving tasks boggled my mind. Since last minute decisions were all mine now, I intended to be a superwoman and do them all in one weekend.

That afternoon I gave away the last of the dried flowers I'd been using as wall hangings. That last hanging was symbolic. The sampler included seven bunches of flowers from my last garden a year earlier, and giving it away was like saying good-bye to an integral part of my psyche. Looking forward, then, a flora and fauna book bought as part of our research for the move proved how little I knew about plants indigenous to St. John. I needed to see and touch them first-hand to make any sense of these strange plants. With no real experience or understanding of my new environment, I'd be starting all over.

Bob's first day took him only as far as Delaware. A six-mile backup on the New Jersey Turnpike had slowed him down. Since he'd decided to take an uncharacteristic risk and not make advance hotel reservations, Bob checked the accommodations board at each turnpike rest area starting mid-afternoon. Luckily he found a single motel under his fifty-dollar-per-day lodging budget and secured their last available room for the night. Bob was stressed out when he phoned that evening.

"Nothing exciting," was Bob's judgment of his first day on the road. "But the hotel budget is making it hard to find a reasonable place to sleep."

It was a stilted conversation, as I tried to pry the details of his day out of him. Traffic, weather, pit stops, and plans for tomorrow were all on my mind. I reassured him that the travel budget was merely a guideline and that his safety and comfort were much more important than a few dollars. He sounded relieved and promised to keep a journal of his thoughts and activities and to phone me every night. With that, Bob ended the conversation.

I said nothing about the fifteen trips I'd made to the condo's dumpster that evening, having made some progress in whittling down our worldly possessions. Nor did I tell him my decision to take a break and relax that weekend. Only fourteen hours into it, and I could not live up to my Superwoman image.

Each night I impatiently waited for the phone to ring and plotted Bob's progress on a map. The farther away he traveled, the more easily he shared his thoughts and experiences. Bob related mostly trivial and somewhat corny tidbits, but I ate them up. Sudden changes in the smells out his car window in southern Virginia, where late spring flowers were in bloom, and his descriptions of the wildflower patches in the Carolinas, were intermingled with the restaurants Bob visited and the details of each meal. Where he dined meant little to me, though, as I'd have two cats in my follow-up expedition and would be limited to fast foods during daytime hours. Still, I encouraged him as I listened closely for some gem of information that would be useful for my own trip south—like road conditions and detours and where and why he'd decided to bed down each night.

Bob's arrival in Florida marked a change in the tone of his nightly calls. Anticipation was growing in him as he neared this milestone. I sent an overnight package to the hotel he'd booked in Ft. Lauderdale. Our new bank on St. John had sent automatic teller machine cards to my parents' address rather than holding them for him on St. John, as we'd requested. I also included some minor items Bob had left behind (and probably didn't need). Bob's audible pleasure at the thought of getting a package from home turned me to mush. In payment, I retrieved some small items of Bob's that had been destined for the garbage bin that night as a gesture of goodwill and thanks.

As we'd planned, I called my landlady to inform her we'd be moving earlier than expected, and offered to split the remaining rent on the lease. Since she'd been adamant about the one-year lease, I expected the worst. But she said that she and her husband had just sold their home and she'd be willing to let us off the hook and return our rental deposit if I could be out in mid-June. That was less than three weeks away, and meant I'd then be homeless for two weeks before my own expedition began. Why did I squander that long holiday weekend by taking a break? I would be paying for it dearly now. Life became more chaotic.

In Ft. Lauderdale, Bob's expedition was also taking a somewhat more traumatic turn. In attempting to check into the wrong hotel before discovering there were four with similar names in town, he'd ended up paying far more than his budget allowed him. Worse still, he hadn't worn much sunscreen during the trip, and his left arm was now beet red.

The sticker shock of staying for once in a fine hotel unsettled Bob. It took an extravagant bottle of his favorite wine and a four-course dinner to calm him. It was well deserved, Bob assured me. Besides, it gave him the energy after dinner to empty essentials from his car, unpack, and begin consolidating and throwing out excess baggage: True to form, Bob had continued to collect travel literature throughout his trip, along with newspapers, comfort foods, etc. Once cleared out, the trash filled all the wastebaskets in the room, and he still had maps, schedules, and notes strewn across his bed when I called.

Bob told me he was trying to iron out the confusing logistics for the next day. Most major roads were under construction in the Ft. Lauderdale area, and he hadn't a clue how to find the barge company. The ninety-degree temperature and sun that day had made the sunburn on his arm even worse despite his using an SPF-45 sunscreen. To add to his woes, I informed Bob that his flight and departure time from Miami to St. Thomas had been changed; the airline had left a phone message on our soon-to-be-packed answering machine earlier that day. So when I told Bob I'd be homeless soon, I got little sympathy in return. The only New England news that interested him at this point was that I'd sent him an overnight package.

My husband survived that next day, and to his credit even created a hand-drawn map showing the way to the barge company, complete with notes on all the detours, so my trip would go a little smoother. He transferred all the gear he would need immediately in St. John to the rental car, and made a test drive to the airport. That night, Bob was excited when he called. Within twenty-four hours he'd be in St. John and, hopefully, calling me from our new apartment.

The next day my thoughts were with Bob, and I wished I could read his mind. Each time I looked at a clock, I thought of his progress. He was on the way to the airport...on the plane to St. Thomas...then on a shuttle van crossing the island. I tracked him in my thoughts as he arrived at the ferry dock in Red Hook and found a porter to help with his abundance of baggage. By my next glance at a clock, I knew he'd arrived, found another porter, and was likely in the process of renting a car. From that point forward, I lost any sense of what Bob was doing and said a prayer of thanks that he'd gone first. Did he find the apartment, or his new boss? Would he call me that night?

That night Bob did call, very agitated and with a lot of phone static. He'd arrived on St. John without incident. But just when my visions had started to blur, so had his progress. His euphoria had been quashed.

"How's Paradise?" I asked innocently enough.

"It's not what we expected," he said. "There was a little mix-up with the apartment."

"What happened?" I asked.

"First, there's more. I went to the Post Office and no packages have arrived." Bob sounded desperate. "Chuck said I sent them the wrong way and not to expect them for four to six weeks," Bob mourned.

Who, I wondered, was Chuck? And which boxes? Bob had sent some boxes for immediate use before he'd left New England, including his computer (so we could e-mail each other) and basics for the apartment like bed sheets and pillows. Before I could react, he continued.

"The place needs cleaning. There's no toilet paper, sheets, towels or anything, and no screens in the windows, and I'm getting eaten alive," he growled.

"Is the..."

"I don't have time to talk," he said before I had time to finish. "The phone isn't working right, and I had to borrow a neighbor's...uh, Will's...cell phone...to call you."

"What are you going to do?" I cut in.

"I don't know yet. Look, I'll try to call you tomorrow if I can find a phone. I'm going to have to sleep on the couch tonight, and it's pretty raunchy. I've got to go. I'll call you when I can." And with that, all I heard was a dial tone and I was cut off.

I hardly slept at all that night worrying about Bob and wondering why we chose to arrive separately. I felt helpless and marooned. Two days later, though, the whole story came together.

Bob's final leg to St. John was uneventful. No one questioned the ski bag filled with tiki lamps and other assorted items. The rental property manager met Bob at the ferry dock and helped carry the luggage down the block to his van, as the porter would only carry baggage to the end of the pier. Along the way, Bob was told a tale of woe about the cleaning of the condo—or lack thereof. The property manager had hired a guy to do it the day before, but apparently he'd gone to the wrong place. Bob had to make do until someone could clean it the next day.

The van was parked next to the Post Office, which perked Bob right up. He asked for a little time to get his bearings before proceeding to the apartment, which the property manager willingly granted, as he had some errands to run himself. Bob made a quick stop inside the Post Office to pick up the boxes of emergency gear he'd sent ahead before he'd left New England. There was no mail of any kind waiting for him at General Delivery. He then sought out Chuck, his new employer at Bestech, to say he'd arrived and was ready for work. Then Bob mentioned the lack of boxes waiting for him at the Post Office. Chuck then gave Bob the sad news that the boxes of emergency goods and the computer probably wouldn't arrive for another month, and suggested that everything be sent priority mail if we wanted to see it within a couple of weeks of mailing. Bob was told to take a couple of days to get settled in and then to contact him again to start work.

Back in the van, Bob and his host proceeded to the edge of town towards the apartment. The roads were steeper than Bob remembered. As the van climbed a hill known as Jacob's Ladder, he was told that it's a good thing we had four-wheel drive vehicles, as the grade made it difficult to drive up when it rained.

I can only imagine Bob's state of mind by the time he crested the last hill to the new apartment. It was quite large, with a fantastic view overlooking Cruz Bay and St. Thomas in the distance. Built into a steep hill, the entire front provided unobstructed views quieted only by the floor-length shutters that acted as doors. But there were no screens to keep bugs out, and keeping out rain by closing windows meant keeping out air. The apartment was filthy, with furniture jumbled together and trash left over from a previous tenant.

Bob kept his thoughts to himself, he later told me. I think he was in a state of shock. He asked for and got a ride back to town under the guise of picking up some essentials before the stores closed for the night. Bob bought a beer to calm his nerves, rented a car, then purchased drinking water, paper towels, toilet paper and cleaning detergent. Nowhere could he locate a place to purchase sheets and towels.

But after the borrowed telephone and quick collect call home to me, things got a little better. The new neighbors took pity on Bob and loaned him a towel and a sheet for the couch and gave him some wine to drink to allow him to mellow out before he headed off to a restless sleep. While Bob was mellowing, of course, I was getting hysterical. I quickly located and moved two big boxes into my car. Inside were items we'd packed—fortunately—months ago, including linens and dish detergent and lots of other things he could use now. The next morning I rushed to the Post Office and paid a fortune to make sure his life would get better by Monday.

Meanwhile, as luck would have it, "St. John Saturday" coincided with Bob's trip to Cruz Bay that next morning, so it was livelier than normal and Bob had an opportunity to touch base with local organizations and businesses and ponder on how he would eventually fit in.

That first day, he managed his first success: a Post Office box in our new company name. In one day! This would become a local legend, as everyone told Bob that day.

Other changes came quickly. One night at the apartment had convinced my husband that I would not be happy living there, so he began searching for an alternative abode that same afternoon. My constant reassurances that I trusted his judgment in this area had paid off for me, while they tormented Bob. He checked at a place called

Connections, at the newspaper, and even at the dry cleaner's looking for leads. Bob made appointments to visit available places the next day. Meanwhile, the apartment we were renting was being cleaned. By the time Bob returned in late afternoon it was better. He bought a bottle of wine as a neighborly thank you for the help he'd received the night before and passed time with our new neighbors, gathering ideas on how to get settled in quickly.

Bob called from a pay phone that night after dinner, much more upbeat than the night before. It was obvious that he was more relaxed. By the end of that conversation, I was once more glad he had gone to St. John before I arrived with the cats in tow. Bob would be very busy for the next few days as he tried to settle in and prepare for our arrival. I suggested that he take some time off and go to the beach (after looking for apartments the next day!) and that he should skip our nightly call the next night. He obviously needed a break and some time to enjoy the nicer side of Paradise.

When we finally talked that Monday evening, Bob's spirits were high. He'd found a new place for us to live. It was in a section called Century Hill, which I couldn't find on any map, but when he told me he could see the rental villa we'd rented on our last vacation from the front door, I was sold. In those two days, my wonderful husband had not only looked at four apartments, and secured one he thought I'd like, but he also managed to talk the original property rental manager into refunding all our monies, including the deposit. In-between, Bob got his bank ATM card activated, went to a job interview on St. Thomas (just in case the job on St. John didn't work out), relaxed at a beach, and bought food and supplies. He'd even taken pictures of the "old" apartment and the new one he'd be moving into, paid a fortune to have the film developed immediately, and had them sent Express Mail in a care package which would arrive at my office by Wednesday. And, he'd gotten his laundry done!

The two boxes I'd sent Express Mail that were waiting for him at the Post Office made his day. Wow! What a difference a couple of days made.

Back in New England, everything began moving forward with more speed than I thought possible. While Bob acclimated to St. John that week, my time was spent ridding myself of our worldly possessions. Now that I had an address to mail to, I put our shipping plan in action. Each person who was to mail boxes to us received an envelope along with their boxes. In the envelope was a one-page flyer with our mailing address and step-by-step instructions on what to do and when. The envelopes also included blank insurance forms for the Post Office; hard, cold cash to cover the shipping and insurance; and a detailed list of the box contents, including shipping weight, requested insurance amount, and total cost. I even included a stamped, self-addressed return envelope for them to use to mail us the Post Office receipts. I was leaving nothing to chance.

Every day before heading to work, I loaded my car with boxes and came home empty-handed. Though I loved our friends, each delivery of boxes and envelopes required socializing as well, which at this point I just didn't have time for. Convinced that I'd still be delivering boxes after the deadline to vacate the condo, I felt rushed. As a result, I did not enjoy each visit as much as I'd have liked.

The care package from Paradise lifted my spirits dramatically, though only temporarily. In it were Bob's travel logs from his trip down the Eastern Seaboard to Florida, a homemade street map to help me through the car-to-barge process, the photos he'd promised, and even tourist literature to give out to friends. With newfound purpose, I emptied the condo, room by room. As I reduced each one to the bare essentials of furniture, I cleaned one last time. Each night I was dog-tired, and anxious for Bob's call from Paradise to keep me motivated. My second week continued like the first.

Then it was moving time. I'd taken care of shutting down the utilities and the telephone and had made sure to have all our mail forwarded to St. John. Bob and I talked every evening about the logistics.

I was now down to those three pieces of furniture—a bed, a dresser and a couch. Once my bed was taken by its new owner, I moved to the couch, but soon that was gone too, and by the last night, I slept on the floor with a pillow and a featherbed that would go to a new home that next day. I'd managed to get all the box deliveries done, and in the process had personally mailed twenty or so boxes to St. John myself. Most would go by parcel post, which meant I'd be in St. John before they arrived.

While I was closing down our life in New England, Bob was preparing the household for our arrival, ordering propane for the stove and getting the telephone connected. He even bought cat food and kitty litter, though we wouldn't be arriving for three more weeks. He cleaned and cleaned and finally figured out the new apartment had only one real drawback: The amount of dust that accumulated in our condo in New England in a whole month was the amount that gathered in a single day at our place in St. John.

Bob adjusted to the rhythms of island life as he worked his way through a constantly growing list of things to do. He picked up his car in St. Thomas, got it registered (along with a new VI drivers' license), filled our apartment pantry with essentials, got a library card, and made neighborhood friends. In between, Bob began work as a contractor for Chuck at Bestech, the computer company at the lumberyard on St. John.

Up in New England I was staying with Birdie while I reconciled myself to the life we'd left behind. Our friends were now blessed (burdened?) with many of our life's possessions, while I had only two suitcases of clothes, two sets of travel supplies for the cats, and two tool chests we couldn't bear leaving behind. There was barely room left in my car for Birdie and her two pieces of travel gear.

Space for the two cats was a problem immediately. It would be dangerous to let them loose in the vehicle, but their travel carriers were too small and restrictive for the long days of travel ahead of us. I needed a way to separate the front and the back of the car so they could have a little room to move around without causing a disaster. After numerous attempts, I hit on an idea that worked.

I bought duct tape, lots of Velcro, glue, and bird netting (the kind you use to keep birds out of your ripening garden) and enlisted the help of my niece to put it all together. The netting was doubled over and the edges reinforced with duct tape. This doubly strong barrier was taped into place from the floor up, along the brace behind the front seats that held the doors in place. The top third was held in place with Velcro, so I could get into the back to reach the cats when necessary. A waterproof tarp covered the luggage and a soft blanket on top became our cats' bed for the duration. As she surveyed our work, my niece suggested that she could squeeze in the back to baby-sit the cats. It was with great reluctance that I nixed that idea. As it was, Birdie and I would be claustrophobic for the whole trip.

And finally, we were off! My phase of the Paradise Expedition moved out with hardly a hitch.

The travel logs Bob mailed me were a constant source of valuable information, with their warnings of construction areas and misleading signs. Challenges for Birdie and myself came from very different sources. Unlike Bob before me, I'd attempted to make reservations for each stop along the route, but found in some cases that no hotel or motel would allow animals. This was true of our first night's destination: We scouted for alternatives at rest area bulletin boards along the way until we gave up, and ended up just sneaking them into our pre-registered "no pets allowed" room for the night.

All this sneaking took a well-coordinated effort, with Birdie acting as lookout while I closed the car doors behind her, opened the top of the netting, and coaxed the little darlings into their travel bags. That first time getting them in was difficult, but I was smarter than my cats. With the bags' air vent flaps down, it appeared from a distance that Birdie and I were carrying only ordinary gym bags. At least that was true if one didn't look too closely and notice the bags seemed to have lives of their own. We felt like criminals as we sneaked the cats through the hallway, but at the same time we got sort of a kick out of it after a long, boring day of driving. Cleaning the room before we left, we hoped no one would find out we'd broken any rules. We even used temporary, disposable litter boxes while in the room, and threw the used ones out each morning in the closest outside garbage bin we could find.

As we traveled, it was difficult to stop during the day, since we couldn't leave the cats in the car given the heat wave that covered the entire eastern seaboard during our trip. At rest stops, Birdie and I took turns going inside places, with the other acting as cat chaperone and entertainer. Finding places to eat lunch was also a challenge, and we usually limited ourselves to fast food along the highway.

We made a few wrong turns when we strayed off Interstate 95 for a change of scenery, but that made the drive all the more interesting. I don't think we added any mileage at all to the trip by detouring from our AAA-recommended route, though the back roads took longer to navigate. But the countryside away from the Interstate was worth it.

While we worked our way south, I imagined Bob was contemplating the future for both of us. It's true we both had jobs, but his was only panning out as a part-time endeavor to start, and my long term prospects as a telecommuter seemed slim. Using an on-island perspective, Bob researched any idea that came his way, from becoming a full-time artisan, to opening a bar, to network consulting. He continued writing his travel logs, which took on a distinctly philosophical tone. In them, he toyed with creative writing as he attempted to describe local sunsets. "Describing a sunset is probably better left to some talented writer," he'd write, "but I'll take a stab at it. There is an interplay of many different shades of gray. There are gaps in the gray clouds where light grays pour through. All the while the silhouette of the islands are in the picture." For my husband this was pure poetry. His travel logs continued, with pages detailing cultural differences he observed between the many layers of locals and tourists he saw on St. John. We were in two different universes.

Meanwhile, for Birdie and I, time flew by. In South Carolina we couldn't resist the signs for unbelievably low warehouse prices on anything we could imagine right off the highway. A bathroom break turned into a quick shopping spree, as we added beach towels and snacks and even new bath towels to my already overloaded luggage. It was a good thing that we didn't dare leave the cats unattended; because of this, our individual shopping sprees were limited to five-minutes. And finally, there was no space left in the car.

Speaking of cats: They were simply wonderful traveling companions. They stayed in the back of the car all the time we were traveling, and although they took turns complaining for the first hour and the last hour of every day, in-between they were no trouble at all.

Except for that little incident in Georgia, of course. My outdoor adventurer wanted out. He'd noticed a small gap in the bird netting that separated their temporary quarters from the front seat, not more than an inch wide. I was cruising down the highway and had just passed a slower vehicle. That's when he made his desperate break for freedom. Suddenly there was a shadow on my left side, while on my right Birdie screamed.

Turning my head, I came face to face with my adventurer as he attempted to squeeze his huge body through the tiny gap in the mesh. I had no choice. With one hand, I firmly grasped his head and pushed him backwards as I attempted to safely steer the car onto the highway shoulder. The cat was as shaken as I was. A little more duck tape convinced him that I was in charge and there would be no escapes to freedom before the expedition was over. The other cat—my little princess—helped the outdoor adventurer over his disappointment by licking his face for a while, and both were on their best behavior from that point onward, though Birdie spent the afternoon constantly looking over her shoulder to make sure everyone was in the right place.

Nightly phone calls to Bob updated our progress as he tried to provide remote advice for our next day's adventures. Meanwhile, new neighbors were eager to answer any questions Bob had about island life. Bob uncovered obstacles to local gardening. Undeterred, he went to St. Thomas and bought big bags of soil and flowerpots in anticipation of my arrival. He had much faith in my ability to overcome any problems.

On a different front, new friends filled Bob in on past hurricanes, swimming pool maintenance problems, island folklore, and even car maintenance and food buying strategies. During odd hours, my husband managed to join the St. John Yacht Club and the St. John Action Committee. He signed on as a volunteer for the VI National Park and even became a member of the newly forming St. John Volunteer Rescue Squad.

Finally, Birdie and I arrived in Florida feeling a great sense of accomplishment—and with a half day of free contingency time on our hands! During that time, we sent our automobile on its way to St. John, secured a rental car, and positioned the cats to enjoy their "pets allowed" suite for a luxurious two-night stay.

Birdie suggested we spend the morning on a gambling boat so she could play a little blackjack and win some money to buy tourist trinkets on St. John. The thought made me feel naughty, but I needed that. We weren't at all prepared for the fun we had. Many senior citizens took advantage of these daily cruises-to-nowhere, and the prices just couldn't be beat. For just more than the price of breakfast, we enjoyed a buffet with live music and were "adopted" by some of the cruise regulars, who passed on gaming tips to us novices. Birdie won enough money to pay for the cruise and all the souvenirs she wanted on St. John. A whole half day without the cats was a vacation in itself, but still I was panicked as we rushed back to the hotel—only to find the little darlings sleeping the day away.

Looking forward to our flight, I was determined there would be no problems at the airport. My cats were each bought a ticket that allowed them to travel as carry-on baggage under our seats. I'd convinced our veterinarian to provide me with a tranquilizer for each cat, and I prayed that the Prozac he prescribed would be effective. Surprisingly, they calmed down nicely just before we boarded the plane and stayed that way until we landed on St. Thomas. Still, they managed to stay awake and aware through the whole ordeal.

In fact, our trip went so smoothly that our arrival on St. Thomas was a letdown of sorts. I kept looking for the local Health Inspector to check our kitties' paperwork and to welcome them to the Island. but no one approached us, and I refused to ask anyone for help, deciding to leave well enough alone.

It was a long, hot walk to the baggage area. When we finally arrived, Bob was waiting there for us, but he was hard to recognize. Normally well groomed, his hair hadn't been cut since Massachusetts and he looked tired. He was glad to see us in one piece. But he saved most of his attention for the cats.

They remembered him immediately and wanted out of their cages to sit in his lap. So while we waited patiently for our bags to depart the plane, my island husband sat against a far wall and sang softly to his pets. He looked like a native St. Johnian already.

Having our own car to ride across St. Thomas from the airport was a unique treat. But I was impatient to get to St. John and hardly noticed the sites Bob pointed out. He'd already found all the supermarkets and department stores and the shortcuts across the island to the ferry dock in Red Hook.

However, there was an unexpected downside to this personalized tour. As Bob swung the car around and backed it to within an inch of another vehicle on the barge to St. John, I started to realize that this occasional part of island life would not be glamorous. We were boxed in on all sides, with just enough room to open our car doors and stand on the deck. To add to matters, there was also a garbage truck on the barge, providing "atmosphere". This was not a pleasant way for Birdie to see St. John for the first time.

"Follow me," said my husband, with a cat bag in tow. He proceeded to the back of the barge where a steel staircase led to a small operations deck. Up he went, without a backward glance. Birdie and I had little choice but to follow.

I went slowly, however, as I was worried about losing my grip on the cat bag in my arms and dropping one of our precious cargoes overboard. Reaching the top, I walked around to the side, where Bob met me at a door. "Let's bring the cats inside here. It's air conditioned and they'll be happier." I got the distinct impression that I was merely an afterthought.

As the boat hit open water, I went outside. Birdie was already there. "This is great," she said. "It's nothing like coming over on the regular ferry," I insisted, wanting her to understand how nice the trip to St. John normally was. "The ferries take you into a beautiful dock in Cruz Bay. It's so picturesque. But on this thing, we'll end up on the other side of the bay, in the Creek with the commercial vehicles, where it's crowded and not very pretty." Birdie's first impressions mattered to me, and I was sure she was disappointed.

"That's okay. This way is fine," she said. "You know what? I feel like Barbra Streisand in that movie on the tug boat in New York." When she stretched out her arms and let out a powerful note, I had to laugh. It would be okay. This was my best friend, and she was trying to ease my concerns.

It worked.

Chapter *9*

Together At Last

An hour later, after leaving the barge and making our way onto St. John, our vehicle rounded the last switchback and crested the ridge to our new apartment. By this point, Birdie's hands appeared to be permanently glued to the seat in front of her. The road was steep and rutted but Bob didn't seem to notice as he rushed to get us all home. I promised my friend she'd get used to the roads, but her teeth were clenched shut and only her eyes shouted her doubt.

Miraculously, our parking space was on a rare plot of flat ground. We gingerly exited the vehicle and tried to get the circulation back in our legs and arms from the cramped ride while stalling the next big surprise that might be in store for us: the apartment!

Both Birdie and I were skeptical, despite the photographs Bob had sent us. After his last attempt at apartment hunting and the roach hotel he'd chosen in Massachusetts, who could blame us? While Bob held open the door with pride, I could see it in his eyes. I knew he knew I'd be hard to impress.

But it turned out to be a nice place, if one ignored the high degree of warmth inside, the stacked boxes everywhere, and the odd collection of furnishings the landlord had provided, albeit gratis. The apartment was indeed furnished, as advertised, but the decor was "early college" at best. The bottom floor consisted of a tiny kitchen with hurricane-scarred appliances, a small bathroom, a dining/living area with a cathedral ceiling leading to sliding doors and a concrete, railed porch. There was also a small guestroom (without a closet) that had a sliding door that opened to the other end of the porch.

A somewhat filthy spiral stairway led down to a postage-stamp-sized swimming pool in the moisture-starved garden area below. Upstairs, a loft area opened up to the small master bedroom, with a tiny balcony just off it and another bathroom. A light layer of dust covered every-thing, and the windows were filthy. But at least these windows had real glass in them, in contrast to the first apartment. After a quick tour, I announced to no one in particular, "It has potential." Birdie gave me a long look, but tagged on a supportive smile; she knew when to stay out of our domestic affairs.

Bob had taken the rest of the day off from work and spent the next few hours filling me in on details of our new life, which I proceeded to forget within minutes, since I had no reference points for the myriad of names and places he described. Besides, the household disarray kept dragging my thoughts back to more immediate matters. And I noticed how Birdie spent the following hours hiding in the crowded, shabby guestroom. Perhaps we were all just overtired, I thought groggily. Everyone was asleep by nine o'clock. The cats both wisely chose the guestroom and Birdie for the night.

* * *

My first full day in Paradise was to be a vacation day for everyone. It was July 4th, and St. John Carnival activities were at their peak. We intended to avoid the tourist Carnival at all costs, since I longed for quiet solitude after frantic months of moving. Bob, anxious to go to the beach as always, was very willing to accommodate. And so our first morning was absolutely perfect. He drove us directly to the north shore beaches and avoided town completely. We passed the fondly remembered plywood fork-in-the-road sign on the way, and even made a few stops for Birdie to take photos.

Birdie was then initiated into the world of snorkeling at Francis Bay on the north shore. It was Bob's favorite beach, and as he predicted, there were only two or three other people within sight. It was a good thing, as my friend is somewhat on the large side and was a bit self-conscious about being seen in a bathing suit.

While Birdie professed to be a good swimmer, I encouraged her to be cautious and take breaks often. But once Birdie saw the aquarium-like environment, my warnings and her self-consciousness had little effect on her, and she had to be coerced into returning to land to rest and unprune her skin in-between adventures.

That very first morning, Birdie swam unknowingly from Francis Bay over to Little Maho Bay. She'd never heard of Ethel McCully or the others who'd followed in her path. By midafternoon, our simple picnic lunch was long gone and we were ready for some refreshments. Congratulating ourselves for having avoided the Carnival Parade, Bob agreed to drive us to Mongoose Junction in Cruz Bay for a welcome cocktail.

We came into town from the north shore, blissfully unaware of what lay ahead. As we topped the last rise, the view gave way to the beautiful downtown harbor stretched out below us on our right. But almost immediately, our attention was drawn to the chaotic sight on the road directly ahead. It was lined by cars on both sides, a line that stretched all the way down to town. Trucks were trying to back up the hill to avoid the jam, while others were trying to go down. But no one was making much progress, and everyone was blowing his horn and using plenty of body language, as if that might motivate others to be smarter, more clever. It was nuts.

Having been taken totally by surprise, Bob suddenly snapped, reverting to his past lifetime as a Boston driver and barging his way past drivers going in both directions, impervious to his female passengers' screams, until he could go no further. A wall of people and an angry policeman stopped him. Undeterred and still a little berserk, Bob backed up and swung the car's rear end into a tiny patch of weeds on the shoulder of the road, just barely wider than the car. He came to a stop only when his front end was completely off the pavement and no longer had any traction—or contact with earth.

I was angry. Birdie was panicked. Bob didn't understand our problem.

Quickly adjusting to the situation at hand, and its location, suddenly Bob was again the nice person we'd been driving with on the north shore road. But now, we were stuck in the middle of traffic at the height of Carnival. The parade had begun hours late, which we should have expected. It was in high gear as we approached, with over ten thousand people crowded into the few blocks that normally accommodated only a few hundred. Quickly trying to get into the spirit of the moment, we just weren't prepared for the crush of humanity.

Dislodging our car from its predicament, we retraced our route backward as the parade wound down, and took a circuitous route back to the apartment, where we watched—with a somewhat different attitude than we had earlier—the fireworks from our porch on that final night of Carnival. The next evening we watched the sunset, then the nightly show of lights on St. Thomas in the distance. The view of St. Thomas was just as spectacular as the Carnival lights the night before, only in a quieter sort of way.

The three of us went beach-hopping that weekend. On the long walk to Salt Pond Bay, Bob gave us a lecture on the flora and fauna. I received my own first-hand lesson in local fauna when I took a quick side trip to a portable toilet near the beach and found a huge furry brown spider inside waiting to say hello. Birdie declined to check it out first hand.

Bob did most of the daily chores that first week. Birdie and I were happy to leave everything in his hands as a reward to ourselves for surviving our expedition south. Our cats also enjoyed the good life. They seemed to realize now that their long ordeal was behind them. The out-door adventurer began his explorations quickly. Within days he'd caught and killed his first gecko, and he purred all night. Our little princess hid much of the time under a bed but occasionally made brave, surprising forays outside. Within days she'd deemed the outside porch a part of her living space and had even taken a defiant belly walk around the entire building. It even seemed that they'd forgiven me for their ordeal in the back of my GEO Tracker.

But with the good came the *less good*: My car didn't arrive for nine long days. We had forgotten to take into consideration a delay caused by the coincidence of the July fourth holiday with Carnival on St. John. Since Bob needed his car for work, I got a rental vehicle for a few days; I needed to get around town to run the small errands that couldn't wait. This added mobility also provided Birdie and me with a chance to explore the island together as only two women could. She seemed more relaxed with me driving, but her white knuckles told a different story.

And there was no way I could convince her to get behind the steering wheel and try driving on the left side of any road. It didn't help when I insisted on a visit to Lamshure Bay, with its remote privacy and ruins and tidal pools. I wanted to show her my own favorite spot to while away a day. The steep, four-wheel-drive dirt road was a necessity that Birdie survived with a clenched jaw and more white knuckles. Thank goodness Birdie and I were such good friends.

By the end of every day we were exhausted, and each day more boxes arrived at the Post Office, bringing unpacking chores in the early evening hours. Although I started out committed to making Bob unpack everything, I quickly decided it was better that I take charge, since I'd mailed many of the boxes myself before leaving New England, and they contained effects I needed as soon as possible. However, Bob loaded the empty containers into his vehicle and brought them to the dumpster a half mile away, which helped to balance the scales. By the end of the week, our apartment was filled with our things, though not all were the goods we needed right away. Those boxes were still some-where out over the Atlantic Ocean—I hoped. As each box was opened and each surprise revealed, Birdie just shook her head in amusement at our well planned chaos. In addition, confiscating the dining room table for a computer desk, my girlfriend and I set up some dedicated office space for myself which I would expect Bob to consider as sacred territory.

* * *

Having my best friend with us for my first week on-island was fun, but it had also kept reality from setting in. On the day Birdie departed, I finally went back to work. My two-week "vacation," which had started with the drive from Massachusetts, was now ancient history, and beach adventures would now be limited to weekends or the occasional holiday. Hi ho. Hi ho.

What a rude awakening followed! Very quickly, the difficulties of being a *very* remote telecommuter became apparent. Since the company had assigned no real firm projects to me before I left, I spent much of my initial time working on-island trying to establish firm working hours while juggling almost continuous use of our single (poor quality) phone line, switching between on-line computer use and long distance phone calls. During certain hours it took up to ten tries to access the 800 number connection to my company's headquarters. As if that weren't trial enough, we lost power for a few minutes at a time on a regular basis. I was productive, but it took real effort on my part to perform even simple tasks. A month passed before I felt comfortable with the situation.

But things didn't stop there. Three days into my new work routine, my automobile arrived on St. Thomas, and I was faced with the task of retrieving it alone. At Cruz Bay, I located the tax office and paid the fee for my vehicle. Then I proceeded to locate the Motor Vehicle Department to secure a one-day permit to bring my vehicle to the island without a proper St. John's vehicle inspection sticker. With paperwork, lots of cash, and a hand-drawn map from Bob, I took a ferry, then a bus, then walked to the shipping company on the docks in St. Thomas.

I filled out paperwork at the shipping company, then caught another bus to the US Customs office. A long walk back, with nary a bus in sight, got me some stamped paperwork and the keys to my car. I managed to drive directly across town to the Red Hook barge dock by instinct alone. Then I faced the stress of backing my car onto the barge while juggling for position with fifteen other anxious drivers. It was an ordeal.

The regularly scheduled barges were the only way to transport a vehicle between the islands, and if the barge filled before my car could wedge its way on board, I'd be left to stew on the dock for an hour before the next departure. This time I was lucky; I made it, and immediately upon arrival at Cruz Bay, I headed to the Motor Vehicle Inspection lane.

The process had taken over half the day so far, and I was not in a patient mood. Parked in the outdoor inspection lane next to a trailer marked with a small official-looking sign, I went inside to present my paperwork; I expected quick approval. I was shocked when, five minutes later, I was being yelled at by the inspector and told that my brake lights weren't working, nor were my back-up lights. A stern warning was followed by my being dispensed forthwith until the next morning, when I was told to return with the lights working. Two repair shops determined that there was nothing wrong with my car.

Late into the evening, I tried to make up the work hours I'd missed.

When I heard that we could give back any of the furniture or other items our landlord had supplied, I was ecstatic. It wasn't that I was ungrateful, but Bob and I had lots of our own things that I would rather use, and we were cramped for space. A chair and many kitchen utensils were quickly removed, followed by linens and framed pictures and a host of other items. After ridding ourselves of these unneeded items, our apartment seemed almost spacious for the next week or so, until our own mailed goods started arriving in large enough quantities to make it seem cluttered again.

During this time, we mostly needed bookshelves. Three different times, Bob brought home small bookcases purchased on St. Thomas to accommodate the growing library we'd mailed ourselves from New England. With a superior bearing, I smugly indicated how badly Bob had misjudged just how many books and computer manuals he'd packed, and how many bookcases he'd need. The truth, however, made me more humble. There were huge quantities of books that needed shelving. But any bookcases we bought had to make their way from the store in St. Thomas to the bus, then to the ferry and then to the car on St. John. A St. John yard sale yielded a fourth bookcase that I quickly confiscated and filled within minutes for my home office needs.

Now that I had my own wheels on-island, I made an effort to drive to town each day to pick up mail and, if lucky, more packages. On the return trips I often stopped to survey the markets for fresh foods. But I found it a real chore very often to tear myself away from the computer and the phone and force myself to take this break part way through the day. Of course, no matter when I left, my boss would decide to call at just that time, or some work emergency would occur which required my personal and immediate attention.

Needing to be available for business, then, the time I spent food shopping quickly became my primary social activity. I also found that when I did check the stores for fresh foods, I would often discover some of my new acquaintances doing the same. There was little I couldn't find or buy on the island; it just took much more effort than on the continent.

I found that each of the small grocery stores on the island had its own idiosyncrasies. One was relatively reliable for vegetables, but another had a better selection of canned goods, while a third was the place to shop for meat...usually. Prices on some items changed daily; most were exorbitant. As a result, I got connected to the human food telegraph and information system on-island. A surprise phone call or whisper from a neighbor could tell you the meat truck had just been spotted heading to one of the markets outside its normal schedule, or there was fresh fish being sold on the dock, or a load of good looking cherries (!)

had just been unloaded at some lucky store. Within an hour or two, no evidence remained that any of these good things had happened.

As I knew would happen (though not so soon), two short weeks after I started telecommuting I had to fly back to New England on business. After only three hectic hours back at my company's headquarters, my new life in Paradise started to fade from memory in much the same way as vacations do. In the hallways, everyone wanted to know what living on St. John was like. I could only shrug and smile and wish I were there. After long workdays in a Northern climate, my evenings revitalized me with rushed visits to my mom or shopping trips to pick up emergency items that my husband couldn't find locally or at a reasonable price. I brought back a knapsack full of fresh corn on the cob to share with new island friends. There was nothing similar in the Virgin Islands to compare with fresh New England corn. The blast of hot island heat stepping off the plane in St. Thomas was welcome, though. This was my home now. It was a good feeling.

Before August was over, island peculiarities had become the norm. The local donkeys that are such a quaint tourist attraction became mere road nuisances to be avoided. My automobile was constantly covered with a thick layer of dust, and I'd begun to think of Mud as the actual color of my car. No longer did I look down on the typical island vehicles that were inevitably dented on all four sides from mysterious sources, and I no longer confused the sound of baying goats with that of babies crying out for help. Sometimes I even bayed back.

And, yes, I was even clued in now to the story—some of it true, some unverified—surrounding a local man named Moses, and his cows. It seems that Moses—a major landowner and farmer on the island—let his cows loose to free-range wherever and whenever they wanted. These huge beasts were a regular nuisance on the only major road crisscrossing the island and were considered a safety hazard by government officials. Often when a resident discovered a new dent on their vehicle, they attributed it to one of Moses cows. By my own limited count, twenty-three people swore to me their cars had suffered this fate within the past thirty days.

The stories started taking on legendary status. But as I thought more and more about it, it seemed to me there were some inconsistencies and irregularities in these stories. For instance, it seemed to me that either Moses had cows that were indestructible (to be able to withstand all those direct hits) or that he had the miraculous ability to multiply his herd on a superbovine basis. At the same time, I just couldn't accept that there were a lot of crooks and liars on St. John taking out their petty frustrations on poor Moses and his cows. Regardless, his cows had now become local legend, and I began to share these tales with our off-island friends.

Most of my own encounters with Nature that first summer were limited by my near-confinement to my home office. I did learn about poisonous caterpillars, spiders, and lizards of every kind after experiencing them firsthand, thanks to my cats. Unfortunately, while my cats seemed to believe that lizards—heads and all—were an Epicurean delight, their little stomachs thought differently. My downstairs neighbor, Karen, told me to be patient with them, however, as the cats would soon learn to leave the heads alone and therefore stop vomiting their catch. Nice.

Surrounded by the exotic scenery, though, I thought it was pretty neat to live in a place where huge termite nests nestled in trees, eating all the rotten wood to minimize the likelihood of forest fires. That is, until my husband and I encountered firsthand a nocturnal swarm. This disaster struck just two months after my arrival. It was a beautiful tropical night, with showers the previous two days making everything smell fresh and clean. Our screened doors were closed and lights were on all over our apartment. At first I noticed only a few flying insects and thought nothing of it; after all, we lived in the tropics, didn't we? And there were always ways for the occasional bug to get in, wasn't there?

But within a half-hour we started to suspect we had a big problem.

"There's some kind of ant crawling around in here," Bob said, sounding a little concerned for the first time. Then panic struck. When we started looking a little harder we saw there were hundreds of the things—on the floors, the walls, the furniture. Bob went outside on the porch to retrieve some bug spray.

"Hey, there's thousands of little wings on the floor out here," he yelled in. Checking the living room floor, I found more wings.

"Remember that book we read that said a sure sign of termites was a mound of fallen wings?" he asked. I never thought I'd need that information. We lived in a very well built concrete condo that was closely maintained.

"Termites?" I asked timidly.

"Termites" was all he said, as we both realized we had no idea what to do about it.

Within minutes our house was filled with thousands of these little ant-like creatures, some of them flying with wings still attached. The situation had gotten out of hand. They were on the walls, the floor, the furniture, and even us. It seemed every minute there were more bugs climbing and flying around the apartment. Bob and I swatted and killed, without exaggeration, *thousands* of bugs. Even when we thought they were all dead, we found more, especially near light sources. It took hours to kill the majority of these pests. Our cats thought it was all great fun.

We slept fitfully that night and, yes, I had nightmares. The next morning, the only reminder of the evening's calamity was the occasional dead bug we'd killed but had missed in our rushed cleanup the night before.

We mentioned our termite infestation to neighbors and acquaintances in the following days and discovered we were not alone in our adventure. Bob's boss, Mark, had ridden his motorcycle right into a swarm on his way to Fish Bay a short time before and got a helmet full of little white bugs. A neighbor told us he'd been driving the night before and found his car headlights were covered with dead bugs in the morning. The more experienced islanders told us to "just shut off all the lights when it happens again. And it will," they reassured us.

It seems the termites had been washed out of their homes by the rains; their missing wings were a sure indication that they'd been pelted by the rain, and one we'd surely never ignore again.

This would be an event that would repeat itself each year, so we would have to learn to adapt.

* * *

Bob decided it was important that we play by the rules laid down by the fine government of the Virgin Islands. He was determined to get a business license for his work as a contractor. But even at best, this would be an overly complicated process. Filling out forms, finding documentation and searching for the proper government offices on St Thomas to submit them to would all take a lot of effort.

So while my husband was proud that he'd completed the process in only a few days, a month later Bob received a letter denying the license. There was no "proof" on file that we'd paid federal taxes to the Virgin Islands for the previous six years. And while the forms had clearly stated this was a new license we were requesting, that made no difference. And only copies of our US Federal Tax returns would suffice to overcome this hurdle. Since the records were in storage over two thousand miles away, getting a license would be quite an ordeal.

Perhaps that's why some on-island folks who were originally from the U.S. mainland didn't bother with all the red tape of business licenses unless they got caught. We were appalled to discover that many didn't even bother with income taxes. It took Bob five queries to find the first soul who did. And that person used off-island accountants to handle all the mess.

Like self-righteous youngsters out to change the world, my husband and I were determined to pay our dues, register to vote, and make a difference. We would be part of the solution, not the problem. At least that's what we thought.

An interesting sidelight, however: Some newly arrived settlers from the mainland brought with them a sort of third world mentality when it came to favorite foods or luxury items. For instance, at some point we met someone who loved pineapple yogurt. Whenever she saw it, she'd buy whatever the store had, hoarding it and leaving the shelf bare. I discovered culprits who did the same thing with coffee ice cream, Pad Thai noodles, and prepared pizza dough. Since the stores couldn't plan for these weird fluctuations in purchases and stock, once an item was sold out it might not be restocked for months. So we got smart: Once in a while, Bob or I would stock up on these very items even though we didn't really want them; we could use them for bartering. And despite our best intentions during the licensing process earlier, that's how we too became part of "the problem." Everyone is.

Bob started out buying coffee ice cream to bribe our neighbor Andre into helping us with some fix-up projects around the apartment. This neighbor, we'd been told, was addicted to coffee ice cream. But one day we tried the ice cream ourselves and we liked it. Shortly after, every store on the island ran out of that flavor. One day, a stranger, seeing me head to the freezer at the Tropicale Market looking in vain for some hidden pint of coffee ice cream, took pity. She spied a pint of Haagen-Dazs Coffee Mocha-Chip I had pushed aside in my frantic search and offered that we might like it even better. We did. Bob and I became addicted.

But soon there was no more coffee mocha-chip ice cream to be found anywhere. It was awful, and nothing else could satisfy our taste buds like a single spoonful of this stuff. Plain coffee ice cream now tasted bland and we could only enjoy it after weeks without the added jolt of mocha-chips. Sure, our addictions could easily be found on St. Thomas, but it was difficult to get ice cream back home to St. John without a major production.

Bob hunted for the ice cream distributor on St. John, hoping to convince him to keep the local markets stocked with our preference. Finally, when Bob caught up with the ice cream dealer one day, he was filling a store's cooler with cherry vanilla, with no coffee mocha-chip in sight.

"If you like that Haagen Dazs coffee stuff, I have something you'll like even better," whispered the ice cream man, as he led Bob to his van. "Try this," he said, whipping out his personal stash of Ben & Jerry's Coffee, Coffee BuzzBuzzBuzz! ice cream. Bob brought home two precious pints.

This was mean stuff, we found out. A couple of spoonfuls of this espresso blend was all it took to satisfy us at first. It was so good that even adding a scoop of coffee or plain vanilla ice cream into it didn't diminish the taste. In fact, a late evening snack usually required "cutting" the Coffee, Coffee, BuzzBuzzBuzz! with vanilla if we wanted to get to sleep that night. But when our two pints ran out, we couldn't find replacements anywhere, nor could we find our trusty coffee mocha-chip alternative, nor the dealer! Bob and I went through serious withdrawal.

We sighted the ice cream man only fleetingly during the next few months, which was, we decided, a good thing, as we weaned ourselves back to sobriety. Since a pint of ice cream cost more than twice the price of a bottle of rum on St. John, we were glad to stop our downward spiral toward addiction before it came to that. We even harbored a little resentment toward the ice cream "dealer" once we regained our sanity. Eventually, though, we discovered the dealer also played in a musical band around the island, and he played so well that we forgave him for fostering our temporary insanity.

* * *

I heard my peers in the States often venture that I probably sat at the pool all day with a cell phone by my side, soaking up the heat. To be sure, there was heat, but it came from the hot sun pounding down on the apartment roof all day. Ceiling fans turning overhead provided only minimal relief. Even friends of ours insisted that our apartment was abnormally hot compared to others on the island, but I doubted them; everywhere I went it seemed just as hot. The continual flow of air from the trade winds kept the air bearable, as long as the windows were open.

But island wisdom also had it that the trade winds brought dust and sand too, all the way from the Sahara Desert, and I came to believe it very quickly. Though only a year earlier I'd been complaining about dirt and dust stirred up by our septic tank replacement, what had then seemed like a real onslaught of grime paled compared to the daily influx I now faced. To add to it, summer brought the added joy of occasional soot arriving courtesy of the volcano on Montserrat hundreds of miles away.

Every morning I swept the floors and dusted, but when the heat built up by mid-afternoon, I had to wedge open the front door for a few minutes so a rush of wind could cool the place down while I worked. If the winds were strong, however, clumps of dust embedded themselves in the ceiling fans and fell to the floor like little bugs. At that point I would have to take another five-minute break to sweep away the new layers of dust that always followed.

Meanwhile, Bob was experiencing his own adventures with work. There were lulls between assignments. At least once a week, he visited clients on St. Thomas, and he was getting pretty good at knowing everyone and every place on both islands. Because of this, he felt he was having to learn the computer repair business from the ground up, but he didn't seem to mind. Still, Bob's work didn't quite keep him as busy as I'd hoped, as this was the quiet season in the islands, and he got paid only for billable work. As yet he hadn't built up a backlog of work to carry him through the slow times. Too often my husband's day was done long before my own and I'd jealously see him down at the pool living the life I—and most of our peers—could only dream about.

* * *

As we settled into island life and started to pay more attention to life around us, we started to notice that people walking along the roadside, both here and on St. Thomas, often carried tree branches loaded with leaves and some kind of nut or fruit on the end. Our curiosity led to questions and research on Caribbean plant life. We learned that the people were carrying branches from the genip tree, whose much-favored fruit was in season. One Saturday we saw a group of young people surrounding a tree near a beach in the VI National Park They were encouraging one of their crowd who was high in the branches reaching toward a branch hanging heavy with fruit.

"Are those genips?" I asked. All eyes turned toward me, and I hurried to correct my rudeness, having jumped right into their conversation with my question. I restarted my speaking with a "Good Morning," and they happily confirmed my guess.

"I've never tried any of the fruit, but I hear it is wonderful," I countered. "We've just moved here," I explained; "do you think I might try one?"

With a unanimous smile, the teens grinned. One gave me a small branch with fruit on it and showed me how to split open the outer shell of the husk with my teeth and get at the small amount of pulp surrounding an overly large seed. My face lit up with a grin as I savored my first genip. To me it tasted like a cross between a grape and a melon. The sweet taste was a perfect counterpoint to the salty aftertaste in your mouth resulting from hours spent beachside.

One genip was hardly satisfying though, and after five more, I was in love. It became my favorite fruit.

From these stops along the road came a number of benefits. Many people on-island walked long distances daily and relied on the kindness of drivers when they grew tired or were in a hurry. Even before genip season, I'd become accustomed to stopping at the side of the road to give others rides on my daily treks to town. While I was trained from an early age not to pick up hitchhikers, on St. John I felt safe. As a result of many of these random meetings, I made lasting acquaintances, got invited to share refreshments, viewed homes in the process of being built, learned island folklore and history, and, most importantly, experienced the pleasure that comes from helping others without expectation of reward.

* * *

Much of the news on-island often didn't get reported in the local newspapers. One example: when a small plane crashed on the north side of the island one day, there was no ensuing newspaper article. I looked for weeks. I was told eventually that since the incident occurred on federal property (in the VI National Park), the Park Service was under no obligation to report the news.

So I learned to rely on the grapevine, which was another reason you stopped to pick up people along the road: They were a great source of information—better, for sure, than those who spent their days in cars. But while I learned lots of the local gossip from hitchhikers, my best source of information for what really happened on a weekly basis came from—of all people!—Bob.

One of the first things Bob had done after arriving on St. John was to join the fledgling St. John Rescue group. During the summer they held weekly meetings at the National Park Visitors Center, which was also the workplace for a couple of members. Not only was he learning first aid and critical rescue skills, but he was also getting an earful of little anecdotes and the sometimes bizarre details of incidents that had occurred on the island during the previous week. Through him I learned much of the real news, and many of the rumors, that never made it into print.

On Friday nights, I was able to confirm even many of Bob's wildest stories through my own growing grapevine. Back in New England we'd always ended a stressful workweek with a quiet and early Friday night at home, gearing up for a weekend of relaxation. Here Friday night was the night to cut loose. Everyone, it seemed, managed to party on that night, even if his or her job required getting up at five o'clock the next morning. Bob and I tried to take part, as it was a good way to meet other locals. Inevitably, however, we were ready to pack it in by nine o'clock, when many were just gearing up for a long night of fun. Still, the neighbors and new friends we met on these excursions enjoyed sharing their opinions on the latest St. John news flashes.

One weekend, our landlords Moe and Bev took us under their wing and treated us to a powerboat ride to Jost Van Dyke, a sparsely populated island in the British Virgin Islands. Once arrived, we spent the afternoon at the Soggy Dollar Bar, so named because until recently the only way to reach it was by boat or by swimming and most folks paid with wet dollar bills. Moe and Bev were the ones who had convinced Bob to join the St. John Yacht Club, a looser social organization than the smaller but more sailor-intensive Coral Bay Yacht Club. These kind folks made sure we were getting flyers in the mail for the regular SJYC parties and introduced us to lots of locals, including some who would become our closest friends on-island. One invitation—to join Moe and Bev on St. Thomas for festivities following an annual marlin fishing competition—opened our eyes to the complexities of this rich man's sport, and as a bonus we saw our first megayacht up close.

But most of the "excitement" in our lives (if that's the right word) was rather mundane by mainland standards. We had car problems on a regular basis; the relatively young age of our vehicles and our constant attention to preventative care made little difference when it came to mechanical troubles. Bob had bought maintenance books for each of our cars just in case we found experienced mechanics difficult to find once the inevitable occurred. But books were of little help when replacement parts weren't available. And books rarely mentioned the kind of trauma caused by island road and environmental conditions.

Bob became an expert at cleaning auto wires, testing electrical connections and tightening bolts. Usually the strange advice we received from friends, neighbors, and, yes, even local mechanics, worked surprisingly well, and a sick vehicle was fixed with just a little elbow grease. We also found we were not alone in being subjected to these mysterious car ailments; they were the norm for everyone. Odd, though: In the States, a breakdown would have put me into a frenzy; here, perhaps because of the closeness of the island, both physically and social-ly, and the fact that we had two cars, it brought only a shrug. But as a two-vehicle household, Bob and I were lucky. In fact, we often loaned out one car to others when they had car problems and needed to run emergency errands.

The flow of boxes from New England had slowed by this time to an occasional delivery. This was a relief, especially after having had four-teen boxes arrive on a single day, prompting our tiny Post Office to take the extraordinary step of calling our home and informing us of the arrival. Bob faithfully checked off each box in the Paradise Expedition Manual, while I cut open the boxes to retrieve our life.

Meanwhile, Bob remained a junk mail junkie. It was a rare day when he didn't receive mail of some kind. Unfortunately, his regular stock of magazines ended up cluttering the small apartment. Occasionally he could be persuaded to drop unwanted catalogs off at Connections, a business in town where a bin was provided for this purpose. Sadly, he often returned home from the store with other catalogs someone else had managed to convince *their* spouse to get rid of.

* * *

I still had big plans for Paradise; there was so much I wanted to do, but it was difficult to find a starting point. Eventually I hoped to become a clay artisan, though my experience was minimal. Then there was the book I wanted to write and get published about our move. My philanthropic goals involved volunteering time reading to young chil-dren and assisting at the VI National Park. I also saw hiking trails, remote beaches and historical ruins I wanted to explore. And I wanted a garden to call my own, just as I'd had in New England.

So in the evenings I began to work with polymer clay, creating minia-ture island images in the art form known as millifore. After a few unsuccessful tries, palm trees, turtles and geckos started to form with-out distortion, and I fashioned medallions threaded with leather strips. A vision of a profitable St. John Saturday danced in my mind. Bob particularly liked the fish medallion I made, and took to wearing it around town as part of his casual work attire.

He came home one night and asked me to make a dolphin medallion for a business acquaintance at one of the resorts. A few weeks later he delivered the dolphin medallion gratis, and returned home that night, surprisingly, with my first commission: two hundred medallions to be used for a marketing promotion at the resort. Since they wouldn't be needed until late fall, the order seemed very reasonable. I was now an artisan. My November target for a St. John Saturday would coincide nicely.

And on the occasional evening and weekend morning when we had time, Bob and I took to the trails. Each outing improved my stamina and increased my desire to learn more about my newfound home. We even made it to the top of America Hill and the ruins I'd seen there for years from the beach. The climb, I had always felt, would be an ordeal, not because of the ruggedness or trail length, but because of the wild lime bushes and ketch-an-keep plants that had overgrown this trail.

Up we went anyway, though the scratches and thorns embedded in my arms and legs would teach me what the VI National Parks "Trail Closed" sign could not: that it had been closed for our own safety. Bob came away mostly unscathed; he had conned me into blazing the trail while he walked behind (under the guise of pacing his hiking strides).

Whenever we went late afternoon to Lamshure Bay on the south shore, we inevitably saw three or more white-tailed deer near the road-way before the beach. We were surprised to find that many locals who'd lived on our tiny island for twenty years had never caught even a glimpse of these creatures. I'm also told there are wild boar on the island, and even a one-day boar hunting season. Given our experience with the deer, the fact that I've never met anyone who's seen a boar on St. John doesn't mean they're not there.

* * *

A business trip to San Antonio and then Atlanta interrupted our late summer island rhythm. My productivity had greatly increased, and I was working forty to fifty hours a week, though getting paid as a part-time worker, and while traveling, my work hours jumped even higher. But I was happy to put in the long hours, since my company was accommodating my life style, and I knew that eventually the number of hours would shrink. Nevertheless, my return landing in St. Thomas was even sweeter than the one the month before. Another snorkeling week-end was about to begin and my life style had become routine.

Before summer's end, Bob announced that snorkeling each weekend was too much effort. He'd begun insisting that we take at least one float with us on our weekend snorkeling excursions to the beach. Instead of snorkeling, Bob immediately headed for the water with float in hand, then plopped down to soak up the sun's rays while tourists took photographs of him from the National Park roadside scenic overlooks in the distance.

I don't blame them; Bob was quite a sight. We'd received our dual-purpose, heavy-duty floats as Christmas presents before our move. These toys were designed to work as sleds or toboggans sliding down snow-covered hills, complete with sturdy handles on their sides and snowflake-patterned designs emblazoned with the words "Authentic Snow Gear." The floats were also designed—or so we had guessed—to be flipped over in summer so that the plain, smooth plastic side would provide a smooth surface to float on. Nevertheless, Ranger Bob preferred to have the "...Snow Gear" emblem showing on the surface, just to amuse tourists with telephoto lenses.

I soon joined him in this weekend fun, but discovered that two bulky snow floats were the maximum my little car could transport. In time, we decided that amusing the tourists was a responsibility, like offering to take group pictures for them with their own cameras. We limited our snorkeling now to those days when we had energy to burn. We didn't feel as if we were shirking, though; some of our neighbors, although surrounded by water, rarely made it to the beach at all. Island life was developing its routine. Until the phone rang late one Sunday night.

Chapter 10

Disruption in Paradise

Fate had dealt my brother in New Hampshire a lousy hand. He was experiencing kidney failure. And as a diabetic, Joe was a poor candidate for dialysis. He needed a new kidney.

My sister-in-law conveyed the news to us. While I'd caught wind that he wasn't feeling well, I never suspected things had become so bad. In fact, Joe's health had gone into a drastic downward spiral during the latter half of the summer. Then the other shoe dropped.

His wife asked that night on the phone if I would consider becoming a donor if that ever became necessary as a last resort.

But I knew it sounded as if a transplant was not really an option for "someday." It would be a necessity in the next year. At the time, the waiting list for kidney donors averaged three years, and Joe's chances for survival if he had to wait that long were very slim. My sister-in-law was being tested as the most likely donor, and so far all her tests pointed in the right direction. I was happy they'd found a quick solution.

Without hesitation, but with confidence that I would never be needed, I agreed to be their last resort.

It was a surreal conversation, one that seemed as foreign to my daily reality as the evening television world news. On St. John, the Flamboyant trees were blooming. They arched across roads and paths like flaming clouds resting on a lining of emerald green foliage. At Francis Bay, a five-foot iguana came by to visit and drink water from the makeshift container I held in my hand. That very day I'd spied my first pomegranate tree heavy with fruit and smiled all the way to town. From the porch that night the full moon's reflection shimmered on the waters separating us from St. Thomas, and the beauty of it made me breathless. Yet I knew that my brother and I looked at the same moon that night.

In early September, I was asked to fly to Boston with the rest of the immediate family for a family meeting with Joe's doctors. Joe's condition had worsened, the doctors told us.

As chance would have it, I had a business trip scheduled for that week and could easily set aside one day of vacation time for the meeting. Janine, Joe's wife, had continued to test well as a potential donor, and we were all anticipating a discussion of when donation would take place, how we could be supportive as a family, and what the odds were of a successful transplant. But the meeting opened instead with a bombshell being dropped.

The hospital staff had just come from their own private meeting, where they'd disqualified my sister-in-law as a potential donor. She'd had breast cancer over fourteen years earlier and, although there had been no sign of a reoccurrence, there was a theoretic possibility that she could pass a hidden cancer cell on to Joe through the transplant. And while this transference had a smaller likelihood of happening than the remote chance that she'd die during the routine transplant surgery, malpractice concerns dictated great discretion. And so, unified in their resolve, the doctors reiterated their final decision to the entire family. Under no circumstances would they take Janine's kidney.

I felt great sorrow as Janine sat in disbelief before us with tears in her eyes. Her hopes for a quick improvement in their quality of life had just been deflated. In a split second, the mood of the room had changed.

Then the repercussions of the doctors' decision sunk in and I noticed that all eyes in the room shifted toward me. Donations from the rest of my family had been summarily rejected for a variety of medical reasons. I was Joe's only hope.

Still, no one even knew if I was compatible, and this was not the forum where I would have liked to begin a serious dialog on the matter, so I kept quiet as other family members asked questions. I learned of the twelve- to sixteen-inch incision, of the hospital and recuperative stay that would be necessary, and the likelihood one of my ribs would have to be removed to gain access to the kidney. It was all a blur. This was no longer a meeting about Joe and his condition, but one about me.

My husband had not flown up to join in the family meeting with the doctors. Given how I had anticipated the meeting would turn out, I felt comfortable that I could relay the facts and findings later. Bob's contracting job at Bestech was just stabilizing and his evenings were filled with a specialized first aid training course as a requirement for the St. John Volunteer Rescue group. Besides, my sister-in-law was going to be the donor and I was just there to lend support.

How I wished now that Bob had insisted on tagging along. As the conference was ending, I finally found my voice. "Uh, it seems like we're all talking about what is probably going to happen to me, since I'm the only possible candidate in the room. But I haven't even been tested yet." With sudden desperate inspiration I added, "And I live in the Virgin Islands, and I'm only here for a few days." I don't know what I expected to happen, but it certainly wasn't what followed.

Within seconds I was shaking hands with my brother's kidney specialist, trying to keep pace with the man as he rushed us through the hallways and down the street while querying me on my medical history. He wanted to begin testing immediately to determine my viability as a candidate.

Still stunned, I was ushered into his private office and led directly to an examination room as he kept up his barrage of questions without a break. Ten minutes later the initial exam was almost complete. Then, given a specimen jar, I was asked apologetically to walk across the filled waiting room to provide a quick urine sample in the bathroom beyond. Entering the waiting room in only my medical johnny, I discovered to my distinct embarrassment my entire family talking up a storm, city blocks away from where I'd last left them.

My brother Don from Pittsburgh was upset that he'd been dismissed as a candidate without a detailed examination, and the whole family was loudly trying to calm him down. I was freaked out that everyone considered me the perfect candidate with no more knowledge than they had about Don, but I kept quiet and hardly broke stride as I rushed past, hoping the bathroom was where I'd been told. I wanted to hide.

The preliminary test results took a week to determine. By that time I'd returned to St. John with a heavy load on my mind. Bob did not take the news happily. It wasn't that he was a selfish person. We'd just gotten settled in our new lives and up to this point Bob was carrying more of the everyday load than I was. Our finances were still in disarray, and my job was tenuous. I suggested we head for a beach to soothe our souls.

The quiet solitude of Lameshure Bay gave Bob the backdrop to speak his mind. He didn't like the idea that I would consider major surgery my body didn't require when there was even a small chance that something could go wrong. Bob reminded me that I didn't eat a completely healthy diet and that I was physically out of shape and had high cholesterol. The ruggedness of St. John hadn't been given the time yet to change my life style and, besides, I hated doctors and medications of any kind and had a low tolerance for pain. He feared the worst. I reminded him the first test results weren't even in, and it was unlikely

I'd pass. Then I pulled the float out from underneath his sunning body and gave him a reassuring kiss underwater to change the mood.

The week passed slowly as I telecommuted, trying my best to stay focused. I did extra chores around the apartment. At work, there were rumors of layoffs in the wind, and I felt sure I was to be a part of them. The VP who'd been my biggest supporter in this telecommuting experiment had left the company, and so had my group's Director. The acting Director had little use for remote workers unless they were direct revenue producers. And my supervisor was under a lot of pressure.

In the evenings, instead of working with clay to relieve the pressure, I did research on the Internet on diabetes, kidney donors, and options, while the cats perfected their ambushing of night geckos out on the porch. The cats were thoroughly enjoying life on St. John, but they were quickly losing a few of their nine lives. Our outdoor explorer ran home one afternoon and into the bedroom with a piece of prickly pear cactus firmly attached to his back. The cactus was almost as big as he was. It took a lot of coaxing to get the wailing baby out from underneath the bed so I could gently disentangle him. Our princess got braver every day in her own explorations. Bob heard her early one evening sliding down the metal roof off our upstairs bedroom porch and caught her just in time before she fell three stories down to the hard surface below. Life was precious.

* * *

When she called a week later with the test results, the social worker with the hospital transplant group tried to put Joe's situation into perspective.

"Don't let anyone pressure you. This is purely elective surgery. Your kidney donation is not the only alternative," she said. Five minutes later we lost power for the rest of the afternoon. Was it a sign from above?

"In fact, it's not a cure, just a temporary solution. It's your decision and you have to do what's right for you, not for anyone else," the social worker confirmed.

Janine disagreed. "Your kidney is the only alternative. This is a life or death decision. It's about your brother's life," was what I got from her minutes after the fans came back on. Her quality of life was going downhill as quickly as Joe's was, she told me. And her frustration over the doctors' unwillingness to accept her as a donor rankled her. To Janine, my personal concerns were trivial.

But the initial tests determined that I shared none of the six genes known to show compatibility between donor and recipient. I wasn't surprised. Joe and I had such different...everything! I just knew we couldn't have compatible genes. However, I found that with today's anti-rejection drugs, this was a minor issue. My blood cells did not attack his when mixed together, which was a more important test. Well, that hardly surprised me at all: My cells were just being overly polite, just like my silence in the meeting back East, and the quick offer to risk my life and happiness in Paradise to improve my brother's own quality of life.

There were more tests to be done, and I was asked to fly back to Boston only two days later to continue the testing process. I nixed the idea. It was unreasonable to ask me to fly to Boston within two days, given the tenuous nature of my job situation, a husband who was grossly unhappy with what was happening, and the little time I'd been given to adjust to the life decision I faced. Suggesting an alternative, I asked that some of the blood work be done locally on either St. John or St. Thomas. Research showed that blood could be taken on either island and shipped overnight to Boston. The mainland doctors were being difficult, however; they were partial to their own labs and would only trust those samples and those results.

We were reaching the height of hurricane season. We'd prepared by buying all the staples recommended by the Red Cross brochures and the local newspapers, and now we'd begun to think it was all a waste of time and effort. While we'd had nary a hurricane so far, we did have the occasional tropical wave, which is the local lingo for a strong storm front. Each tropical wave brought torrents of rain along with strong winds. Sometimes the rain seemed to be coming at us horizontally. When this happened, a small hole from a rotted corner of our kitchen door brought regular pools of water onto our tiled floor. In addition, the noise drowned out conversation.

While we were grateful for the natural filling of our cistern (the concrete water containment area built beneath our building), each rain shower fell so fast that much of the water rolled off the roof without making it into the gutter system that led to the cistern. This was our sole source of water for bathing and cleaning. Only souls living in downtown Cruz Bay had access to the island's public water supply.

My next business trip included a vacation day spent at the hospital; the day after, both my arms were covered with bruises from the needle work. But I almost didn't get there at all. Hurricane Erika had just grazed the Virgin Islands the night before I was scheduled to leave St. Thomas. It hit us with minimum force, hardly more than the occasional tropical waves we'd already experienced. By the next morning the rain had stopped, but when Bob drove me to the ferry dock to catch the early ferry to St. Thomas, the ferry dock was deserted and there wasn't a boat in sight. A half-hour of talking with the few locals milling around led us to the commercial barge dock at the Creek, where all the barges and ferries were lashed together as protection from the now distant hurricane. No one knew when any would start running again. Although the water was rough, the sun was peeking through the clouds as we made our way back toward Rendezvous Bay and our apartment.

Two hours later, a phone call to the ferry company confirmed that the first ferry would leave at noon. I was able to change my plane reservations and was told the airlines had not cancelled any flights. When I finally arrived at the airport that afternoon and passed through customs, I was greeted by a crowd of tired and annoyed travelers.

They had good reason. Despite the telephone claims of the airline, no planes had left the ground all day and, once through US Customs and Immigration, those people were confined to the gate area. The food concession areas were closed due to the hurricane scare, and everyone was hungry. Apparently the airport personnel were doing what little they could. An airline ground crew member offered to play Good Samaritan and go down the road to a snack shack to buy food, but he needed cash up front. Many were wary, but their hunger won out as most gave him their orders and their money.

An hour later we boarded the plane to San Juan and the airplane propellers began to turn. The Good Samaritan hadn't arrived back with food; some grumbled and others sighed, while one person made disparaging comments on being robbed on his way out of town. Most smiled, however, when the back door suddenly opened to reveal the ground crew hero with bags in both arms and one held under his chin.

He apologized for the delay, explaining it was difficult to find any place open because of the hurricane. As he passed out food, he offered sandwiches and meat pates—ground meat encrusted in a flaky pastry—as an alternative to unavailable hamburgers. Most people were extremely grateful; when one person grumbled about a necessary but creative substitution to their request, I felt a strong urge to do this person bodily harm. The airline worker deserved a medal.

Eventually I made it to the hospital in Boston, taking the tests a day later than planned. Each test was affirmative. I was a surprisingly healthy person, unlikely to get diabetes in the future and, assuming the final tests were positive, a great candidate for kidney donation.

The doctors and my brother Joe were all hoping for an early October operation. I was thinking more like late February. By then, my husband would have a strong local support system and our tenth wedding anniversary and the romantic ski trip we'd planned would be history. Most importantly, I wanted time to live a little of the life we'd found in Paradise. Then I'd be ready to take a risk.

The pressure to make a final decision and commit to a timeframe was strong. Joe's doctor explained the medical reasoning for doing the operations quickly, and it was clear that late February was not a good option for Joe. My own Internet research bore this out. He also said I should not feel pressured to make any decision I was not comfortable with. Fat chance. I was comfortable with none of it.

I talked out the issue with my multicultured hitchhiking acquaintances. Some thought it was a wonderful gift to give, while others said they wouldn't do it for anyone. It appeared most West Indies natives fell into the latter camp, although everyone seemed to know someone with diabetes. The rumor that I was giving my brother a kidney began to move around town, and soon even strangers knew. Like a local celebrity, I received preferential treatment in places formerly closed to me. "Make room for the brave kidney lady" was the startling reassurance I heard one afternoon as I tried pigeonholing my car near the post office. "Yo da ki'nee lady - Go'd be wi'd yo," greeted a hitchhiker another afternoon, one I'd never met before. My husband was experiencing similar treatment. He was slowly accepting the inevitable.

I knew it was childish to want to be selfish and self-centered and stay on as I was, unaffected, on St. John. Wasn't that why we came here—to indulge ourselves in The Good Life? If I had to donate a kidney, then, I wanted my parents, my husband, or even my friends to take the decision out of my hands and insist I get it over with. But I knew it was my burden to decide my own fate.

I spent an entire day driving on the back roads of St. John searching for a sign. But there was none. Even the fork in the road sign, now in dire need of a new paint job, only seemed to make matters worse, despite a long hard stare from me.

Finally, I put the question to myself: "If the tables were turned, would your brother give you his kidney?" I was sure I knew the answer. But I asked him this question anyway, and directly. Joe's answer—"I wouldn't be able to with my medical problems"—however unsatisfactory on the surface, only solidified his unspoken answer in my own mind. Yet if I didn't help my brother, I knew I would have difficulty living with myself.

The last test before the operation required minor surgery. Logistics required that it would have to be done just days before the final kidney procedure took place. I decided that if this test was positive, I would go through with it. I knew I was doing it mostly for me and not just for Joe.

The decision, then, was made. October it would be, but a week later than everyone hoped. A weight was lifted from my shoulders.

Bob got us free tickets to take a ride on the Atlantis submarine as a thank you for helping out a business acquaintance in St. Thomas. His weekly work hours had become steadier, his client base was continually growing, and his local popularity didn't surprise me any more. The boat trip across the harbor towards Buck Island was relaxing. It was my first time in a submarine of any kind and I had high expectations. While the excursion through coral reefs and marine life was fun, it barely compared with a nice afternoon snorkeling on St. John. But who could complain?

On the ride home, I made promises to Bob. Five days in the hospital, ten days to recover nearby, and then I'd be home. Bob would go to Boston to see me through the final test results, then leave for home without staying through the kidney surgery, which would only make him a nervous wreck. He'd return two weeks later to bring me home. My sister-in-law had planned to return to her full-time workload as a lawyer a short week after surgery. Published recovery time ranged from four to eight weeks, with most people falling into the latter camp. I wouldn't even try to live up to Janine's superwoman estimate and push the recovery.

I was determined to minimize my family involvement during the ordeal. Birdie had offered to let me recuperate at her home after surgery. It was the perfect solution. I wanted to wallow in my own pain and not be constantly reminded of my "great sacrifice," as my parents were calling it, or even the gratefulness of my sister-in-law. I wanted normalcy as soon as possible, and my best friend would surely comfort or cajole me into it.

Bob met me at the hospital in Boston at the completion of the last test, and we tried to carve out a weekend together before the big surgery. While waiting for me to be discharged, he walked the halls of the hospital selling raffle tickets for the St. John Volunteer Rescue group to the nursing staff. The Rescue group was hoping to raise money for its first "Jaws of Life" toolkit on St. John. This had become a big priority with the recent influx of enclosed recreation vehicles and the hourly cross-island bus service St. John now enjoyed. No one had worried about extraction equipment when only open-sided jeeps and open-air taxis had been the norm. The hospital was a perfect place for Bob to share island woes and play on sympathies. Within minutes he'd sold all the tickets he'd thought to bring north with him.

Our weekend together was a blur. It was the first time back in New England for Bob, but even under happier circumstances he'd rather have been on St. John. Most of the time we were there, it was cold and wet and miserable. I sent Bob home at dawn the day before the kidney surgery so he could prep for a first-aid test and get his mind on easier things.

Birdie took that last day off. She decided we both needed a diversion and suggested we travel to Connecticut and spend the day at a gambling casino. We'd spent a day like this once before and had lots of fun, but this time it was a bust. Neither of us could stay focused, and after a couple of hours we gave it up. We were both subdued the entire way back to Boston, where I'd stay overnight until my 5 AM check-in at the hospital. I was a little glad when she left, as I needed to face my fears alone.

* * *

The surgery went fine for both Joe and I. Amazingly, I got to know my oldest brother better in those few days in the hospital ward than I had in my forty-some-odd years on this planet. With a seven-year age difference between us, we'd just never been very close. He didn't understand why I'd moved to Paradise, and I didn't understand why he hadn't followed his dreams. In the end, it was our common paranoia and misery that united us.

My brother insisted on morphine to ease his pain, then other prescription drugs to continue the dulling process. I was more afraid of side effects than anything else, and opted for an epidural short-term and then simple Tylenol, hoping I'd recover faster if I wasn't doped up. I wanted no Tylenol-3 or Tylonol-2, just simple, basic Tylenol. Joe complained that I was trying to be a martyr, but I retorted that I was being cautious, fearing that any side effect might keep me in the hospital longer than necessary.

It wasn't that the pain was unbearable three days after surgery, but I knew it would be bad soon. When I wanted another dose of Tylenol one hour before the prescribed six-hour interval had passed, the nurses acted like I was a drug addict. Stopping by my brother's room on the slow shuffle back to mine, I whined and told Joe it was unfair. His spirits were high, just as he was from all the drugs, and he found the situation humorous. I threw a pillow at him and left Joe laughing as he took his fine Percocet. Ten minutes later, I was unsuccessfully trying to get comfortable in my bed again, when I heard a loud commotion in the hallway.

"I don't care if it *is* just aspirin, you cannot just take drugs from the drug cart. Your sister will have to wait another half-hour. Now get away from there." Shuffling preceded Joe's shy arrival at my bedside. "I tried," he said with a grin. Wow, my brother tried to steal drugs for me! I *loved* this man.

I was out of the hospital in five days and was determined to return home on schedule. Bob called almost daily to cheer me up with news from Paradise. He sent a homemade get-well card with a photograph of my favorite rocking chair on our porch overlooking the gardens and St. Thomas in the distance. Inside, the card told me that my husband and even the cats were proud of me and missed me and were waiting anxiously for me to come home and watch the sunsets with them. It was the sweetest thing.

Birdie opened her home to me and made sure I had food to eat and things to read. But she didn't overly pamper me. By the third day, I only hurt when I laughed, which unfortunately was often. Every evening we traded adventures from the summer months and I brought her up to date on everything happening on St. John. I had plenty of time to paint gold "St. John, USVI" inscriptions on the hundred-odd medallions I'd brought North, and to worry about how I'd find time to get the other hundred completed for my first deadline.

Joe recovered faster than I did. The volume of medications that would be his future depressed him, but his personality was back and I was glad. I was embarrassed that I had been so afraid to give him a kidney and that I'd considered a few months' disruption in my life to be such a big deal. On the phone every day we compared recovery pains and I was disappointed when there were indications he felt better than I did.

I accomplished my mission to get home two weeks after surgery thanks to Bob's playing "Sherpa from the Himalayas," carrying my entire coterie of luggage. A plump pillow in the taxi provided added padding for my side. The doctors had insisted that I lift no more than five pounds for a couple of weeks, and then not lift any significant weight for a solid eight weeks. Even the taxi driver on St. Thomas was extra kind as he tried hard to avoid the numerous potholes and minimize the jolting. As he avoided each one, the driver turned to me with a grin and asked if I was okay. I made Bob give him an extra big tip.

At home, our neighbor Jay, who'd volunteered to cat-sit for a few days, also had a warm meal waiting on the kitchen counter for our arrival. It was just what we both needed. The next morning, an orchid plant that smelled like chocolate arrived as a welcome home present from the St. John Rescue folks, and five people called to welcome me back. I was humbled and felt undeserving of all the attention. What had seemed like a horrible life decision a month ago now seemed trivial. I was happy and home and my brother now had a brighter future. And in two more months I'd have everything behind me, while Joe would have a lifetime of adjustments and medications ahead of him. But life, nonetheless.

I still had one more challenge ahead. My workplace was having its yearly kickoff meeting the first week of November. It was only one week after my return to St. John. Bob grumbled, but I promised to make porters carry my bags, and I would travel as light as possible. The trip was worth it. While I was uncomfortable part of every day, I was being productive again.

Since my return to St. John five days earlier, I was ready to stay put for a while. In fact, I was in a panic. I still had eighty medallions to make for my first commission and we needed a host of other craft items to fill even a tiny booth during St. John Saturday. If I put off the November event, I knew it would be a long time before I got around to doing it again. Raw materials were strewn everywhere in the living room and kitchen, and I worked feverishly. Even waiting for my company's 800-number computer connection to the mainland gave me the two minutes necessary to accomplish some small task.

Meanwhile, my recovery continued at an accelerated pace. The worst part involved my surgeon's insistence that I stay out of the pool as well as the ocean. When he first told me I had to refrain from taking a dip in the swimming pool for six to eight weeks, I balked. He'd just finished telling me that I could resume normal showers a short week after surgery. He'd lived his life in Boston, and it showed. Normal showers on St. John? Incredible.

It took all of my patience to explain to this urban doctor that I lived on a little island where water is scarce. "A short dip in the swimming pool followed by a navy shower with as little water as possible is our daily norm," I complained. "And as it happens, my regular dip in the pool is the least strenuous part of the whole chore."

The surgeon was hard to convince. So I tried a new tactic, asking why he didn't want me in the pool. "You'll strain yourself and won't be able to resist the urge to swim," he said.

"Our pool is tiny. We can barely float, never mind swim. Besides, I'm not a tourist, I'm a native. I'm very happy to spend just five or ten minutes floating there," I persisted.

Finally he acquiesced. "Five minutes max, after four weeks. And only the pool. Ten minutes, in six weeks. No ocean for at least eight weeks so you won't be tempted to strain yourself. And you must immediately dry off afterwards and keep the scar tissue out of the sun."

I barely survived the weeks without a dip in the pool. While I was careful and immediately changed to dry clothes, my sea baths started two weeks earlier than the doctor ordered. It just wasn't worth a phone call to Boston to convince him I could be lazy in the water.

St. John Trivia

The only true "native" mammals living on St. John today are a handful of bat species! All of the others – including mongooses, rats, and donkeys – were brought to the island by boat. Small white-tailed deer, originally brought to the island in the late 1700's, have adapted well and can often be found around sunset near Big Lamshure Bay in the south part of the island.

Goats are found in their greatest number on the east end of St. John, where they often lay in groups along roadways and take naps. Donkeys, until recently a common form of transportation, roam almost everywhere.

Chapter 11

Every Day is a Holiday

Bob and I had much to be thankful for, so this first year on-island we wanted a Thanksgiving we'd remember forever. Two years earlier we passed the holiday on St. John with a traditional feast at a waterside restaurant in the heart of downtown Cruz Bay. This time a restaurant just wouldn't cut it. I pondered alternatives as I readied for my first postsurgical dip in the pool on a hot November afternoon. Then I looked down at the pool.

"Unbelievable" was not exactly the word that came out of my mouth, but it sums up the sight that faced me from our porch: A mysterious green algae had grown overnight in our pool, and it looked very ominous. But it could not deter me from my goal. I considered the alternatives. I made a decision.

Down the spiral staircase, I took a left turn instead of the usual right toward our pool. Across the trellised bougainvillea and down another flight of stairs, I came face to face with my neighbor's pool, clean and inviting. Thank goodness Moe and Bev had built two pools on the property, one for each nearly identical building. The lower pool was slightly longer and narrower than our own, but suited my purpose just fine. My neighbor Jay sat in a corner soaking up the sunrays. Her grin betrayed her closed eyes as she taunted "Go to your own pool, lady," while contrarily patting the chair next to hers in invitation.

Jay was always philosophical and creative when she was relaxed, so I posed my Thanksgiving dilemma and hoped for the best. I wasn't disappointed. "Wouldn't it be fun," she proposed, "to invite everyone who lives here to share in a Thanksgiving pot luck dinner at the pool?"

"Have you seen my pool?" I countered. I described it.

"Yuck," she frowned back. "But the odds are good that at least one of the pools will be in okay condition. Besides, with enough food and drink, it won't matter. Andre can cook a big ham for the occasion."

"And I'll roast a turkey," I offered without thinking.

On a roll, Jay suggested we could invite not only everyone who lived nearby, but also some people we knew who'd only recently moved here. And then there were the few boat people we'd both become friendly with, for whom cooking a turkey dinner was nearly impossible. Everyone would be asked to contribute some food or paperware item. The men would round up tables and chairs, and tarps for shade.

As for me, I would only have to make a turkey, I thought to myself. *In my oven from hell*, I realized as the warm pool water finally soaked through and softened my brain.

Our stove was a small gas job, about thirty inches wide, with barely room for four burners on top. The kind you find in studio apartments. My stove knobs didn't even have writing on them. I'd laughed when I first saw them, until my guessing at temperatures resulted in a couple of inedible meals. I'd visited Bev to make a paper template of her own stove knobs, and wrote the appropriate markings onto my knobs with permanent ink. Another failed meal brought me knocking at Jay's door to make a template from a stove identical to mine. It still didn't matter. My oven really only had two settings. "On" and "Burnt." Still, I looked forward to the turkey challenge to prove I was smarter than my tiny hellhole of an oven. It would be a unique Thanksgiving. I was feeling better.

And although it wasn't yet Thanksgiving, I was already anxious to unpack all the Holiday goods which were in the last of the unopened Paradise Expedition boxes. But as I looked around myself, knee-high in packing materials, I realized that maybe I had less desire to decorate than I thought. After all, our apartment was finally beginning to have a lived-in feel to it, and the thought of over-decorating for the holidays depressed me. On the other hand, I did want some Christmas and Hanukkah trivia and I hoped to get Bob to cut down a local version of the fresh-cut Christmas tree he'd traditionally provided from the New England woods.

Jay was in a completely different quandary. Ted, who lived below her apartment, had cut a twenty-foot-long Century plant for a traditional island Christmas tree before deciding it was too big to be useful in his apartment. With Jay's cathedral ceiling, the tree made a perfect focal point for the living room. But, she lamented, most of her Christmas decorations were stuck in Rhode Island due to a family squabble, and her house would be abnormally bare for the holiday season. Another neighborly chat with Jay, this time at my newly cleaned pool, solved both our dilemmas.

"I have more decorations than one person on St. John should be allowed to have. I'd be thrilled if you'd take some to use in your apartment." All had been unpacked and needed organizing anyway, but I could see the doubt on her face.

"You don't need to worry about any getting destroyed, as we expect that during the holidays. There are enough decorations to do justice to your tree, with enough left over for the smaller one I hope to have," I pleaded. "Really." I added for emphasis.

"Only if we have a holiday party at our place to show it off," Jay compromised. "And Andre and I will take care of everything. We'll celebrate Hanukkah and Christmas and whatever and invite all the neighbors and our friends."

It was perfect. (Better her place than mine, I thought. My apartment would stay rather clean and we'd get a party out of the deal. That's the Christmas spirit, I thought!) So Christmas was well under control before Thanksgiving even arrived. I set to work on other things I had on my mind.

Bob had signed me up for booth space at the next St. John Saturday event, which was to be held two short days after Thanksgiving. I needed more goods to sell and I needed them fast. Enlisting Jay's and her daughter Jessie's help, we made little princess crowns made of foil and ribbons that were sure to be a big hit with the kids. I made doorknob hangers like the "Do Not Disturb" signs found in hotel rooms, with island scenes I designed on my computer. Birdie helped us from New Hampshire by critiquing the designs I e-mailed her via the Internet. Even Bob got into the spirit of things and laminated and trimmed these unique items. He borrowed a couple of doorknobs from friends in town and mounted them on a board as a display rack.

Digging into my craft supplies, I came up with a large batch of earrings with a Christmas theme, the ones that Birdie had delivered to my garage a year earlier. With sudden inspiration, Jessie and I gathered seashells and spray painted them gold. We tied them in mesh bags, added a blue ribbon to each, and tagged them as Island Hanukkah Geld. Attached to each ribbon was a short explanation of how pirates in the Caribbean had stolen all the local gold, and so, true to St. John's unique style, we offered this new version of the traditional holiday gift. It was silly, but so were we.

Meanwhile, Thanksgiving was two days away, and I'd forgotten to buy a turkey. But by noon on Thanksgiving Day, I'd been hovering over my temperamental oven and our turkey for hours and I was tired. Just that morning Bob told me he thought we were about to run out of propane gas for the stove. We hadn't filled it for six months and the gas company was closed for the holiday. I prayed the gas would last until the turkey was cooked.

Maybe being low on gas helped. Or maybe it was constantly opening the oven to make sure the broiler hadn't suddenly turned itself on. But by some strange miracle, the heat in the oven stayed just perfect, and the turkey came out plump, juicy and *unscorched.*

The party was a lively one. There was enough food for an army. An open tent provided shade for the food, and a motley and eclectic combination of lawn furniture was spread throughout the garden. Lots of people showed up, with some seated on the edge of the pool while being occasionally splashed by the younger set. There was music for every taste, and the good times flowed freely. So did the spiked cups of Jell-O that never seemed to run out.

Andre's ham was a big hit, which was a good thing, since he'd mistakenly chosen a spiral cut style at a St. Thomas supermarket. Given the price of goods there, the ham ended up costing a full day's pay. Everyone insisted, however, that it had been worth his pain.

The only low point in the festivities was the army of fire ants that lived near the pool. It was hard to believe such tiny creatures could cause such excruciating pain, but the second they found any exposed flesh they bit with all their might. Even they couldn't spoil the fun for long though. By nightfall, exhaustion overtook our fun. Bob and I went home, determined to call it a night. A short while later, though, we were drawn back by the laughter from the lingering crowd below. Again and again we were drawn downstairs to join the last of the party die-hards taking dips in the pool and philosophizing in the darkness.

* * *

The urge for an island Christmas tree inspired me to solve several problems at once. The story goes something like this:

The day after Thanksgiving, I woke up insisting to Bob that the cutting had to be done immediately. Bob was caught off-guard and was still in a festive mood from the day before. In fact, he'd already gotten tools and gloves together before he remembered he was still supposed to be grouchy. But by then it was too late for him to back out or pretend he felt other than excited about this new adventure. And so he stalked down the dusty road. I followed in high spirits, thinking, some things never change.

A traditional St. John Christmas tree meant (for some) the dead stalk from a Century plant. The gem Bob chose was growing a mere two hundred yards above our apartment on a hill, but getting to it required a gingerly hike through the bush. Once we'd arrived, we found the stalk was not only dry but also twisted and slanted and not overly attractive, while only fifty yards further up the slope was the tree of my dreams. I begged and I pleaded and I sang Christmas carols to my husband while pointing to the tree I wanted. Bob turned a deaf ear and began sawing away at its twisted sister.

Surprisingly, though the Century plant was extremely strong and hard, it weighed very little. I was able to carry my end of our fifteen-foot tree with just three fingers, which was a relief, since I was under doctors orders to carry little weight. Bob and I walked down past a beautiful, late-blooming Century plant that had tempted me on our walk up the steep hill. But we'd resisted, since we'd both heard horror tales from people who'd cut down a fresh stalk. That beauty wasn't worth the oozing sap that would follow a few days later. It was a great way to ruin anything on or under the tree.

We startled some tourists coming up a switchback, and they almost stalled their car on the steep road as they slowed down to stare at our strange lumberjack antics. Back at the apartment, Bob cut off the bottom of the long stalk and placed the remaining eight-foot-high island Christmas tree top into our patiently waiting tree stand. (Finally, I had been vindicated in mailing it to St. John.) Still, there would be no need to water this "fresh" Christmas tree. I put the bottom part of the stalk into a large bucket, which we then filled with stones. Bob was directed to cut back its branches of seedpods to a mere eight inches out from the central stalk.

Suddenly it hit me. Instantly I had the display stand I'd been searching for to hang the foil fairy crowns for the St. John Saturday crafts fair. It was crooked, but it would work. Bob fumed.

"You tricked me into doing two chores today, when I only promised to do one," he whined.

"And rather painlessly," I commented a little dryly.

Holiday season chores always seemed to bring out the child in my husband, in good ways and in bad. St. John Saturday was only twelve hours away.

The craft items were a big hit the next day. Jay and Jessie both came down to help set up. Bob graciously helped to unload the car, knowing he'd have hours at the beach without interruption that day. Conscious of my recent surgery, I welcomed his assistance. While Jay had to go back to work for most of the day, Jessie stayed, even finding a friend to help out and keep her company at the same time. Steel band music from the bandstand in the park set a festive mood that day. My fellow vendors were pleasant, and the holiday spirit was everywhere. Bob's desertion was quickly forgotten.

Our neighbors, Ted and Katie, were selling Christmas wreaths made from the seedpod-laden Century plant branches. It was recycling at its best. Ted had been making a few dollars on the side cutting down traditional island Christmas trees for seasonal residents who didn't want to walk through the bush this year. The wreaths were the by-products of cutting the trees down to size, since branches can extend over twenty-five feet down the length of the tree. For added variety, Katie had made some beautiful wreaths, threading together the empty seedpods of the ever-abundant tan-tan trees that sprout up on roadsides everywhere. Their booth was a big hit and was photographed for posterity, appearing in the next *Tradewinds* newspaper.

In-between customers, I started dancing with the Mocko Jumbies that provided entertainment for the tourists. Mocko Jumbies were costumed dancers on eight-foot-high stilts. Imagine my surprise when I

165

realized that one directly above me was another of our talented neighbors who'd moved here two years earlier. As each ferry arrived with more visitors from St. Thomas, the Mocko Jumbies moved closer to the docks to provide a special welcome and to direct them back towards the park. I did my part by offering to take photographs of tourists and Jumbies with the tourists' cameras as they passed by.

Meanwhile, my own sales were respectable. The youngsters helping in my booth were a boon, especially when a short sun shower threatened to ruin my goods. As is typical, the first drop of rain signaled a downpour to follow mere seconds later. Quickly we whipped out plastic to cover everything but ourselves, knowing the shower would be over in just a few minutes. The sun stayed shining throughout.

Along with a free lunch chosen from a nearby food vendor, I rewarded my little helpers with their choice of souvenirs from my own booth. One selected a necklace and the other a key chain, both made from polymer clay. The day wound down as the sun was setting. Bob returned and packed the car without complaint and took credit for being a good husband. He'd found a beach he'd shared only with the birds and the sea life to while away the hours, but I think I had more fun that day.

The next day, we both spent a quiet day at Jumbie beach on the north shore, with no responsibilities and no intrusions. Somehow even the boats knew to stay away from the little cove that day. I took my first sea-bath in months, two weeks earlier than the doctor had ordered. It was heaven. Palm and sea-grape trees provided shade, our picnic basket yielded delectable grazing, and a good book helped pass the time while Bob sunned himself on his snow float. There was no place I wanted to be at more than St. John that weekend. It wasn't even December, and yet the holidays were now in full gear.

The little gifts I gave my crafts fair volunteers were a big hit in the schoolyard the next day. The whole sixth grade class begged my young friends to find them some they could buy. After school, Jessie came knocking on my door, interrupting a business conference call, and asked if she could bring a selection of clay trinkets to school for her friends to choose from. After a few minutes' patience (which I'm sure seemed like years to my eleven-year-old friend), Jessie left with an eclectic selection and the promise of a finder's fee she could use towards her own holiday spending. It was another strange success for me as an artisan.

Following up on our newfound relationship, Jessie personally asked me to attend her small school's Christmas pageant. Along with the invitation came an admonition to wear "real shoes and a dress too." This child had always seen me in sandals, or else barefoot, and the only dresses she'd seen me wear were the flowery, floor-length shifts I'd come to prefer over shorts and a T-shirt (for comfort's sake). The night of the event I went all out and wore an outfit more suited to a formal summer's concert in Boston. I wore high heels and added makeup and jewelry to complete the attire. Jessie hardly recognized me, and even her mother couldn't stop staring.

The pageant was great fun, starting with darling preschoolers in their angel garb and seasonal songs, in both Spanish and English. My favorite was their rendition of "The Twelve Days of Christmas," with a decidedly island twist: "Nine Harried Tourists... Four Swaying Palms... And a Donkey Braying in a Hog's Plum Tree." It made me laugh so hard I almost fell on the floor with the three-year-olds.

Exactly eight weeks after surgery—the time specified for my official recovery—I was confronted with an unplanned business trip to California. It was mid-December, and the trip might bring an opportunity to find a few last-minute gifts for Bob. Convinced I'd babied myself enough, I decided to carry along my notebook computer so I could keep up with my normal workload between meetings. The travel between the USVI and the West Coast of the US was long and tiring, and I relearned respect and sensitivity for the tourists who make the long trek to visit our islands for their vacation.

By the time the return flight disembarked on St. Thomas, my side was aching from the weight of the bag I carried; my computer couldn't be checked as luggage like the rest of my load. Besides, the welcome basket of goodies that had greeted me on my arrival at my hotel in California from a company in San Jose was filled with local delicacies too fragile to pack.

Minutes after arriving home, with relaxing being my sole goal, Bob reminded me that it was Friday night and we had two parties to attend. He was ready to celebrate, since that very day he'd been offered full-fledged employment with Bestech, along with almost fantasy benefits and security that came with no longer being a mere contractor. Reminded that no business trips were scheduled for the next seven weeks and that the holidays were upon us, I got my second wind, and within minutes I was ready to party.

I sat in the passenger seat of my own Geo Tracker as Bob began the slow roll down the switchback towards town. The seat was at an angle, with the backrest reclined, which is my husband's preferred riding position. I didn't bother to make it more upright before reaching for the seatbelt to secure myself in. As my right arm, buckle in hand, reached across to find the buckle latch, a sharp pain jolted my body. I screamed. Bob braked the car, and though he was driving at a snail's pace, it was by the barest of margins that my head missed the windshield.

Just as suddenly as it started, the pain was gone. I tried again with the seat buckle only to reach the same painful conclusion. Perhaps the notebook computer I'd traveled with *had* been too heavy after all. Nevertheless, as we found out, after eight weeks of babying myself, I'd pulled the slowly healing inside stitches at the back end of my scar line. For months after, though with slowly decreasing levels of pain, I'd pull them again and again, resisting the urge to call my brother to see how he was holding up. The scar tissue, I would find out, was permanent. I rode illegally through Cruz Bay that night without a seatbelt and frankly, I found out, I didn't give a damn.

Our two parties that evening were marked with the diversity that had become our lives. First was the annual Holiday party at the local sail-making business where the crowded fun was already underway. The insides of the warehouse-style workspace had been lined with fresh palm fronds and Christmas lights to create a festive atmosphere. Hordes enjoyed a sea of food and beverage while others danced to the music or chatted away in clusters. A water cooler had been turned into a margarita dispenser; that was my first stop. Within minutes, I'd forgotten my pains. Bob and I mingled comfortably with the multi-everything crowd, some in cut-off jeans, and others in pressed slacks or dresses. Too soon, someone asked me the time and squelched our fun: we realized we were overdue at our other engagement...

Which was a large vacation resort near our home. While we knew it would be an upscale dinner/dance, we were unprepared for the formality of the occasion. Beaded gowns and—yes—even tuxedos adorned the outdoor gala event. There were sandals at this party, but the only shorts were those paired with crisp blazers and ties. Each place setting at the dinner tables included a party favor. These were extravagant seasonal ornaments discreetly marked with the initials SJYC and the year, as a take-home keepsake. A live band performed, while Bob and I danced under the moonlight. I drank enough so that I remember no more pain that night.

* * *

Our neighbors had no experience with Hanukkah. Bob sought to change that by inviting guests to participate in the lighting of the Menorah each night and sharing the history and traditions of the holiday with all. Some traditions he made up as he went along, but everyone had fun, and the sense of community we all felt made me keep quiet. I'd lined our porch with miniature Christmas lights, and discovered my downstairs neighbors, Ricky and Karen, always lined the pool area and gardens with lights too. A large electric Menorah crowned our upper porch for all in the valley to see.

Actually, you couldn't see much from the road, but at night our backyard was an enchanted place that made me smile all month long. Every tree and bush was covered with lights, each with its own distinctive color, creating a nighttime rainbow of delight. Inside, our Century plant tilted somewhat left or right, forward or backward, no matter how Bob tried to turn it. It seemed to have a mind or its own about these things. Even with lights and decorations and tinsel, it reminded me of a Charlie Brown Christmas tree. But when we turned out the living room lamps...then it was truly spectacular. With the glittering porch and garden below as a backdrop, it was the most beautiful tree we'd ever had.

Jay remembered to include Hanukkah decorations in her apartment for her as-promised holiday party, which pleased Bob tremendously. It seemed that a good portion of the island managed to stop by and spread good cheer. There was no dancing at Jay's party, but the long day and night of good food and plentiful drink and lively conversation interspersed with dips in the pool left little room for much more.

* * *

A week later I was searching for a different kind of party as I danced between the docks in Cruz Bay Christmas Eve morning. My husband's older sister Eve and her family were scheduled to visit us, just for the day. They were on a Caribbean cruise and the ship would dock in St. Thomas, only five miles away. Bob and I had been psyched for their visit.

These wonderful people had neglected to tell us what ship they'd be on, however, and by the time Bob got around to calling them to ask, they were already on their way. The local newspaper told us there would be seven ships in port on Christmas Eve.

On the designated day, Bob headed to work convinced they wouldn't show up, but told me to call him if they ever did. I drove down to the barge dock in the early morning, hoping they'd arrive soon.

It was my first real experience with cruise ship excursion routines. The barge dock where most cruise ship passengers disembark is at Cruz Bay Creek, which is out of sight of the regular ferry dock. I'd noticed cruise ship crowds there many times while driving past, but I didn't appreciate the magnitude of the operation. It was like a well oiled machine, with employees from the cruise ships, the ferries, the tour companies and the taxis all working in concert with each other.

With arms waving in patterns as though they were directing aircraft, workers chanted and pointed, "Annaberg over here, Trunk Bay over here, Island Tours over here." A continuous mass of tourists poured off ferryboats lined up next to the barges and followed directions like they were used to the routine. There were, of course, a few strays, but they were quickly intercepted and directed to the correct waiting lines. It was amazing.

But Bob's relatives were not there. As the empty boats departed, so did I. I rushed to the ferry dock where the hourly ferry was coming in. There were no relatives on the regular ferry from Red Hook, but seeing a coming ferry boat divert towards the Creek, I returned to my earlier location, knowing more cruise ship passengers were arriving over there. I repeated this dance throughout the morning, finally giving up.

The phone rang just as I walked into the apartment, saddened and exhausted. It was my brother-in-law's secretary on the phone from Massachusetts. The family would be landing at the regular ferry dock in five minutes. Town was at least ten minutes away. Bah Humbug. I was not a happy camper.

By twelve minutes later, I'd phoned my husband, parked my car on the dock, and was kissing and hugging Eve and our other long-lost relatives. We piled into the car. Then, after dodging tourists driving on the wrong side of the road and waiting patiently for a water truck to ascend Jacobs Ladder (an atrocious hill on the outskirts of town), our caravan of two cars got everyone to our home, smiling. It was Christmas Eve.

Bob's relatives had exactly two hours before they had to take a return ferry to Charlotte Amalie, as their cruise ship was docked at the Sub Base rather than the normal Havensight location where most ships arrived. The Sub Base meant an even longer trip back.

That two hours was a blur. Bob quickly made sandwiches for the hungry teenagers while I gave their parents a penny tour of our apartment. Then we all got back into the vehicles for a whirlwind tour of St. John. Up over Gift Hill we took them, as they hung on for dear life. We made a quick stop at the ruins at Catherineburg where I told them about—but didn't have time to show them—my favorite windmill site, with its tunnels and gravity-fed molasses storage pits. A roadside over-look showing islands in the British VI over the north shore was our next stop. Onto Bordeaux Mountain we took them, where they marveled at the view of Coral Bay.

Unfortunately, we were too concerned with their time constraints to drive them back to town via the slower north shore route, through the National Park. Instead we took them back down Centerline road while entertaining them with stories about cows and donkeys and goats. And then they were gone. It was hard to believe they'd been here at all. That evening, I looked out at the glittering lights of cruise ships settled off shore for the night, and wished them all very happy holidays.

While Bob and I spent Christmas day quietly together, the day did not end all festivities for us. Still to go, there were Kwanza and New Year's Eve and Three Kings Day (celebrated by islanders with great importance and parades and pageants). Every day seemed to bring another holiday. Before we came up for air the second week of January, I was partied out.

Chapter 12

**Everyone Needs
a Vacation**

In the middle of high tourist season on St. John, our first overnight guests flocked to us from the continent for a ten-night stay. Unfortunately, we were also in the middle of a drought. Navy showers, using as little water as possible and turning off the water while sudsing up, were the required routine. It wasn't so much the cost of buying a truckload of water that worried us as it was facing the wrath of neighbors who had to chip in for each meager truckload. Bob and I are always quietly paranoid about having extra bodies using the cistern.

Still, the guestroom was cleaned up and readied, and as a special touch, the Century plant display rack from our St. John Saturday fun was painted and recycled into an eccentric hat stand in the corner. Bob caved in and bought a round plastic patio table on St. Thomas that could easily seat four people on the porch for dinner using our still-strung Christmas lights and some table candles.

I'd offered use of my Tracker to our vacationing guests for day trips, since working in my home office often meant days with the vehicle sitting idle. Bob grumbled that using the car this way wasn't worth it, especially when I had to take the barge to St. Thomas to replace worn brakes in anticipation of the visits. Still, I caught Bob cleaning his own car and prepping the back seat for added guests just before they arrived. Sure, he complained, but he was always ready for visitors.

First came my sister-in-law Dee (from New York City) with her long-time girlfriend Shelly (from upstate New York). Dee had been with us on St. John during our family vacation two years earlier. She knew that St. John wasn't truly the end of the world, so we expected her to show up with just a small carry-on bag for luggage. Instead, Dee and Shelly each disembarked the ferry carrying two huge suitcases along with a large carry-on bag for each of them. My little Geo Tracker was so overloaded it had a hard time making it to the top of Jacobs Ladder, even though it hadn't rained for days and the road was dry. If that road had been wet, we never would have made the hill. As I drove, I brushed aside their comment that they'd brought some food stuffs for us and just shook my head, laughing at how two people could arrive so overpacked for a place where a T-shirt, shorts, and a bathing suit was all it took to dress day-to-day.

Imagine my surprise—and shame—when the first large suitcase was opened and I discovered wall-to-wall food and household items. The next suitcase surprised us even more. It too had been filled with food-stuffs, but the sugar and the cornstarch and the flour had burst from their packaging, causing a cloud of white to rush out at us when the baggage lid was opened.

The inside of the luggage was a disaster. Even more amazing was the sheer quantity and variety of food items that Dee and Shelly had purchased. Even if Bob and I hadn't bought any food since we'd arrived on-island, we'd now have a well-stocked pantry. They left nothing out. Finding room for it all took creativity; it took months to eat our way through most of the foodstuffs.

Dee and Shelly were dream guests. They not only brought us a huge supply of foods, but they also cleaned and cooked and accommodated our every whim. The first day was overcast, but it still gave me an excuse to sneak a day off from work and play tour guide. I showed them all around St. John, pointing out the usual sites, but interspersed it all with local trivia, like pointing out the cotton plants now growing wild on the other side of Bordeaux Mountain, but that had been planted by slaves in the 1800s. After some prodding, Dee took the wheel and got the hang of driving on the left. I started her out on the north shore of the island, near Annaberg, where there was little traffic. To her credit, she only panicked her way to the right side once. I knew that for the rest of the week, they'd be on their own, so it was good they learned how to drive here now.

Every day was an adventure for the girls, and Bob and I tried not to cringe explicitly at their tales each night: They took a wrong turn heading out of town and were nearly to Coral Bay before realizing their mistake, guessing how to get back to our apartment via a relatively direct route in the dark. They explored areas I couldn't bring myself to take my poor, vulnerable car to.

But at least our water shortage fears were unfounded. The girls showered sometimes at Trunk Bay or the Cinnamon Bay campground after their beach time, and both were out and about for most waking hours. Our fears seemed totally ungrounded, except when Shelly insisted on cooking for us and used valuable water for the clean-up. And when Dee decided to stick around one morning to clean the apartment from top to bottom, including the porch. Nevertheless, we were truly sorry when they had to return to the States.

* * *

The same day Dee and Shelly left us to return home, I left town for Atlanta. But at least I knew I'd be back in a few days. On the last day of business in Atlanta, anxious to get back home to the USVI and away from the cold weather that seemed everywhere on the mainland, I discovered what a small world it is.

The day after I was scheduled to leave Atlanta was my sister-in-law Janine's birthday, and I called her local florist in New Hampshire for a quick gift. When I gave my billing address, I expected the usual surprised exclamation and questions. Instead, I got an unusual "Sure, I understand." It seems the owner of the flower shop was on St. John at that very moment; he'd be there for another six weeks, as was his custom every winter. I asked where he was staying, and to my surprise, the address was right down the road from our apartment. Everyone who worked at the flower shop, in fact, had been to St. John for a vacation in the past year. When asked where we lived on St. John, I replied "Century Hill," since street addresses mean nothing on this island.

"Oh, you can probably see his roof in Chocolate Hole from there. Say hi to the Boss for us."

As it happened, the florist was still on St. John when our next vacationers—from New Hampshire too!—arrived.

* * *

But first, Bob and I took our own vacation.

Our excuse was our tenth anniversary. We'd planned to spend some days cross-country skiing in Vermont, as we'd done for part of our honeymoon. (In fact, our very first date was spent on a cross-country ski trail, with my future husband trying his best not to laugh as he attempted to teach me the sport.) The rest of our anniversary trip would be spent visiting friends, shopping, and getting health checkups.

Two weeks before the trip, Bob began to balk. He'd adjusted so well to St. John that the idea of cold weather had tarnished his desires. It was a call from Janine that reaffirmed our plans. Joe would turn fifty on our anniversary. His wife was planning a surprise birthday party while we were scheduled to be up north; conveniently, the party would take place the day before our resort reservations in Vermont. It was to be a big event that she hoped would raise Joe's spirits and help him forget his medical problems for a few hours. We couldn't refuse.

This would be the first time we'd left our cats alone for more than three days since we'd moved to Paradise. We were very concerned about them being cooped up for a whole week with only relative strangers to care for them. Jessie, our eleven-year-old neighbor, volunteered for the task (to be chaperoned by her mom, Jay). Since she had a cat of her own, and her mom would be there to ensure regular feedings, we left our babies in her care.

For our first night up north, we stayed with our good friend Dan, who was now sharing a home he'd bought with Jo, the lady who'd survived the West River camping weekend with us the spring before. They'd be visiting us on St. John a few weeks later and, like many first-time visitors, they were anxious to discuss their plans with us. Bob tried to explain that the timing of getting from the plane to the ferry would depend on their understanding of the concept of island time. But they couldn't grasp our lack of concern over which ferry they'd be on.

The next day was hectic. Early in the morning, we drove past the home of one of my co-workers to drop off my notebook computer for a long-needed upgrade. Then we stopped by Birdie's to have coffee and pick up some party items that she'd kindly prepared for me. Afterwards, it was on to my mother's house to visit with a brother and his wife, who'd flown in from Pittsburgh for the surprise party that evening.

Bob was tasked with the chore of spending the afternoon with Joe under the guise of working on his home computer to keep him occupied, and then to get my eternally late brother to the surprise party on time. Meanwhile, I was frantically running around town to buy party decorations, then rushing to the rented hall to set it up and decorate; Joe, meanwhile, had been told I was out clothes shopping with his wife. In the cold of New England, St. John was fast becoming a blurry memory.

By 6:30, everything was ready. Over seventy people were gathered in the rented hall, including the friends I'd visited with that morning. All were chatting freely and enjoying the poster-sized tongue-in-cheek collages representing fifty years in the life of my older brother. The DJ was warming up and the hors d'oeuvres were moving nicely. My niece, wanting to know everything about St. John that she had missed out on during her whirlwind two-hour Christmas tour, stood lookout with me for Bob and Joe at the other side of the huge restaurant complex. Joe expected to find his wife and I waiting there for a quiet dinner foursome with Bob.

The moment I spied Bob and Joe, I sent my excited niece through the restaurant to the adjoining rental hall to spread the word. I slowly guided the men through the restaurant to the closed door that separated the restaurant from the rented hall. It was only when I stood back and suggested that Joe lead the way that he got suspicious. Before Joe could react, I pushed the door open ahead of him and a rousing *"Happy Birthday!"* greeted him. All he could do was stand there motionless and stare.

The party was more fun than I thought possible. There was a trivia contest on the life and times of my brother, and strange dance contests to boot. Friends and family I hadn't seen in years were all there. While it was my brother's night, it also seemed to Bob and me a sort of pre-anniversary party for us. By the time we reached my brother's home late that night for what would be a short night's sleep, I was exhausted.

Early the next morning Bob and I departed for our three-day skiing vacation in Stowe, Vermont. The day was perfect for a long drive, with the sun shining on freshly snow-covered trees, while the roads were dry and held little traffic. The inn at Stowe was fabulous, as always. Late afternoon tea and cakes followed by a Jacuzzi bubble bath and a quiet fireplace supper of Mullagatawny soup and wine brought a fine end to the day. It was the antithesis of our life in the islands.

Trail conditions on that first day of cross-country skiing were perhaps the best we'd ever encountered. True to tradition, my husband skied with me for the first twenty minutes, then rushed off to the farthest reaches of the trail system while I enjoyed a slower pace, absorbing the quiet nature around me. We were on the Von Trapp Family trail system, which was famous for the family that founded it (of *Sound of Music* fame) and the pristine variety of sights and trail, it offered the day-tripper. By early afternoon, we were tired and traveled to town to do some shopping for local gourmet goodies for our friends back on St. John.

The next two days flew by fast. One evening Bob and I went to the local movie theatre. When we tried to remember the last time we'd done so, we were surprised to realize it had been a full year earlier on our last visit to Vermont. There was no movie theatre on St. John, and the practicalities of going to St. Thomas to get to a theatre always seemed too daunting. Too soon, we had to leave.

My mom was scheduled to have back surgery the day we returned from Stowe and I wanted to be back in New Hampshire and near the family. My mother's surgery went well, and my brother from Pittsburgh was in residence in my parents' home to keep a watchful eye on my elderly father. By late evening, Bob and I were at Dan and Jo's again. It would be our home for the next two days as we waited to keep doctors' appointments and stock up on household goods we couldn't find in the islands.

On that last day before returning to St. John, we said our good-byes, picked up my newly upgraded computer, dropped off a thank-you bouquet of flowers to Birdie, visited my mom in the hospital, and then said good-bye to my dad and brothers. Then Bob and I were off to Massachusetts and yet another visit, one night with some island enthusiasts. After a fine send-off dinner and good conversation, we were just settling in for the night when my husband suggested I call St. John to talk to Andre and Jay—and especially Jessie—to check on our cats. Andre answered our call.

"It's about time you called," said my anxious neighbor. "We tried tracking you down for the past twenty-four hours, but you were nowhere to be found."

I was sure there was an emergency of some kind. "Sorry, Andre, but we weren't sure where we'd be yesterday until the last minute. What's happened?" I worried.

"It's what's going to happen. Here's what I need you to do. You need to put on your coat, and get into your car and find a supermarket. You're in civilization up there, so that should be easy even at nine o'clock on a Saturday night. I want you to go inside the market and buy me a box of Drake's Ring-Dings... a *big* box". Ring-Dings? The emergency was that the man wanted me to buy some kind of *snack cake*? "And don't bother coming down here unless you have a nice big box with you. I've been dying for some Ring-Dings for ages. Then it hit me. You're coming back so you can bring them."

For some strange reason I found myself grinning and agreeing. My husband, hearing my half of the conversation, was shaking his head in disbelief over what was about to occur. As I hung up the phone, I confirmed his disbelief.

"I'm going out to find a convenience store. Does anyone want to join me?"

My somewhat dazed and confused hosts declined my invitation, but they made me a map to the closest store. My husband grumbled, but put on his coat anyway and handed me the car keys. A few blocks later, I discovered his reason for giving in to Andre's request so easily, and even joining me. While I reached for the only box of Ring-Dings in the store, my husband was also reaching—in his case, however, for his own preferred snack cake from the Drake folks: Yodels.

"Hey, if you can go out at all hours and get Andre some Ring Dings, then I can get some Yodels," he responded to my raised eyebrows. The cashier rang up the purchase. "And I don't know how you think we're going to get these home, but my Yodels better not get crushed," he demanded. Master packer that I was, one day and three thousand miles later neither man was disappointed.

I'd felt badly the next morning as we quietly abandoned our sleeping hosts at all of five in the morning to catch our early flight home; we'd spent so little time with them, and yet they'd been so kind. (They had barely laughed over the Ring-Dings and Yodels. I knew they'd fit right in living on St. John.)

Bob and I were anxious to get back home to peace and quiet and the same bed every night. Before the plane from Boston left the ground, we'd made a firm decision to take our next vacation in Arizona or New Mexico—in fact, anywhere we knew no one and had no obligations or schedules to keep. We'd had enough of holidays for the moment, and now we had commitments back in St. John to keep.

* * *

Bob and I had started an Adopt-A-Trail group on the island. It began innocently enough: a casual conversation had turned our attention and thoughts to the VI National Park, which covers two-thirds of the island. The National Park survives on a tiny budget, with little funding available for upkeep and maintenance. Since the whole of the US Virgin Islands is allowed only a non-voting delegation in Washington, vote-trading with other Representatives to get the Park budget increased is nearly impossible. But Bob wanted to hike and I needed the exercise, and we thought it would be a good idea to do some volunteer work at the same time. We'd seen Adopt-A-Trail programs in other National Parks, and given the financial crunch the VI National Park Service lived under, it made sense to try and help them by offering our services. When Bob mentioned our plan to our neighbors, they were immediately enthusiastic to join in, and things just grew from there.

As part of our initial effort, we settled on the Brown Bay Trail, mostly because Andre and Bob went for a hike there one day and came back enthusiastic. While the trail was pretty rugged and long, the portion from the East End road to the beach on Brown Bay was reasonable as a project, they both agreed. It was overgrown but still passable and led to a rather remote beach. In just two weeks, twelve friends had decided to participate with us in the program. Once everyone had signed the park-required volunteer forms, we were ready to begin—or so we thought. It seems that the only day that everyone had off from work on a regular basis was Sunday, which would make it difficult to get on-site assistance from Park personnel. But we were determined.

That first day we made it to the trailhead at eight o'clock in the morning. Since we all lived on the other side of the island, we got up very early to make it there in time, and it showed. Only a few of us had brought machetes, and even fewer knew how to use one. Bob and I had received our "his" and "her" machetes for Christmas from our friend Dan in New England, and we were anxious to try them out. No one had brought work gloves, and quite a few people wore T-shirts and shorts, as they no longer owned long pants suitable for the job. Still, Bob thought he was very prepared. On principle he carried a huge back-pack loaded with towels, water, emergency first aid kits, etc. He should have brought more Band-Aids.

The first third of the trail was uphill all the way. The kids from Colorado in our group were hugely annoying to us older folk, as their twenty-something bodies bounced up the trail with little effort. As for me, I was winded within the first five minutes, and I wasn't alone in my pain.

Everything was overgrown, and in some places it was hard to believe there was a path under there at all. Both Bob and Andre received much ribbing for their having concluded earlier that the trail was "passable." A Park Ranger joined us for a short time on that first day to teach us how to use the park-loaned tools safely and to provide advice, but even he was smart enough to fall to the rear.

"Start at the top of the ridge," he encouraged us "and leave the beginning of the trail alone for a while. That will discourage tourists from using the trail until it's in better shape. Perhaps I can get the Park to use heavy equipment to clear the first part at some point." It wasn't exactly a promise, but it was an encouraging pipe dream we could all hang on to for a while.

We learned to use (and *abuse*) our machetes that day, and although the Ranger suggested working only a small section of the trail at any one time, once he left everyone hacked their way to the beach. I think we all just needed that sense of accomplishment to get us going.

There were no plants that needed protection, we'd been told. "Just be careful of the thorns," warned the Ranger. And there were *billions* of thorns, and they scratched us all. We encountered baby goats in the bushes, and even a donkey munching on groundcover in a ravine. At some point, Andre detoured everyone for a few minutes to see an old plantation gravestone he'd discovered; it was of a little child, the sole occupant in an elaborate but decaying graveyard.

The final stretch to the remote Brown Bay beach was littered with old piles of broken conch shells, discarded by the fishermen who occasionally worked this area. Jessie was the first to discard her outer clothes on the sandy crescent of beach and to head for the water. It was shallow for a long way out, and much of the shoreline was lined with a bed of sea grass, home to thousands of baby conch. The fish were bountiful too, but what blew us all away was how close the island of Tortola seemed from this north-facing beach. We knew that after the abolition of slavery on Tortola in 1838, a number of slaves from St. John had made their way across the rough currents of the Sir Francis Drake Passage that separates the islands. It was easy to envision slaves picking this very spot in Brown Bay from which to make that desperate swim to freedom.

We ate an early lunch and, refreshed from our swims, hauled our gear back up the overgrown trail, only to collapse with fatigue at our vehicles on the other side of the ridge. We all then committed ourselves to returning the next week, and then every other week after that, until the trail was up to official park specifications.

But two people never returned, and one of our group had been unknowingly injured. Apparently, one of the Colorado kids had unwittingly uncovered and hacked away at a small, unusually formed Manchineel tree near the beach. Wherever this relatively rare plant was found on the island, the Park Service marked the trees with bright red paint and placed dire warning signs near them, noting that a simple touch from the tree's sap could cause extreme burns, and eating its apple-like fruit could even cause death. Apparently, the National Park Service had overlooked this mutant Manchineel tree.

The injured Colorado kid came back the next week with his tale from the health clinic and with a local expert on native foliage. Together they found the offending Manchineel tree, and the whole group cleared the surrounding area and marked the tree's presence with a small wall of broken conch shells and driftwood. Someone found some charcoal from a fisherman's beach fire and a couple of washed up pieces of plank with which to make a warning sign. Another person found a length of red plastic tape on the beach carried by wind and water from who-knows-where, and we used it to rope off the offending plant from unwary tourists. We were proud of our efforts. A couple of visits later, anyone could traverse the Brown Bay Trail without even the threat of thorn scratches from more benign foliage.

* * *

Finally, Dan and Jo made it to St. John. I wanted everything in the apartment to be perfect for their arrival. Bob figured they were so enamored of both St. John and each other that my efforts wouldn't really matter, so he refused to chip in and help! The day before the couple were due to arrive, I spent the whole morning cleaning, trying to remove any lingering trace of cobwebs or dust balls that I knew could easily grow inches wide by dinner time. Halfway through putting fresh towels in the guest bathroom, the phone rang.

"Hey Buddy," my friend Dan began in apparent high spirits.

"Where are you?" I asked. "Are you ready for Paradise?"

"I was going to ask you the same thing. Where are you? Do you know what day this is?" Dan plodded on.

"Sure. I'm getting all ready for you. I'll be waiting for you at the airport tomorrow." The guy was obviously *too* excited about getting here. And he had called me, so of course he knew where I was.

"Well, we may not still be here tomorrow. We've been waiting for you already for two hours." Did he mean what I thought he did? "At the airport," he finally added.

"But you're due tomorrow, not today. Bob wrote it on the calendar." Nevertheless, the itinerary we'd posted on the refrigerator door told the real truth, and the calendar was *wrong*.

"I'm sorry, I'm really, really sorry," was all I could think to say.

"She's on island-time," I heard him chuckle as he hung up the phone.

Dan and Jo made it from St. Thomas under their own steam. A contrite and humble hostess was there to greet them on the St. John dock, babbling about island-time and how their vacation would be uphill from this point forward. They'd come for a ten day visit and were determined nothing would prevent them from living their fantasy.

And they did it all. Swimming and snorkeling and exploring every day, as expected. Their romantic evening walk along the grounds of a lush St. John, was followed the next night by an even more romantic sunset dinner high up at Chateau Bordeaux overlooking Coral Bay and the East End. For both Bob and I, though, most days were business as usual, and we were jealous.

On the only day Bob and I both had free from work, Dan and Jo wanted to treat us to a day of fun and play. Those normal pleasures of floating at a beach didn't meet their criteria of "something special," however, so, we turned to the local newspaper for ideas. *A FUND-RAISING FLOTILLA*, the ad screamed. The Moravian Church in Coral Bay was to be beneficiary of the event. The church's history of kindness to local boaters needing shelter and assistance during hurricanes and other disasters ensured a strong turnout. Each donation provided event participants with a sailboat ride to Norman Island in the British Virgin Islands for a day of partying and beach fun. Even Bob got excited, and the next morning he bought four tickets to the event for an outlandishly small donation.

We gathered at the dock in Coral Bay at eight o'clock in the morning to board a sailboat. It was first-come, first-served, and Dan made sure to get there early. The sailboat we ended up on carried only ten people, including the captain and his mate. Dave, our captain, made us feel comfortable right away, and offered to let anyone volunteer to help with the rigging and the steering and to learn something new about sailing. Our Norman Island destination, thought by many to be the site of Robert Louis Stevenson's *Treasure Island*, was a three-and-a-half-hour sail away. The boat didn't even have to make the normal detour to Tortola to clear customs. Customs agents had volunteered to meet the flotilla in a bay on Norman Island itself to handle the formalities, and again on the dock in Coral Bay, so we'd lose no time from the festivities.

There were over twenty-five boats participating in the event, and though ours was first out from Coral Bay, it was by no means the first to arrive at our destination. For the queasy among us, powerboats were provided to make the journey a much quicker one, and some sailboats had left directly from other places already filled with friends and relatives of the captains.

Once we arrived, , there were tables waiting for us heavily laden with free food on a sandy beach on Norman Island. T-shirts and drinks were being sold for a small sum to contribute to the church funds. A huge fishing boat from Maine (of all places!) sat in the middle of the Bay, providing a stage for live music to be enjoyed by all.

We snorkeled in fabulously clear water, the surface as smooth as glass, and saw new varieties of fish and corals in amazing colors. In the food line I was surprised by how many people greeted me by name as they tried to decide between hamburgers and chips or fungi, rice with beans and other local fare. Live entertainment from the floating stage got even Dan and Jo to lift their heads out of the water a few times. An occasional cloud cooled things off for a few minutes at a time.

On the return trip, Dan took the wheel and piloted the boat for a while. That night Jo and Dan told us they'd decided to move to St. John themselves in a couple of years. They didn't expect our reaction.

"You visited Maho Bay this week, didn't you?" Bob asked, catching my eye. Puzzlement was written all over their faces. Yes they had, they agreed.

"Hmmm," I added with a smile, but said no more.

Dan and Jo then both proceeded to babble about the reasons they'd fallen in love with the island and why it made sense to make a drastic change in their lives, but we hardly listened; we knew better. Bob and I exchanged secret looks and chalked another one up to the Ethel McCully syndrome—the overwhelming desire to jump ship and spend the rest of your days on-island. We were now convinced the legend was real.

The next day we took them to the Brown Bay Trail along with our motley crew of locals. Our numbers had dwindled to a core of six to eight people who managed to bring visible results to the trail. Like many volunteer groups, we'd lost any real enthusiasm for the hard work after our first few visits, but we kept at it. Besides, the trail had become an escape of sorts from our daily grind, and while moving rocks and cutting away the jungle, we shared weekly gossip and philosophized on every topic imaginable. It might not have been a biweekly *vacation* by any stretch of the imagination, but it was therapeutic.

Since the trail's numerous thorny ketch-an-keep plants clung to me so often, I'd become known as "Ketch-An-Keep Karin." Bob was in his glory as Ranger Bob again, and Andre had become Machete Man. We also had the Colorado Kids, the Rake Queen, and the Lopper Lady, who took all her pent-up aggressions out on the stubborn trail growth. Only Jessie was without a nickname—until Dan bestowed the perfect one on her.

It happened by chance. The East End of St. John is notorious for it's large, free-roaming herds of goats. Jessie—the only real kid in our crew—loved to mimic their cries. "Watch this," she told Dan and Jo as we approached our first herd in Coral Bay on the way to the trailhead. "I'll make them move."

"Baaah-baaah," she intoned, and sure enough the goats moved out of the way. Dan was not impressed and told Jessie it was probably just coincidence.

"Oh, yeah? I can make them answer me," she said indignantly. Around the next curve, five goats gave her the chance to prove it. "Baaah-baaah-baaah," cried Jessie.

The returning chorus of "Baaah-baaah-baaah" caused raised eyebrows from all the adults.

"Lucky..." Dan said, which brought smiles from most, but a mild punch in the shoulder from Jessie. I pulled into the parking area at the trailhead and was greeted by three more goats wandering past. Jo asked if the goats would bother us when we got out of the car.

"No problem," said a smug Jessie. "I'll just tell them to lay down. Baaah-Baaah. Baaah," she called out and sure enough the goats moved out of our way and then lay down in the middle of the road. Everyone was amazed, but Jessie just bounced out of the car and up the trail.

Dan called out "Pretty good, Goat Girl." That was it. The name stuck, and whenever the Adopt-A-Trail group got together, it just wasn't the same unless Goat Girl made the trip with us.

* * *

Bob's mom and some of his extended family arrived in St. Thomas for a one-day cruise visit just a couple of days after Dan and Jo left the island to return home. Rather than attempting to get to St. John for just a few hours visit, his mom wrangled an invitation for Bob and I to join them on the ship while it was in port. It was our first experience on a large cruise ship. We got to the dock early and observed the slow process of docking and the disembarking of the day-trippers. On board, we got a tour and spent the day relaxing and catching up. Bob's folks were relieved to see us so happy and healthy; we felt the same way toward them. Still, it was disappointing that we couldn't show them our home, but before the end of the day they promised to visit St. John for a week the following year.

The visit had had an unlikely impact on Bob, who'd always demurred from taking a cruise himself, claiming he'd be bored and spend all his time eating. A visit to the health club, a walk around the running track and the pools, and a look at a typical daily activity schedule had caused this change in attitude. He even suggested we take our first cruise before the year was out and visit other Caribbean islands. "Check out the neighborhood" was the way he put it, I think. Besides, after our recent trip north for my brother's party, he was determined to vacation where it was warm.

* * *

One night as we were having dinner on our porch with a couple who'd lived on St. John for a few years, the conversation naturally turned to the hectic tourist season and local craziness. The tourists seemed to have invaded Cruz Bay, making it difficult to park in town and making ferry rides a crowded affair; but they also added regular color to our normally dull lives. I commented that I thought it was our duty to be nice to every tourist, even if we were having a bad day.

"Then I guess I shouldn't tell you about my almost decking a tourist from the ferry," said the normally sweet and bubbly Mary seated next to me. We just *had* to hear this one!

It had all started when she was returning to St. John one afternoon after a hot, frustrating morning measuring canvas awnings for a client and picking up a shipment of cushions that was a staple item for their manufacturing business. The foam cushions had arrived days late, and production was behind schedule. Ferrying the materials to St. John was the only way to get them into the shop without further delay. As it happened, though, the hourly ferry was overflowing with tourists and luggage all heading for a week of fun on St. John and, as is normally the case, the ferry crew required all luggage and packages to be left dockside, to be loaded onto the ferry by crewmen.

Mary was very anxious that her shipment might get soiled, and though she begged the crew to be extra careful, they treated the foam as roughly as they did everything else. Twenty minutes later, Mary attempted to take the cushions with her as she left the boat. "No!" they yelled at her.

After all of the passengers had disembarked, the crew formed a human chain and tossed stored items piece by piece onto a pile on the dock. Mary's customized foam cushions landed in the middle of the pile. To add insult to injury, a big, brawling tourist began to climb over the pile to retrieve his own luggage without waiting for it to be all sorted out.

"Stop it please!" shouted Mary, as she reached for his arm. The man continued his own hunt, stepping all over one of my friend's cushions.

"Those are my cushions you're stepping on," she said through clenched teeth.

"Bug off!" was the answer Mary heard, as the tourist stepped onto another of the cushions to get better leverage.

"Wanna bet?" Mary snarled as she snapped. Readying with a right hook, she wound up to punch the man squarely in the face and knock him off the pile. Luckily for her, Mary's husband had come down to the ferry to help her carry her load, and at precisely that moment extricated Mary and her cushions from what had become an ugly situation.

"When did this all occur?" I asked in a sweet voice.

"Six weeks ago, so I think we're safe," Mary said. The whole incident was so out of character for Mary. We all chuckled.

"Great. I hope the guy didn't get your name or the name of your business," I chimed in. "Any day now we're going to read a letter to the editor in Condé Nast Traveler or Caribbean Life complaining about the unfriendliness of the natives. It'll probably make headline news in the local paper."

"Mary needs a vacation," Bob murmured after they left. *Don't we all, and all the time*, I thought to myself.

St. John Trivia

June is Hurricane Preparedness Month in the USVI. Most take the hurricane season seriously, stocking up on water, canned goods, plastic tarps, and prescription medicines.

Many St. Johnians are addicted to the Weather Channel on Cable TV, especially during hurricane season. Local newspapers publish hurricane-tracking maps early in the season, showing longitude and latitude coordinates for each island in the Caribbean. Tracking the storms from the time they form off the east coast of Africa is a favorite local pastime.

Hurricane season in the USVI lasts from June until November, with the greatest likelihood of storms occurring in September and early October.

Chapter 13

Going with the Flow

In-between visitors and holidays, our time was spent more serenely in the daily existence that makes St. John special. A romantic dinner took little effort whenever Bob or I wanted it. Plugging in the Christmas lights that lined our porch railing and adding two wind-protected candles was all it took to add ambiance to our outdoor dining room. Our sunsets were always spectacular. When the sun set, the nighttime lights of St. Thomas in the distance and a background gratis chorus of nature's nightlife made our porch a very private Paradise. Later, we often lay in our hammock in the dark and watched the stars spanning the heavens. We never experienced such spectacular shows of nature in the States. St. John nights always made us want to linger, even more than our redwood swing set in New England. And we never lost the awe our private views inspired.

It had been three months since I'd bought a funky coconut bird feeder made by a local artisan near Salt Pond Bay and hung it from the edge of the porch. My island neighbors assured me that a little sugar water in the bottom would quickly attract lots of birds. With two cats and a memory of the timid birds in New England in mind, I wasn't hopeful.

Even according to island-time, I was overdue in filling the bottom of the feeder with the sweet mixture. Finally, I went ahead and prepared the sugar water mixture, and within minutes it one morning, a lone bananaquit perched on the feeder's edge, enjoying a morning snack.

When I glanced out in mid-afternoon, there were no less than six bananaquits crowded around the feeder, with lots more chirping in the bushes nearby. I looked for my cats. The princess was enthralled. She was seated on a table just five feet away, staring with a mixture of disbelief and joy. But having had no experience with killing birds, she was content to sit back and watch. And our outdoor adventurer couldn't be bothered: The birds were too small and too fast for his taste; besides, he'd cornered a small lizard at the end of the porch. Priorities were priorities.

Bob's regular weekend priority was to find beach privacy. He liked the idea of nude sunbathing, but only with great discretion, since that activity is illegal on St. John. We discovered that adjacent to many beaches were small sandy coves that were out of view and inaccessible except by swimming or by boat. And so one day we packed everything in waterproof containers or dry bags and tied them to a swimming float for the short trip to complete privacy. This would become our routine from that day on. But we didn't rough it on these occasions. We'd float a beach umbrella, snorkeling gear, books, a cooler with lunch, and even binoculars and a camera to our private coves. All the creature comforts.

Then Bob and I bought a kayak. The only surprise here was that it had taken Bob so long to convince me to do it. The kayak was a used heavy plastic one, designed for two people. Gear was meant to be hauled using ropes, and the tie-downs were attached at various points throughout the length of the boat. Unfortunately, the kayak had seen better days. The tie-downs were loose in some places and missing in others, leaving small holes that made it easy for water to get into the boat.

"A simple ratchet tool and some new rivets will easily fix it," Bob assured me.

It took months to find a ratchet tool that worked. Nowhere on St. Thomas or St. John could we find the right size ratchets to do the job. A business trip to the States and a visit to a stateside hardware store were necessary before the problem was solved and we could kayak to our private hideaways.

Finding tools and hardware was a tiny part of the local shopping challenge. You may recall hearing in the news that the landmark J. W. Woolworth's Company had closed its doors nationwide across the U.S. forever. On the mainland, its passing went unnoticed by many. But everyone on St. John felt the effect of the store closing on St. Thomas. This Woolworth's had been a profitable store, frequented by most everyone, and now only a K-Mart remained to provide a variety of everyday items at reasonable prices. Rumors quickly spread of some company moving in to fill the Woolworth's space; everyone had a favorite to fill his or her personal needs and desires. In the end, however, K-Mart decided to open a second store. So much for competition.

My business trips off-island had been cut back to a reasonable every-six-weeks-or-so, while I'd become the neighborhood conduit for odd purchases that were difficult to obtain in the tropics. For instance, on one trip I'd brought back a purple plastic ski jacket zipper for Bev's local dry cleaning company, a stainless steel clamp for Matthew, a paperback book sought after by Jay, and the inevitable Ring Dings and Yodels for Andre and Bob. Of course, I also regularly brought back odd grocery items that were priced much cheaper in the States. I was not alone in this endeavor. Every time someone took a trip off-island, even if it was just to St. Thomas, they offered to procure items that friends needed—or just wanted. This was always with the understanding that the goods would be purchased only if time, availability, prices, and transportation made it possible.

As an avid reader, I had anticipated books would be scarce on St. John. The island had a single small bookstore with retail prices considerably outside the range of a ferocious reader. As it turned out, though, I found my paranoia was unfounded: Since others shared my pleasures in reading, a round-robin approach to book lending became the norm. Occasionally, recent releases came courtesy of Birdie or visiting friends from off-island. Pickles Deli and the Sea Breeze Café in Coral Bay were two of the many businesses that offered a free bookshelf, where passing tourists left an occasional gem they had read on-island and had finished. I sometimes recycled books of my own by adding to these collections.

* * *

Local ways could often appear painful to the uninitiated. Take normal house-building, for instance: a fairly successful endeavor on the Mainland, someone educated us about on-island struggles with a tale about Mark and Marsha—St. John residents for a few years—and the house they had attempted building on the island.

While many had tried to convince them that the difficulties and delays they'd experience in building a house on-island weren't worth it, Mark was determined to succeed. As the story goes, things were going well, and his roof was even halfway completed when the roofer didn't show up for work one day. When found at a local bar, the roofer said the weather called for showers so he couldn't work, but he'd be back the next day. That next day was perfect, weather-wise. There was a nice breeze all day. Occasional high clouds brought regular relief from the normally hot island sun. Yet again the roofer didn't show up. Neither did the plumber, who'd been dependable up to now.

Finally, three days later, the roofer returned to the site and continued work as though there'd been no delay. But there was still no plumber. The owner was furious, and demanded reasons for the delay. Wary of the owner's anger, the roofer mumbled his explanation. The weather had gotten so good that he'd gone sailing down-island for a couple of days.

"First the roofer, then the plumber," Mark could be heard growling, mostly to himself; "at least one of them is back," he spat out.

The roofer, overhearing Mark's complaints, just grinned. "No problem," he told Mark. "The plumber, he be here soon," the roofer assured the owners. "We'd be on his boat."

This was a classic case of applying mainland standards to island customs because, believe it or not, the roofer and plumber had good reputations for dependability. Their behavior was acceptable within the local culture and their job skills were beyond reproach. Our friend learned the hard way that ignorance of island ways could be detrimental to the sanity of any relocated continental.

* * *

Bob and I had initially shied away from buying food at the numerous small food booths located around town, primarily because no one ever posted signs to explain what was for sale. Shela, who lived in a little house near our apartment, ran a small booth called *Shela's Pot* directly across the street from the ferry docks in Cruz Bay Park. She always seemed busy. But I had avoided doing business there over concerns that my queries would be considered rude.

Wanting to participate more fully in island life, I decided the risk was worth the gain, and I asked her why she didn't put up signs. "Wouldn't you sell more if you did?" I asked naively.

"If it's good, you don't need to," she scolded me with a smile as she offered me some chicken soup for a little cold I'd been suffering. "Every day, I sell out," she explained.

I was going to suggest that she could make and sell even more if she put up signs, but I already knew what she'd say. Shela cooked what she could make, transported it via taxi, and stored it in her small downtown stall. Increasing her product would have meant increasing her overhead for a car, more storage, and more help. More importantly, increasing sales meant she wouldn't be able to "lime away" the time she could spend talking with her customers, and to her trade it just wouldn't be *Shela's Pot* any more.

So now, whenever I had to send a fax, I'd make sure I passed by *Shela's Pot* and say "Good Morning." Since my company headquarters opened late in the morning by St. John time zone standards (the daylight savings time change in the states meant it was mid-morning before I could reach anyone at my office by phone), morning was a good time to run errands in town. St. John never adjusted its clocks, as most didn't feel the need to add this kind of stress to their lives. For me, it meant early morning hours were relaxed, though it certainly added a challenge when I worked with West Coast folks by phone.

As I mentioned earlier, I did most of my work via computer. To log on to my computer at my company's headquarters, I had to connect my notebook computer to our apartment telephone line, dial the long distance number for my company's computer connection, and—with luck—hope to get through to it without being interrupted by a Spanish recording telling me all the circuits out of the island were busy. Then I needed to use a credit card-sized device my company had given me to get past computer security and log in. Then I could begin my workday.

As it happened, I'd passed all the foibles when the little security device died one day. This meant that, since it would take about seven days to ship a new device out to me, I could not get my e-mail for at least a week. Why a week, you ask? Well, the company said they had to verify my problem before they would send a replacement by mail; they would make no exceptions and by-pass their security processes. In fact, it took over two days of arguing just to get them to agree my device had indeed stopped working and I needed a new one sent by Express Mail, which would take not one but three days to arrive on-island. Meanwhile, I would have to do most work via telephone or fax. There was one positive effect this breakdown had, however (if you could even call it "positive"): I could now imagine the disruption a hurricane would cause in my work-life. Then, telephones and faxes might not be an option.

Once I received the new card, and anxious to catch up on my e-mails, I locked both cats outdoors for the first time, closing the screen door behind them. I needed uninterrupted work time without the risk of a cat jumping onto the keyboard for attention. Soon I was involved with work, and didn't notice how the time had flown by until my shoulders began to ache. As I broke my focus on the screen in front of me, suddenly something swooped by me through the air. My immediate thought as I cringed in fear was that a piece of the overhead fan had broken loose. But I heard no crashing sound, and so I dared look up. I noticed nothing wrong at first. Then I saw "it," up in the master bedroom loft, precariously circling the large ceiling fan and swooping down toward the bed occasionally, trying to find a way out. It was one of the island's large hummingbirds.

I ran up the stairs, opening the living room screen door on the way. Both cats at first jumped back for safety before quickly bouncing inside. When the hummingbird first entered, they had pasted themselves to the screen with their claws, watching the tantalizing show wide-eyed, though at first I'd been too focused on my computer screen to notice this. It seems that I'd had a hummingbird in my house for perhaps two hours.

Opening the screen door in the bedroom had no effect on returning the bird outdoors, nor did turning off the fan: The bird only flew in larger circles, until it was swooping down to circle the large living room fans. My cats thought it was all great fun. They both sat down on the middle of the living room couch and were watching with awe and fascination.

I opened the remaining doors in the apartment to try to lure the bird outside, and even turned off the downstairs fans, then watched helplessly as the bird continued its efforts. I think now it saw my non-threatening moves and changes in the atmosphere of the apartment as an open invitation to explore. And it explored everywhere, though it appeared to be a little confused by where the wind (from the fans) had gone.

This was one of those rare days when no trade winds blew on-island, and without the fans, it was hot. Both cats sat on the couch panting, with their tongues hanging out (but probably for a reason different than the heat). Shooing and moving, shuffling and waving, I moved around the house like Isadora Duncan, but it was a long half-hour before I could coax the hummingbird out of the house.

By this time, the cats were playing dead on the living room floor, either in disappointment or from heat exhaustion (I couldn't tell which) and wouldn't move until I turned on their ceiling fans again.

* * *

After a good rain, the hummingbirds would take baths in the water-filled leaves of an almond tree that climbed beside our porch. Unlike the early winter months, a lot of rain fell in early spring, and every week some new and peculiar flower came into bloom and a new exotic perfume filled the air. My garden on the porch was finally beginning to take shape. A rooting from an asparagus fern, bromliads, a couple of small palm trees, a ficus, some hanging ivy and a wandering jew started from cuttings, anthuriums gratis of my landlord, and a lone orchid received as a gift—all gave our porch a decidedly cozy, tropical, and exotic feel. My husband began training the ubiquitous bougainvillea nearby to weave gracefully through the porch railing to form a natural sun barrier that would minimize the afternoon heat all summer.

My landlord even gave me a couple of tomato seedlings, and visions of a heavy crop of fresh fruit filled my brain. In fact, the tomato plants grew unbelievably fast, and when they bloomed with their yellow blossoms virtually covering the tops of each plant, my excitement mounted. While watering them, I would think back on our life in New England and how visits with neighbors during the summer months often included offers of strawberries or squash—or tomatoes. Especially tomatoes.

But my old approach of "stick the seedling in the ground and stand back" wasn't an approach that would work in Paradise. I encountered new species of insects and fungus that threatened my plants, and a "blossom drop" phenomenon that no locals seemed to be able to solve.

Bob was supportive, even testing out a theory he had that these plants needed cooler nighttime weather by lugging the very heavy pots into an air-conditioned room inside our apartment for a few nights. But nothing worked. For months I hung on to my bug-infested but constantly flowering plants before finally giving in to the inevitable.

Whenever I got really depressed over hoping for my own vine-ripened tomato, someone else's generosity soon made me forget. A hand of fat, short little bananas, a pile of guavas, mangos, limes, and herbs—these would arrive gratis from some local friend, who was as grateful that we took these gifts as we were of receiving them.

When a banana tree bears fruit, it bears a lot of fruit. I experimented with local fruits, including them occasionally in recipes I'd previously restricted to New England-grown bounty. Bananas and mangos were also good picnic fare for the beach, though we always seemed to have too much. So we shared whenever we could find a willing tourist.

Like most people on St. John, we truly appreciated the tourists, even when they made downtown parking difficult and crowded our restaurants and beaches. They kept the island fresh and alive and made us smile. Bob and I liked to make the tourists grin, which they did regularly when we offered to take their pictures with their own cameras. At the beach, in the parks, in restaurants, on the dock—wherever we went we met fascinating people that way. And on the white sandy beaches, I loved to share island trivia with them.

"Do you know what makes all this beautiful white sand?" I would ask them, whether they wanted to know or not. Often their answer was "no," but some offered that they thought it was "the waves breaking the coral" or "broken sea shells" or "rocks being worn away." And while all these sources did help create the sand, much of our beaches came from a very different source.

"Parrot Fish poop," I would respond with a laugh. "This is true," I'd tell them, because it was. And the looks on people's faces were filled with amazement—and perhaps a little disgust—as I suggested they try floating face down when snorkeling and watch to see if my story was true. As often as not, they'd follow my suggestion, then stop back by with big grins on their faces, nodding agreement and appreciation (however distasteful!) at their newfound knowledge.

Bob and I also looked forward to playing like tourists at the local pig roasts and beach parties that were often held on palm-tree-lined Oppenheimer Beach on the north shore of the island. A popular site for these events included the small house that sat right on the beach owned by the Territorial government: that building, with its broad porch, its steps leading directly into the water, and a kitchen and two bathrooms, could be rented for a nominal fee for private parties.

Special events meant lots of cars lining the narrow National Park road above the property, but at the most upscale parties, free open-air transportation was provided from Hawksnest Beach, where parking is more abundant. Typically, a truckload of borrowed Tiki lamps provided lighting for these evening extravaganzas. Sometimes the events were very private weddings or birthday parties, while some were more public fundraisers for some good cause. Often they were word-of-mouth parties for bunches of locals to get together, when someone rented the space just as an excuse to enjoy a day at the beach. For us, these highlight a special quality of island life—as if island life needed a party.

But life on St. John is not always fun and games, or even as mundane as I sometimes like to think of it. Occasionally a crisis, whether real or imagined, shakes up our world. As when one quiet day my neighbor Shela stood at my door calling out "Inside! Inside!"

It took me a minute to remember that some folks on St. John still lived in places that had no doors, and that calling out "Inside" was a culturally proper alternative to knocking.

"Inside! Kah-rrin, are you d'ere?" Shela called again, in an unusually urgent way. Her propane tank had just been filled, and now the smell of leaking propane was overpowering throughout her small home up the hill from our apartment. She was afraid of an explosion. I quickly lent her our phone, but it wasn't much help, as I had no idea who to call. Luckily a friend of Shela's drove by my open door at just that moment and offered to check out the problem.

He found that the tank had been filled so completely that the sun pouring down on the exposed tank had expanded the gas and it had no where to go but out through a built-in safety valve. Everything was ok.

But running out of cistern water was a more common, and equally traumatic, event for everyone on St. John, since it meant no water for flushing toilets, taking showers, or cleaning dishes until the water trucks came. It was the tropical version of running out of winter furnace oil in New England. It cost a small fortune to have a water truck provide your cistern with just enough water for a month or so after no rain.

Of course, occasionally the problem was not a lack of rain, but that someone sinned, as they did in Andre's apartment building one day.

The building had just gotten a water delivery a week earlier, and at great cost, but suddenly the cistern was empty again. Everyone assumed a leak in the cistern below the house had caused the problem. Moe, our landlord, didn't find this theory either likely or amusing, and wouldn't entertain it. So before even checking out the cistern, Moe personally checked out the apartment building inside and out to get answers, meanwhile growling at everyone. Finally, he sniffed out the problem.

It turned out that a new tenant had a toilet that sometimes didn't stop flushing completely, and without realizing the problem this could cause, the tenant had left town for ten days with his toilet continuously leaking water. Eight thousand gallons of water had escaped in one week this way, and no one had even noticed.

Unfortunately our water bills weren't tax deductible, and it was tax season. Bob and I found a local accountant, Maureen, to help us survive income tax season; she played a base cello in a band we often went to see on Friday nights at the Tamarind Inn. With her guidance, we learned about the nuances in the tax codes which made it advantageous for us to live and work in the USVI. We also paid a bundle for our sins during the past year.

Even so, when it was all over, Bob and I had a little money left over to allow us—even to help us step up our efforts—to play in Paradise. And so we did. With two other couples, we rented a powerboat for a day and tooled around St. John, with each of the men taking a turn at piloting. Only one of us had any real experience with powerboats, however, but the seas were extremely calm that day, and everyone's confidence was running high.

Normally, the waves crashed hard against the high cliffs on the south shore of the island, so the calm today gave us a rare opportunity to explore. We pulled very close to the point at Ram's Head to make a quick snorkeling stop. I felt very much under control when Andre told us the depth gage indicated we were still in fourteen feet of water, even though it appeared we were very close to the rocky shore.

Later on, however, someone pointed out that that the boat did not come equipped with a depth gauge, and that Andre had been reading the tachometer—the gauge that measured the boat's engine's RPMs. The water was far shallower than fourteen feet. Despite the fact that we were still well off-shore and the sun was high in the sky, my whole body shuddered at that discovery.

After our near collision with disaster, we made our way out to Norman Island in the British Virgin Islands for lunch. Our restaurant was a floating ship anchored in a quiet harbor, a crowded place where the drinks were strong and the food hearty. Halfway through our cheeseburgers, Bob's boss and his wife popped on board from a small inflatable skiff with an outboard motor; they'd come over from St. John just for lunch. It is very unusual for anyone to cross even that small stretch of sea in such a tiny craft, but with the rare calm waters on this particular day, it was even easy to envision someone water-skiing all the way to St. Croix that day.

Over time, Bob and I became savvy on the local boating regulations. As knowledgeable locals, then, we got a little steamed when pleasure seekers proved themselves either too inept or too determined to break the boating rules, especially when they anchored boats too close to shore or blocked the marked entry channels.

When this happened, it was often most effective to simply comment out loud (*very* loudly!), "I hope the Coast Guard doesn't catch those boat people outside the markers. Did you know that they might get their boats confiscated?" Moments later you typically saw these boats moving on to other, less public waters. Unfortunately this strategy didn't always work, and we all cringed a bit when we thought about how these stupid people were destroying the reefs and shoreline that had drawn them to this spot in the first place.

But I'm sure the policeman, too, cringed when I parked illegally across from the Post Office, as I did one day. Parking in town was always a challenge, but up to this point I had been blissfully unaware I was breaking the law through some of my parking habits.

As it happened on this particular day, on its first loop through, my Geo Tracker found a rare open parking space inside the lot along the road across from the Post Office. The ferry was about to leave for St. Thomas, and I considered myself lucky.

Upon returning three hours later, my first St. John parking ticket waved at me from my windshield. "Parking in a 30-minute parking zone," read the indictment. But, I thought to myself, I'd parked in this same lot a hundred times before without getting a ticket. What had changed?

It took me long minutes of searching to find the "posted sign" mentioned on the ticket. Even so, it took a hard scrubbing from a rag in my car to wipe the grime off the sign and decipher its warning. Apparently this one row of parking spaces was earmarked for short-term parking, while the rest of the lot was up for grabs.

And yet, as I discovered, the car next to mine as I recalled had been parked there *when I parked*, but *it* had no ticket. This discovery suddenly had me feeling like an outsider, like someone who had just arrived on the island: like *a tourist!* Two wrongs don't make a right, I reasoned and reminded myself, and I was in the wrong. So I decided to pay the ticket right away, which was another new adventure in island ways.

The policeman had written on the ticket to pay at the Boulon Center. So I went there to pay, only to be confronted with a locked door and a sign informing all that this was indeed the place to pay fines of various sorts, but that the next time it would be open for business was three weeks away. I would be out of town on business by the time the office opened again, so I took a short walk to our fine new police headquarters a block away.

It was my first time in this new building; it had only been officially open for a short while. I was impressed by the thick, bulletproof glass partition and encouraged by the smiling officer behind the barrier. Walking right up to the grill (which was placed at an awkward height), I offered to pay my fine directly to him, since the Boulon Center office was closed. He looked the ticket over, thought for a moment, and then told me the ticketing officer was wrong and probably from St. Thomas (whatever that meant). Nervously, as he eyed the new overhead security camera, he said they didn't take monies at the station and redirected me to the Motor Vehicle Inspection Lane down the road. At the Motor Vehicle lane, I was assured that I could pay parking tickets there. However, the computers were down and it was suggested that I return the next day.

That next day, I made sure I had enough cash, along with a blank check and even a credit card, to cover all possibilities. One of the girls behind the desk told me there was a little problem. The girl who is allowed to take monies was out on break and wouldn't be back for an hour or more. Despairing, I started to head home when I passed Jay's place of work, where she too was taking a break. She motioned me to stop and chat.

When I told Jay about my parking ticket woes, she just rolled her eyes and laughed. Most people didn't bother to pay tickets right away; they waited instead until they were due for their yearly inspection. At that time the computer would show their outstanding fines and people would either pay up in full or sell the car to some unsuspecting person, who would then have to pay the fines before they could register the car. Anyway, said Jay, she'd bet me five dollars that I wouldn't be able to pay the ticket on my next try.

At the Motor Vehicle lane, the girl who took the cash was back in the office, but she wouldn't take my money because the girl who was responsible for writing out the receipt was at lunch and wouldn't be back for another hour. I returned to Jay's to pay off my lost bet and kill a little more time. Some time later, I returned from my considerable aimless wandering to find the receipt girl back at the office, where it took only about two minutes from beginning to end to actually pay my parking ticket and get a receipt.

It was about that time I started figuring out—on my own and through people like the receipt and ticket girls—how some of the confusing signs posted on the roads worked. Like the one that ran between the cemetery and the beach across the street from it in Cruz Bay. One sign facing toward town read "No parking from 8:00 AM to 6:00 PM Mon-Fri," while on the other side of the same pole another read "No Parking," nothing more. As relaxed as people were—and were expected to be—on the island, they sure were expected to spend a lot of time reading, examining, deciphering, washing, interpreting, and searching street signs!

As if to rationalize the cultural idiosyncrasies of the ticketing process on the island, I fantasized all the way home about how every law breaker would be ticketed and would be expected to pay their fines right away, and how the local government would then have a surplus of funds available to improve efficiencies and signage and make the world a better place. How there was probably a master plan behind these idiosyncrasies. How things probably made sense in the long run.

But closing my car door at home, I suddenly snapped myself into focus, and allowed my last thought to be *"That* will never happen!" Then I let my mind move off to thoughts of a quiet evening in Paradise.

* * *

Bob and I had just settled into our bed when we noticed flashing lights reflecting off our bathroom window along with the unusual sound of gathering people. Guessing it was the police ticketing a car that had sat at the side of our road for weeks, my husband went to the window.. "It's a fire!" Bob called out.

Rushing to his side, I saw fire trucks and firemen milling about as they attempted to extinguish a transformer fire at the top of an electrical pole near our building. No matter what they did, they could barely reach the source of the fire high up on the pole. Our electricity went off as the firefighters sought to gain control. Because of the strong wind blowing in that night, we immediately considered the possibility that the fire might spread. But after a few minutes the firemen seemed to have the situation under control.

Without electricity and the constant movement of a bedroom fan, the room was stifling, so I stepped out onto our balcony, from which I could no longer see the firemen at work. As I looked in their direction, however, I could barely make out the pink glow in the black night. I also saw a red spark falling to the dry ground below us and assumed my neighbors were also awake and watching from their balconies, and that someone had thrown a cigarette butt off their balcony.

It annoyed me that anyone would be so inconsiderate to drop a lit cigarette onto the ground, which was so dry from the lack of rain. But then, looking in the distance, I saw two, then five, then many more sparks floating downwards, some landing hundreds of yards down the gut (the ravine) below our property. I realized our neighbors weren't smoking at all, that the wind was sending sparks across the gut and that the situation was a dangerous one.

But the firefighters kept at it, and seemed to be gaining on it, and a restless hour later the fire was out and no other fires had appeared below our house. The next morning I discussed the previous night's excitement with my Parrot-Head neighbor (surrounded by Jimmy Buffet memorabilia) who lived in a studio apartment diagonally below mine. It was a wild event, she agreed, and assured me that the firemen were as conscientious as possible with the sparks the night before.

She said this with a shrug and a sense of certainty that had me curious, so I prodded her a little. Pam told me she had awoken from the commotion as we had, but had stayed inside until the fire was almost out. A little relieved and wanting to check out the fire's aftermath, she had unfortunately chosen this moment to light a cigarette while standing on the outside staircase in the dark of night. Not a smart move, I thought. Sure enough, a firefighter, seeing only the red glow on the side of the stairway, turned his hose in that direction and utterly drenched Pam.

Our stout concrete walls had prevented Bob and I from seeing or hearing this calamity. But my Parrot-Head friend wasn't angry at all with the firemen. "They were just doing their job," she admitted with a wry and somewhat embarrassed grin.

"At least they brought their own water," I added. I had obviously begun to think like a St. Johnian, accepting the bizarre without a thought, but with precious water always in my consciousness.

"And the lawn and bushes got a nice free soaking," my friend added, not missing a beat, with a smile and a flick of her cigarette.

* * *

Not everyone on St. John had the amenities that those living in our building did. Some even lived without electricity, or even four walls to call home.

Exploring the East End of the island in our kayak one day, Bob and I encountered numerous remote sandy coves accessible only by small watercraft and hidden from the eyes of larger boats. With an occasional paddling, we drifted from one cove to another, finding each more picturesque than the last.

Rounding a small outcrop of rocks, we discovered one tiny cove that was spectacular. Bob murmured that this would be the ideal place to hang it up and live off the land. The cove was edged with a shallow reef on one side and sea grass on the other, while the center was pure white sand leading up to a perfect beach. Sea grapes and palm trees lined the beach, and rising from the steep hills I could see a mighty papaya tree.

But then there was more. Bob had noticed that, tucked almost out of sight, there lay evidence that someone—probably until just recently— had been living a remote life here in the bush, using only the most minimal of goods: A hammock, boards for a bench, an old wooden cable spool for a table, and a well-used grill. Nearby, a pile of recently crushed conch shells, the remains of a fire, and coconut and mango remains told more of the story.

Looking hard, we let the lazy current move us slowly away, on to another undiscovered patch of Paradise. *It can be done*, I thought quietly, as the bits and pieces of a life moved back into their quiet anonymity.

Chapter *14*

Peculiarities in Paradise

I'd heard about the phosphorescence in the sea waters surrounding these islands long before ever experiencing the phenomenon. In fact, I'd probably been seeing this strange occurrence without even knowing it, when an evening ferry home to St. John, for instance, coincided with the new moon. On those nights, when the lack of moon glow made the night especially dark, I'd noticed that if the seas were choppy, you could see whitecaps clearly a good distance away from the ferryboat. But not until I'd experienced the phosphorescence at Cinnamon Bay did I pay much attention and notice that the whitecaps actually glowed in the dark during these nights.

Cinnamon Bay, one of the larger bays on the north shore of St. John, is the site of the island's largest campground. Bob and I had camped here for ten days on a vacation to Paradise many years ago. Since our move here, though, we'd almost ignored this wonderful place except to attend a few special events held on the premises. When the seas were up, the waves could be rough, and we preferred our bathing sites to be as calm as a pond.

One weekend St. John Rescue was asked to provide on-site assistance for an "enhancement weekend" at Cinnamon Bay Campground. The event was geared toward at-risk kids and their single-parent households from St. Thomas. Most participants would be camping out for the first time, and Bob and I were asked to stay overnight in the campground along with the families. It turned out to be a very memorable experience.

The parents and children were appreciative of the smallest gesture of kindness. A peaceful first day passed, with the only injury being a scraped toe in need of a band-aid. Bob offered alcohol swabs to a diabetic minister who'd forgotten his own supply, and I soothed a crying child who'd forgotten where her mom was. But for the most part, we weren't needed.

As the sun set, we interacted more freely with the campers. Most participants had no idea how to start up the propane-fed lanterns that marked the entrance to each tent site, and one mother asked us for assistance. Enlisting a young "lieutenant" from among a crew of children nearby, my assistant and I quickly solved her problem.

Seconds later, we were asked to do the same for another lantern on the other side of the group camping area. Before we could light that lantern, we were inundated with additional requests. My lieutenant was a big help as he introduced me to the campers and led me through the various tent sites. Before it was over, I'd lit over twenty lanterns and had reached the status of minor heroine.

Bob, meanwhile, had remained at our own site and began getting requests for cups of ice: Every child wanted at least a cup of ice to take to their bed that evening, initially to suck as a treat, and later for the inevitable drink of water they'd want late into the night. Returning from my own mission of sorts, I found Bob surrounded by six toddlers holding out their cups to him; he looked a little overwhelmed. I began to help him while chatting with the children. With each handout, I reminded the children to say thank you, which brought wide eyes from some, but smiles and "t'ank yo" to Bob from all. Thank goodness the ice chest the VI National Park Service had provided was large. We must have given out fifty cups of ice before the campground quieted for the night.

Once we'd settled down a little, Bob and I found the evening was too young for us to consider turning in for the night. So we stood and took a walk down to the beach, where someone had left out two chairs overlooking a rocky barrier to the shoreline. It was dark and peaceful around us as we sat watching the sky filled with more stars than we had ever seen before. Occasionally, a meteor flashed by, adding momentary excitement. But within a few minutes, it was the water that captured my attention.

There was no surf that night, yet out of the corner of my eyes I caught a movement of some sort. I began searching the waters, and within a moment or two was rewarded with a sudden glow from the water, like a green light bulb being turned on and then off from beneath the water's surface. A few minutes later it happened again, in two different spots in the water. The glow was obviously caused by nocturnal fish of some kind, we thought.

Neither Bob nor I felt sleepy. Our apartment was almost five minutes away from a beach, which on St. John meant we were a long way from the waterfront, and we wanted to enjoy our nocturnal beach time. So there we stayed, sitting quietly on the quiet beach in the middle of the night.

After a while, we headed out for an isolated spot on the sandy beach for a nighttime dip. My husband was barely a shadow walking away and into the calm water. Seconds later, his feet were surrounded by an eerie glow. But the glow dissipated soon after it started, as my eyes caught Bob's stationary silhouette. While taking my first steps into the water after him, I looked down. As I moved, my body churned the water, and with each movement the water glowed with thousands of tiny green lights as minute marine life attempted to escape from my path.

Bob and I sat quietly on the sandy bottom in knee-high water and pondered this new wonder. He slowly moved one hand along the surface, resulting in a wave of glowing phosphorescence. I mimicked his movement and we both sucked in our breaths. It was amazing. Each movement brought a glittering glow that most of us would only imagine could appear in a science fiction movie. We played with our microscopic friends that night for a long time, experimenting with them, awed by their beauty and the beauty of nature, as a meteor shower overhead provided added entertainment.

After that, whenever I traveled by water at night, I had new respect and admiration for the invisible nightlife surrounding me.

* * *

Respect for our island's environment is something no one on St. John ever takes lightly. Earlier, while Bob and I were in the final planning stages of our move to Paradise, a major change very nearly occurred on the island that may have had enormous repercussions, with total disregard for the needs and sensibilities of those who live here.

A USVI territorial government agency, we were told—one with little or no clear understanding of the idiosyncrasies of tiny St. John—had decided to put a traffic light on the road near Cruz Bay. To a vacationing visitor, this may have seemed like a reasonable answer to the problem of chronic traffic jams that continued to occur on this island of few stop signs, few police, and no traffic lights. The traffic light arrived on-island a day before its scheduled installation. Its arrival was all it took to start a storm.

Once word got around of a traffic light's arrival on the island, St. Johnians were appalled. After all, no public notice had been given to residents, and after only scattered discussion, the locals were quickly united in their belief that a traffic light would be an eyesore and would only exaggerate the island's traffic problems. Besides, tourists came here to get away from urban trappings such as traffic lights. Luckily, the region's Governor himself was on-island that afternoon for a speaking engagement. It was amazing how fast the local grapevine worked.

Within what seemed minutes, a grassroots group of outraged citizens confronted him and insisted that he order the traffic light to remain uninstalled. The Governor was overwhelmed with the visible public outrage. At the same time, his office was informing him that it was being inundated with faxes and phone calls insisting he act immediately. The Governor responded by calling for an immediate halt to the installation.

What came next is surely peculiar only to St. John: Apparently, since the traffic light had been paid for and the box opened, the equipment couldn't be returned. For a while, the three-tiered light fixture found a home in some office at the public works department, until someone came up with a better plan. It was decided that the traffic light would be mounted as the main—and only—ornament high in the middle of the concrete side of a public works building. Its display, set back from the road off Gift Hill Road near the Centerline Road intersection, ensured maximum visibility, reassurance to any St. Johnian who knew the story that respect for the island mattered.

* * *

Sometimes it took the united efforts of both man and nature on St. John to create a legend.

On the North Shore Road in the VI National Park, a huge boulder has stood solitary along the shoreline-side of the road for what most figure to be about a millennium. This two-story-high boulder, which came to St. John via a volcanic blast that helped shape our neighborhood, is known as Easter Rock. The rock is a well-known landmark on the island, but it was a very tall tale that gave it its name.

According to local legend, in the predawn hours every Easter morning for centuries, the egg-shaped rock would roll down the steep gut below it and into the sea. Then, still before dawn, it would magically roll back up into its regular spot, wet and dripping, until the rising sun dried it before most mortals noticed it had been wet. That was the story.

But some people seem to want to take legend to legendary lengths, so just before our first Easter on-island, some friends tried to convince Bob and I to join them in skipping our normal sleep and helping them to dowse the rock at four AM so early rising tourists would not be disappointed by the legend.

Now, it was one thing, Bob and I figured, for us to hide Easter eggs around our yard back in Massachusetts for neighborhood tots to find during our annual Easter egg hunt, but we really had to draw the line here between a child's fantasy and an adult's lunacy. So we decided, even filled as we were with the love of island lore, that it was time to consider leaving legend to others.

* * *

While the legend of Easter Rock is a quaint anomaly that is regularly pointed out to willing tourists, locals more often find themselves wanting to memorize the whereabouts of the ubiquitous potholes that pepper our island roads. Most of these potholes have been there for years, and while our vigilant road crews spend a good portion of their lives repeatedly filling them with stones and dirt, the results of their efforts typically last only until the next evening's shower. At this point, their work is washed away, sometimes replaced by small rocks falling down from the hillsides above.

Braking for potholes or fallen rocks, by the way, is a clear indication to St. Johnians that the driver is a tourist. Residents instinctively swerve to avoid any large obstacle without any change in speed.

This is generally true, though there are bizarre occurrences to the contrary. One night, I remember, a strong rainstorm and some recent construction had toppled a huge boulder onto a seaside road. The boulder was at least ten feet high and wide enough to cover almost half of the narrow road; no small rocks or gravel had accompanied it. Once discovered, all locals merely swerved around the strange sight during their normal roller coaster rides to and from town. The boulder appeared destined to become another St. John landmark. But a week after it had appeared, I braked to a stop—in amazement—as I reached the rock, where I observed the back end of a jeep jutting out of the boulder, looking more like a monument than a car crash.

On my way out of town later that day, I found the boulder gone, but the jeep was still very much there. With no explanation.

Another road story: In Paradise, everyone took care to avoid harming God's creatures, no matter how disruptive this might be to their lives. One day, as my car did a little dance around an abnormally large pothole, I had to jerk it to a quick stop to avoid hitting a mama hen and her brood of chicks, who had decided at that moment to leave their pothole nest to cross the road.

I discovered just how far some people took this responsibility one night on St. Thomas. A friend and I were a long way from the Red Hook dock in a relatively rural area of the island. This friend offered to give me a ride to the dock where I could catch the ferry home, but she had a large ice cooler on the passenger's seat. I expected her to simply transfer the container to the back of the truck. First, though, she moved a small distance from the vehicle, then opened the cooler to let hundreds of little frogs escape.

"Normally I do this right away when I get here, but I was rushed tonight," she explained.

"Frogs?" was all I could think of to say to her.

"Yes, it's part of my apartment building's FRP... Frog Relocation Project," she chuckled. "My apartment building is designed with a nice little open-air courtyard in the middle, which contains a small water fountain. The frogs just love that place."

"Sounds nice," was all I could think of to say.

"But have you ever heard the sounds these little guys can make?" she said, a little defensively. "It gets so loud some nights, none of us can sleep. So every other night or so, one of us takes a pool net and fills an ice cooler with frogs, then we relocate them out here where there's a little more space for them and peace and quiet for us."

With the empty ice cooler now in the back of the truck, my friend got into the driver's seat and pulled a screwdriver out of her glove compartment. "This is my key," she said with a grin as she proceeded to jimmy the screwdriver into the steering column shaft; she turned it, and the engine sputtered to life with a cough. In the space of only a few minutes, I had gone from disbelief (about the frogs) to belief and even admiration (about the frog story) back to disbelief (with the screwdriver/key).

In moments we were at Red Hook, where I was informed I would have to open my vehicle's door from the outside to get out of the truck. Her truck, I found, was a typical "island car", falling apart both inside and out. But it had great brakes. Someone leaving the island had bequeathed it to her for free, and that made the clunker beautiful to both of us.

Arriving early at Red Hook meant time to stop at Senor Pizza—my favorite pizza parlor. It was housed in what had been a steel cargo container in an earlier life. A covered porch for the picnic-tabled seating area, along with some green, red and white paint and the omnipresent Christmas lights for *ambiance,* disguised its origins. The pizza was great, but the place was more famously known as the home base for the VI Olympic Bobsled team. Their street-side sign displayed a picture of a lone bobsled, while photographs on the inside proclaimed the store workers' fame and provided a basis for the legend.

Down the block, Duffy's Love Shack brought tourists and locals together like no other place on St. Thomas. The solitary bamboo structure, situated in a strip mall parking lot, housed plastic palm trees and other orders of tackiness that only seemed truly perfect and appropriate at Duffy's.

Duffy's owner was the son of the Duffy who was an integral part of the Mamas and the Papas rock band legend. This establishment was an endless beach party. The food was always great and the drinks were wonderful. A tacky island memento came with every drink, and for a little extra money each drink came in a specially designed plastic souvenir mug. For even a bit more money, the plastic souvenir became a ceramic souvenir. Duffy's T-shirt is a popular keepsake that I've seen in airports throughout the US. Some St. Johnians have entire collections of coconut, monkey, and parrot mugs courtesy of island guests who had stayed with them and who had had a memorable evening at the Love Shack.

Back on St. John, Skinny Legs was the gathering spot for many Coral Bay events. Beyond the bar, a bare area led to Coral Bay itself and provided a natural space for small concerts and fundraising activities. Some people insisted that this was the spot where Jimmy Buffet actually came up with the initial idea for his song "Cheeseburger In Paradise," and many insisted the burgers here were the best anywhere in the world. I liked the place for its unique artwork—a hanging mobile made of driftwood titled "Lost Soles of Coral Bay." From each dangling string hung a long-lost sandal or shoe bottom someone had left behind.

There were other long lost souls on St. John, such as those who'd created the petroglyphs that tourists trekked to see on the Reef Bay Trail. Some soul-less people were rumored to have developed a marijuana plantation out in the bush on the northeast end of the island, complete with an automated irrigation system; if the rumors were true, they might still be there, since I've never heard any rumors that they'd been caught. In addition, the local music scene was filled with soul of all kinds, from the steel drum bands to the strong reggae beat that made local St. John bands a regional legend. And our churches sometimes attracted tourists to the uplifting sounds of congregations in perfect harmony.

While our roads were few, some drivers had a tendency to speed along the few relatively flat stretches they could find, so for safety's sake, St. John roads included a few speed bumps. To understand why these barriers were placed where they were, it helps to know who lived nearby or what school used to be in the area. When increased traffic necessitated installing larger speed bumps—near Cruz Bay, for instance—someone had decided they weren't really bumps at all anymore: The large yellow caution signs proclaimed "Speed Hump" for these monstrosities. And judging from the underside of Bob's car, the signs were appropriate, to say the least.

In fact, peculiarities were so plentiful on all our islands that I just couldn't understand why some tour operators ran tours that bordered on the mundane. On St. Thomas, for instance, a common tourist complaint was that the tour guide told them little beyond what they could have read in their tourist guides, and stopped only where T-shirt vendors were located. On St. John, some tour operators simply embellished the mundane with extra words and stopped wherever there was a rare flat stretch of road.

Often these open-air tourist taxis, with their crowded bench seats, would wind their way out of town and past the switchback toward our south-shore apartment. As they passed around that last curve, I would hear a variation on the inevitable "And on your left are wealthy condos, each with their own private pools." Each would then slow to a stop on the level patch of road directly in front of my door, as the loudspeaker continued "and on your right is Rendezvous Bay with its million-dollar villas." And the drivers always failed to notice, it seemed, that most tourists continued to look left at my front door, hoping for a peek at a wealthy condo owner. It was highly annoying.

After three such tour visits in one morning, I understood the rage my friend Mary might have felt when that tourist had walked all over her cushions at the ferry dock. I was mad. That afternoon, I saw a taxi driver waiting for a fare at the Cinnamon Bay Campground. I asked him if he took people on tours, especially past the overlook to Rendezvous Bay. His smile and nod were all I had to see. I told him he was wrong and crazy to think any of us in those apartments were rich. Yes, we were paying a premium to live there, but it took most of our money to be able to do so.

"Half of the apartments are studios, for goodness sake, and don't even have real refrigerators or stoves. And have you ever seen the pools?" I insisted. "They're the size of a postage stamp." I fumed, but bit down on my tongue so as not to admit we called them dipping pools, for fear of adding more fodder to his tour dialogue.

"Why don't you talk about the trees or the animals or something?" I asked. "You're good—a good tour guide, right?" I asked, changing to another tack. "I'm sure there's something else you can say in place of making up tales about how rich we all are. Tell them how all those small rusting cement mixers in front of everyone's homes is the St. Johnian's version of a lawn ornament. Maybe you can make up a story about how rusting abandoned vehicles add precious minerals into our hillsides. No one ever talks about those things."

The poor man didn't know what to say. He was amused and shocked at the same time. Now sane, I tried to save face, gave him a big smile, and said "Think about it. And keep bringing those tourists around," as I inched my way back to my car.

On my way home I decided perhaps the taxi drivers needed some help. For weeks I pondered what to do. On a business trip to the west coast of California, I found a large, official-looking metal caution sign painted yellow, like those used to slow down traffic on roadways. The sign read "Iguana Crossing," and showed a picture of one of the critters, just to eliminate any possible confusion in the minds of those unfamiliar with the animal.

Perfect, I thought. We had iguanas nearby our house, and although the local dogs would occasionally find and eat iguana eggs, I knew there were a couple of adult iguanas around that the dogs had learned to leave alone. Four thousand miles that sign traveled in less than one day, yet it took months of island-time planning before it was hoisted in place near our front yard.

Soon, the tourists noticed the sign and began pointing and taking pictures, even though no taxi driver ever mentioned the sign in his tour. I also resisted posting the sign I really wanted (but didn't have the courage) to put up: "The Sum of the Gross Incomes of the Tenants Who Live Here Is Less Than the Salary of Your Taxi Driver." While the tourists might not have understood, the sign would have entertained the neighbors.

* * *

Getting a local driver's license gave me the jitters. I knew I was long overdue to apply, but the thought of the compulsory written test scared me. The test questions and answers required that I think like a local; many continentals failed on their first attempt. I was advised by others to remember that the speed limits I might be asked about on the test were the limits posted ten years earlier; moreover, I would need to memorize the formal names of highways on St. Croix. Friends prepared me to quote that one could obstruct traffic only "a little while" when stopping in the middle of the road to speak to a friend, and that a necktie is an important safety device, to be kept in the glove compartment in my open-air vehicle. I discovered that drinking while driving was not illegal, but you *could* get arrested for not offering to take an injured person to their home, or *wherever else they wanted to go!*

The afternoon before I took the test, three visitors and I went swimming at Trunk Bay. When we left the parking area for the Bay, I accidentally left my small black purse with my stateside driver's license on the soft-top of my Tracker. Unaware of my mistake, we headed home—a good thirty-minute drive away. A couple of hours later I discovered my loss and panicked. I drove in the dark back to Trunk Bay with a flashlight and a prayer. The purse was nowhere to be found. Slowly I headed home with a wrenching in my gut, as my mind pictured the disaster I faced when I took my driver's test the next morning. Without a valid license, I would also have to take a driving test, which, despite my perfect driving record, I knew that for some obscure reason I'd fail.

About a mile from Trunk Bay on my way home, however, I saw a magnificent sight right there in my headlights: My black purse hung from a tree over the road, where some kind soul had found it and placed it, in the island custom, for me to find. My money, my credit cards, and—most importantly—my driver's license were all intact. I wasn't surprised.

On my way back to town I saw a lone man with long dreadlocks walking along the road. I slowed to offer him a ride, but he waved me on with a smile, and I could only guess that he had been my savior that night.

Bob and I came to accept dreadlocks just as we'd come to accept that some island women were afraid to let raindrops touch their bodies. Good dreadlocks required a lot of attention and care, we found out. And the long-standing superstition that rain on a woman's belly would cause a child to be born sickly was a belief that no one messed with. We learned to say "Good Night" in greeting after a certain time in the evening rather than as a parting gesture. After a while, these all became the norm for us.

One could easily recognize newcomers to the island by the thumb they stuck out when hitchhiking. Everyone who'd been on St. John for even a few weeks got used to pointing in the direction they were going with their index finger instead. In time, we gave hardly a thought to seeing people dressed in clothing that was finely stitched from burlap and adorned with cloth remnants to give it style. And we got used to seeing elderly ladies on Sunday morning walking long distances under the hot sun in beautiful snow-white dresses; these ladies always greeted us with a smile, but rarely accepted offers of a ride.

Having someone on a street corner offer me a hibiscus for my hair for no other reason than my hair was unadorned was something I came to accept with a thankful smile. Even island vehicles were often adorned to represent the personality of their owners, using some quirky decoration attached to the grillwork, or some ornament on the windshield. Some decorations were easy to figure out, like the Pillsbury doughboy that topped the baker's car, or the tiny hammer belonging to a local carpenter. Others made you wonder, like the Barbie doll from hell or the toilet bowl carefully perched to catch the rain. My downstairs neighbor had a live cactus growing from her car, while one lively grandma we met managed a daily fresh floral bouquet on hers.

Bob and I decided that we, too, needed to make a statement. My husband chose his ornament rather quickly: a plastic Smurf in a kayak, which he just happened to have with him. I, on the other hand, had no immediate and automatic sense of personal identity. An airplane could represent the travel I took regularly, but that was definitely a non-island kind of thing. I didn't want to use a model of a small computer, since it hardly represented my personality. And while my Brown Bay trail name was Ketch-an-Keep Karin, only a few locals would recognize this native thorny plant hoisted on my vehicle. Besides, I wasn't sure that was a reputation I wanted to promote.

After long and careful rumination, I finally settled on a goat skull I found one day in my island travels; it had no real meaning for me, and confused everyone, and while it really didn't have anything to do with me, it somehow seemed perfect.

* * *

Our friend Marvin, who had a little sailboat on the front of his car, told us he'd gotten a ticket for failing to halt at a newly erected, though poorly positioned, stop sign one day. As he was telling us about it, we all waited to hear the St. John twist his little story was sure to have. It seems Marvin had told the ticketing officer he thought the stop sign had been put in the wrong place; his own logic made it seem to him that the sign should have been placed on the intersecting side road, he explained. But he agreed with the officer that he'd broken the law and humbly accepted the ticket.

The next morning Marvin received a phone call from the police. He was told to tear up the ticket he'd received the day before. The policeman had checked, and sure enough the sign had been placed in the wrong spot.

It was often difficult for police and other public officials to deal with peculiarities on St. John. Often police were assigned to the island from St. Thomas and had no understanding of local landmarks or traditions. The intersection up on Gift Hill on St. John, which for years everyone knew as the Fork in the road, was one such example. When a grass roots crime prevention group started in the area, the police insisted that all intersections needed to be fitted with *official* road signs, so police could ensure fast and accurate response to calls.

And so a sign went up on the opposite side of the intersection from the plywood fork. Curious as to what it said, one day I slowed my Geo Tracker to read the small, black words that were hardly visible on the new white road sign.

It read "FORK IN THE RD."... of course.

St. John Trivia

The three-story police station in Cruz Bay boasts the island's first and only working elevator. After the ribbon-cutting in 1998 to officially open the building, some of St. John's leading citizens took advantage of the Open House to enjoy their first elevator ride.

St. John's first bona-fide criminal got a free ride a few months later.

Chapter 15

The Quiet Season

As summer approached, we looked forward to the seasonal downswing in tourists, longing for the empty beaches we'd enjoyed the previous summer. Bob looked forward to encountering less traffic on his regular trips to St. Thomas. But before it could happen, we would have to survive Carnival time on St. Thomas and the months before St. John would host its own Carnival.

As expected, when St. Thomas' Carnival time arrived, Bob encountered parking lots turned into Carnival venues, new places for parking cars along the waterfront, and increased traffic throughout. Companies he visited were working with skeleton staffs, as many employees took vacation or sick leave to take part in various events during the month-long party. Because Bob had to deal with these inconveniences all week long, there was no way I could convince him to return there with me for an evening or on weekends to enjoy the festivities ourselves.

I resigned myself to reading about the venues in the daily papers and watching the various parades on TV. On the last day of the festivities, I had to travel through St. Thomas to the airport for a business trip and left an hour early, fearing big crowds in town. But downtown St. Thomas was all but deserted; it seems everyone was sleeping off a long party the night before and was preparing for a longer final-night finale later on that day. I'd missed the St. Thomas Carnival completely our first year on-island, and so I promised myself we'd take part when St. John's own Carnival came around this time.

The St. Thomas fireworks that last night were spectacular—or so I was told. Even Bob couldn't resist watching this grand finale from our balcony across the water. He even invited neighbors to our apartment for the event, since our balcony had the best view in the neighborhood. I got to see pictures of it in the paper when I returned home from my trip, but by then no one wanted to talk about Carnival anymore. A classic *day late and a dollar short*.

Bob and I celebrated his twelfth month on-island by doing what we'd learned to do so well: packing and unpacking. This time I didn't argue, though, since May is hurricane preparedness month in the USVI, and Bob was determined to prepare early this year. We reviewed our pantry staples and made lists of things to stock up on just in case a disaster should strike. We checked batteries and organized candles. We sorted camping gear to make sure emergency essentials were easily available. We bought cases of drinking water and lots of bleach and other cleaning supplies. And, of course, we made sure we had plenty of food for our cats and us too.

Prior camping trips had given us plenty of experience in preparing appetizing meals from simple basics. We tried to think of every contingency, like the need for comfort foods and foods with differing textures. If a hurricane struck, we were ready with pancake mix that needed only the addition of water and of sweetness from our stock of maple syrup. Crunchy things like potato sticks and crackers were a necessity, helping to break up any potential boredom we would experience with typical canned foods. Our pantry soon overflowed with staples enough to feed our whole neighborhood for weeks.

As the tourist season dwindled, I started taking pottery-throwing lessons on St. Thomas, though commuting to and from class always posed a challenge. While the VITRAN buses at the Red Hook dock ran irregularly, the open-aired gypsy taxis were even less dependable. The air-conditioned taxi vans that picked up and dropped off tourists at Red Hook were an expensive option for going to class, and there were even fewer options for returning to the dock afterwards. Luckily, I was able to find someone at the pottery studio to drive me through the dark to Red Hook after each class; after that, I needed only to contend with a forty-five minute wait before catching the next ferry to St. John.

After a time, I began to enjoy, and even to look forward to, that waiting time. Arriving forty-five minutes early for the ferry, only the taxi drivers were around. Most played dominos or cards to pass the time away. I always gave a "Good Night" greeting to them when I arrived and sat on the edge of the dock to watch the fish feeding in the glow of the bright lights overhead. The fish were attracted to the lights and gave me quite a show. Sometimes I'd see stingrays or flying fish fleeing from their prey; it was mesmerizing. After a while, the tourists began to appear in small groups, and once they'd sized me up, proceeded to interrupt my commune with nature with their reluctant questions.

Glancing at my clay-stained casual clothing, it usually only took them seconds to figure out I was a St. John resident. Typically, they always asked the same questions: where to eat, where to swim, where to shop. In time, I actually learned to enjoy trying to figure out what would please each of them. Other times, the men working the dock taught me local slang; it was here, in fact, that I learned the three-part and five-part handshakes that were unique to our area.

Most locals arrived at the dock right at the last minute, their timing down pat. In time, I'd come to know quite a few regulars, and every week I met a few more. Waiting for the ferry, we played a kind of St. John Trivia Time, which took the place of our Friday evenings out in Cruz Bay (this had dwindled with the end of tourist season). On the docks of Red Hook, I found "belongin'."

* * *

On the weekends, Bob and I saw fewer and fewer people generally on the beaches, but more and more that I knew personally by name. Because the seas were mostly calm, Bob and I spent lots of time floating our weekends away. Despite our hurricane preparedness, rain was hard to come by, and we wavered between being glad for the good weather and hoping for rain to fill our cisterns.

Just when it seemed that a long, lazy summer was fully upon us, St. John Carnival arrived to give us a jolt.

A taxi driver on St. Thomas described the annual Carnival scene with acute accuracy. "You know how I know its Carnival on St. John?" he asked. "When I see Cruz Bay in the distance dip down into the water from the weight of the people. That's when I know for sure it's Carnival time."

He wasn't far off the mark. On tiny St. John, Carnival time brought huge crowds of people. For weeks before the beginning of festivities, signs of preparation appeared as locals prepared their Carnival booths, repaired the roads, and added a touch of new paint to their buildings. Our Carnival this year coincided with the one hundred and fiftieth celebration of the Emancipation of slaves in the Virgin Islands, and therefore Carnival on St. John was expected to be even larger than normal.

For weeks there were special Carnival and Emancipation celebrations meant to disrupt our tranquility. Calypso and Carnival Queen contests, band jams, and food fairs were the traditional crowd pleasers. Carnival Village, with its food and alcohol booths, took over the parking lot across from the Post Office. The bandstand in Cruz Bay's park (along with every other empty or level space near Cruz Bay) became a regular site for dance and musical events. Every night the Village came alive and stayed that way until the wee hours of the morning. The ferries extended their hours of operation, and larger ticket booths were put up in Red Hook to handle the influx of visitors.

Bob and I managed a couple of rare nights out during the workweek, just to dance to the beat in Carnival village and sample various devastating local alcoholic concoctions. We also bought local crafts from artisans in the park. Tourists on their first visit to the island found it hard to believe that St. John was known as the quiet island. During Carnival it became a wild and crazy place.

I was determined to join in J'Ouvert, a traditional early morning march to the beat of loud music through the streets of downtown Cruz Bay. This started around four o'clock in the morning the first day of Carnival. My friends copped out, deciding instead to "sleep in," so I blissfully decided to join them in sleeping through the event. Moe and Bev, living downtown, were not so lucky: They were woken at five o'clock in the morning, sitting bolt upright in their bed, thinking a riot had broken out. But it was simply J'Ouvert beginning its march through their neighborhood.

On July fourth, Carnival came to a climax. Bob was hoping to go to the beach that day, since everyone within five hundred miles would be in Cruz Bay to watch the parade. But Bob, as he quickly found out, didn't have a prayer of beaching it that day. Apparently, peer pressure from the neighborhood convinced him to be a good sport and help line the sidewalks with the rest of us.

While the parade was scheduled for late morning, this was St. John, and our arrival in early afternoon still gave us plenty of time to select a prime viewing space. My neighbor Jay and I managed to spend some time visiting the crafters in the park and playing tourist for a while. We bought matching straw hats and went off to admire the newly erected Emancipation statue that had just been unveiled that day. The statue— its mirror images proudly erected on St. Croix and St. Thomas that same week—had been placed at the front entrance to Cruz Bay Park to welcome all visitors to St. John. The statue was the bust of a former slave; in one hand he held a conch to his mouth to blare the news of emancipation, and in the other he held a raised scythe. The statue was reminiscent of the logo for all Emancipation celebration events throughout the Territory that year. Sporting our new straw hats, Jay and I even posed for pictures with the statues.

By mid-afternoon the streets were lined with crowds of people, and the parade finally began. Spectators occupied every inch of free space along the roads, and even fit themselves onto nearby roofs and trees. People from our neighborhood sat in their lawn chairs, content from their various lunches, which they'd culled from the multitude of food booths found everywhere downtown, comfortable under hastily rigged umbrellas to shade the sun.

As the parade passed by, we spotted Mocko Jumbie troupes and a myriad of princes and princesses propped and waving from their sponsor vehicles. Trailer beds with live bands playing from them made the ground shake below our feet. Handcrafted floats were interspersed with every kind of marching group you could imagine, and the costumes they were wearing were absolutely wild.

The parade moved past, starting and stopping regularly, and each short break in the action gave Woody's, the bar/restaurant across the street, a chance to send over fresh drinks and snacks to the hot and weary spectators among us. They were doing a phenomenal business, reminiscent of any night during tourist season.

One Post Office worker who marched by was decked out in an outrageous costume of feathers and streamers and was barely recognizable. His broad smile—not typical on the job at the Post Office—made him more unrecognizable than his costume did. One troupe carried fruit baskets and burlap sacks balanced on their heads as they bounced to the beat of the music being played just behind them. Hours after it started, the parade was over, and we all headed home to get ready for the finale later on.

As part of St. John Rescue, Bob had to help out that night during the fireworks display. He was stationed on the waterfront near the fireworks barge in the harbor. All boats were warned to leave their moorings, "for safety's sake," and most took heed. Though he hated crowds, Bob had ended up right in the thick of things. I, on the other hand, found a more secluded place to view the event—at a small party in a beautiful house perched above Cruz Bay. When the fireworks began only a few minutes late, it surprised all of us. I was duly impressed. Besides beginning practically on time, they were spectacular.

But it was the fireworks' grand finale that confused us, since rather than the expected huge climax, the fireworks just seemed to dwindle away. The whole party had been poised for a final, huge display of pyrotechnics, but it never came. Only the smoky remains of previous fireworks still filled the night air, until that too drifted away into the distant beat of music. Bob later told us that some of the fireworks had accidentally fallen onto the deck of the barge and had gone off in a horizontal direction, and that the fireworks slated for the grand finale had fallen into the water itself.

In a way, I suppose, this near-anticlimax was a better ending than had been planned. It left us all wanting more, wanting an even bigger celebration next year.

* * *

After Carnival, St. John became a sleepy place again. There were parking spaces to be had in Cruz Bay, and it was possible again to find beaches with no other soul around. I marveled that most of the few tourists still present thought our summers to be hot. They sweltered in the hundred-degree heat, while gentle trade winds seemed to us residents to keep our weather just wonderful.

Summer brought warmer waters and calmer seas, just perfect for weekend floating in Paradise. For the first time in our lives, summer didn't pass too quickly. Work on the Brown Bay Trail slowed down, as the sun made the days too hot for that sort of physical work, even in the cooler early morning hours. Besides, this particular summer there were other adventures to keep everyone entertained.

An archeological dig began at Cinnamon Bay, just a few feet away from the beach's edge. It was a ceremonial Taino Indian site, and just a few inches below the surface bits and pieces of shells and pottery dating from the fifteenth century had been found. Under the guidance of professionals, everyone on-island was encouraged to volunteer and participate in the dig. It was fun sorting these bits and pieces by size and type; sifting sand through screens was something that brought back childhood play.

My friend Jan and our "Goat Girl" Jessie were the most consistent participants we knew of at the dig. When Jessie uncovered a shell pendant one day, she was on top of the world. And when the site's chief archeologist gave her a commemorative T-shirt for all her hard work, her feet hardly touched the ground as she pranced around the neighborhood to show it off.

One evening the women on the island enjoyed a girl's night out when an island-wide fashion show was held at the world-class Caneel Bay Resort. It was an evening filled with fun and entertainment and it gave everyone a chance to dress-to-kill without husbands to worry about. Best of all, it was a fundraiser for the Safety Zone, an organization dedicated to providing a safe haven for domestic violence victims.

The Friends of the VI National Park also offered an unusually inexpensive snorkel tour of the British Virgin Islands, and Bob and I were first in line to enjoy snorkeling at the Baths on Virgin Gorda. We even found time one weekend to spend a day of shopping on St. Thomas and have dinner at a Chinese restaurant near Havensight.

As a bonus, the island completed considerable public roadwork and construction that summer. But we all dreaded the change to make the South Shore Road a one-way lane out of town, adding a long two-minute permanent detour to anyone's rush to catch a ferry from our south shore apartment. Worse still, anyone who wasn't in that sort of rush typically stopped each morning at Ronnie's Bakery for a quick coffee and pastry on their way to work. Now, everyone had to drive to town, then head back out of town on the one-way road to make the stop. It took months, and some serious creativity on Ronnie's part, for the bakery's business to recover from the detour. Die-hard fans of Ronnie's such as Bob, however, were happy with the inconvenience, since parking was easier and the early morning construction crews didn't gobble up all the fantastic pastries before Bob managed to get there.

No one minded the temporary, five-minute detour caused by the anticipated repaving of the hill known as Jacobs Ladder. At present, when it rained or a water truck dripped water on the road, making it wet and slippery, many vehicles couldn't make it up to the top. Besides, I was tired of driving behind trucks that would lose their payload halfway up the hill. Knowledgeable locals got used to stopping at the bottom of the hill to wait in safety while trucks carrying large loads attempted the climb. When these trucks stalled, they had no other option but to back slowly down the hill and try again.

Occasionally, a taxi would stop on an angle at the crest of the hill to drop off passengers. They were oblivious to any unwary driver behind them or cresting the other side of the hill. And once tourist vehicles stalled, tourists would occasionally attempt to turn around halfway up the hill, often resulting in disaster when their vehicles tipped over halfway through their turn. In addition, the road was narrow and there were no sidewalks, so many unfortunate locals had no other option than to walk up or down the steep hill regardless of traffic. To make matters worse, halfway up the hill lived a variety of goats and chickens that liked to cross the street at their own whim.

That summer, Jacobs Ladder got repaved to a smooth, blacktop finish; it even got roadside walkways added for the walk most of the way up the hill. Unfortunately, it was barely widened enough to accommodate these changes, and worse still, the road was not regraded before it was repaved, so the steepness of the grade remained, as did the danger of striking someone walking just over the crest of the hill. But at least the potholes were finally gone, making the trip up or down lots more manageable.

* * *

Like many islanders, Bob kept a close eye on our cable TV's weather channel all summer long. Surprisingly, the few tropical waves and tropical depressions that formed anywhere near bypassed us with little rain or wind. We occasionally dipped into our hurricane supplies, but only for odd items to consume and only out of choice; we became more and more convinced that there'd be no hurricane this year. Little Hurricane Erica from last season was quick becoming a dim memory of our overkill preparations last year.

Then one day a tropical depression appeared off the coast of Africa. Its mass was large and it quickly picked up strength. Although all our tropical waves and depressions started this same way, somehow everyone on St. John knew that this was the one storm that could really impact us this year. The mass, which became known as Tropical Storm Georges, gained strength and stayed its path; still days away from our island, it became a full-fledged hurricane.

At this time I was back in Massachusetts, but even I knew in my heart that Georges would be coming to St. John soon. With still a couple of days to go, Georges had gained so much strength it was quickly escalated into a category five hurricane. The news brought fear to everyone, since a hurricane of such magnitude is very rare and extremely destructive.

Everyone, including Bob and I, remembered the meteorological wrath brought to St. John in 1995 when Hurricane Marilyn, a mere category two hurricane, passed through. The hurricane had brought tornadoes along with the wind and the rain, and the destruction still remained in evidence to this day in some places.

I arrived back home on a half-empty airplane, energized with the need to prepare for Georges' destruction. But the first thing I did was to tape our hurricane map for the region on a wall in the apartment. The map had been saved from a *VI Daily News* edition at the beginning of the hurricane season. Once it was up on the wall, I marked it up with the latest storm coordinates for Georges.

Bob and I moved our outdoor furniture into the swimming pool, which is standard prehurricane procedure. We brought the wind chimes, birdfeeders and hammocks inside and packed them away. We then shrouded our bookcases in plastic and packed all our clutter in plastic bags. We sent off a round of e-mail messages to family, friends, and my workplace, then packed the computer and related equipment away in two layers of protective plastic. We cleared the tops of all tables and counters and reorganized our kitchen cabinets to make space for our small appliances. We taped our kitchen cabinets shut and wrapped everything else in plastic.

Then we piled the living room furniture against an inside wall, well away from the windows and doors, and covered the heap with a huge tarp. We made our floor space as bare as possible, just in case we had any flooding. The master bedroom was next, and suffered similar treatment; then we encased all our clothes in plastic—except for those few things we kept out for immediate use.

We didn't limit our efforts to just our own apartment. Bob and I helped neighbors and businesses wherever we could. The island that weekend was a beehive of activity. We squeezed in a short hour at a beach for a sea bath, knowing it would be a while before we could bathe again. The empty beach spoke volumes about the approaching storm, and so we cut our visit short. Long into the nights that weekend, we prepared for the worst, and although Georges had slowed down and had been downgraded to a category two hurricane, it was still coming right at us. No matter how I viewed the changing map coordinates, we were in for quite a storm.

The emergency supply containers we'd organized in the spring came in handy, since we didn't have to search for flashlights or candles or radios or foodstuffs. So while stores in town stayed open late, we were already prepared and didn't have to deal with the crowds. On Sunday night, with the hurricane less than twelve hours away, everyone we knew was cooking up a big batch of stew or chili or some other concoction in quantities large enough to last them a few days. Exhausted by our own preparations, I was in no mood to cook. We turned off the propane flow to our stove for the duration.

Invitations came in from five different people for Bob and I to stay with them if we weren't comfortable at our own apartment. As part of his St. John Rescue routine, Bob got a hurricane curfew pass that would save him from being arrested if a state of emergency were called. He then went to the designated St. John shelters to check in and help out, but the shelters had yet to open. Most people just hunkered down at home. And finally sometime after midnight, so did we.

The main force of the hurricane hit us just before mid-day on Monday. We'd lost our telephone and power and assumed everyone else had. The first big gusts toppled a tan-tan tree next to our building; we'd been trying to convince Moe to trim it back for months. There was no question that the hurricane had arrived.

Bob and I retreated to our apartment's guestroom, with its three concrete walls. We coaxed the cats in with us. The fourth side of the tiny room was mostly a sliding door made of safety glass, but it was in the most sheltered area of the property and we hoped for the best. While Bob and I were adding the final touches of comfort to our well-sheltered cubbyhole, Jay and Andre were having a party. Their building was much more protected than ours, since two-thirds of their apartment was backed up against a hillside.

Soon, the front side of our apartment began getting barraged by constant, strong winds. Outdoors, the wooden enclosure for our propane tank blew off and onto the ground. With our neighbor Karen helping, we brought the loose boards into our apartment before they were lost forever; what one person could normally do, it took three people to do now because of the winds. Soon after the enclosure blew down, some unknown object outside flew against our kitchen window and broke it. Our outside door and all the windows were pulsating, and water began seeping under the door.

In our protected guestroom, the sounds of the storm were distant. A couple of hours into the hurricane, our neighbor Andre came up the spiral staircase next to our cubbyhole. His apartment had no phone outage and he and Jay were concerned about our safety. The walk from his building to ours was relatively protected from the winds, but Bob and I both thought he was crazy to be out during the storm.

"Is this where the hurricane is?" Andre asked in a little boy voice as he took a little walk around our porch toward the front of our building. Two seconds later he got his answer: As he rounded the last corner, a blast of wind and rain almost knocked him over. Just then one of our gutters flew by. Andre quickly retreated to the relative safety of the back porch.

"Want a little tour of reality, neighbor?" Bob chided as he led Andre into our living room.

"Gee, you guys are overprepared," Andre said as he spied our tarp-covered furnishings against the inner wall. Then Bob showed him the long blades of grass that had somehow wrapped themselves around the inside of our front door, and the growing puddle on our living room floor that a mass of beach towels stuffed against the door were trying to keep at bay. I showed him the broken window in the kitchen and the inch of standing water in the downstairs bathroom. Andre was duly humbled and convinced. He helped Bob shore up the kitchen window with duct tape and more plastic, then suggested we visit the party down at his place. Bob and I declined. It was time to wring out the towels and add more protection to barrier the water flowing into our apartment, both upstairs and down.

At the storm's worst, water flowed halfway across our bedroom from the lone bathroom window upstairs, despite our regular attempts at towel wringing and sponging. The downstairs fared little better, as each of the windows on the front side of our house leaked like a sieve. At some point, we noted that the ceiling was creaking and shaking in the wind, as the storm attempted to rip it apart. The loudness of the storm made it difficult for us to talk to each other, and we worked the towels quickly, anxious to finish our mopping and return to the relative safety of our guestroom.

Our cats were smart enough to stay in the guestroom, where it was relatively quiet and safe. But our crazy neighbor Andre returned once again. This time he had a rope attached between him and his daughter Jessie, and he had strangers behind them.

"Everyone wants to see the hurricane," he said as he led the party around the side of our porch.

"You're crazy," I told them all. "The eye of the storm is just south of here right now."

A few seconds later the winds were too strong for anyone to do more than peek around the corner without being blown away. We knew that those people with the most curiosity were most likely to be harmed than we were, so we urged them to "get a life"—in other words, to go home. They just hadn't grasped the extent of danger that flying objects could cause.

The darkness that night was oppressive, and our candles and flashlights and radio were our only companions. Each time new storm coordinates were announced, I took a flashlight into the hallway and marked them on our hurricane map. Our cats were happy to stay in the guestroom and cuddle next to Bob. The storm continued late into the night, and somehow we both finally dropped off to deep, exhausted sleep.

Chapter 16

The Grass Is Greener . . .
After It Rains

The next morning, the stuffiness of our room woke us early. Quickly, Bob and I made our way out of the room, then outside. Our swimming pool was almost black from the soil and leaves and other debris that the storm had deposited, and the pool furniture was invisible under the sludge. The rain was long gone, and the passing clouds promised a beautiful day. Bob and I searched the hillsides around us, but could see only one home with any apparent damage.

Some things had changed, however, since now we could see houses that had previously been hidden by the dense foliage. The palm and papaya trees and most other plants had been stripped bare of their leaves. It was hard to believe that less than twenty-four hours had passed since the storm had arrived.

Bob and I were not alone in our explorations: Karen, Ricky, Jay, Andre, Jessie, Pam and our other neighbors had also emerged into the sunlight and were gingerly dodging fallen wires as they surveyed the damage. Some came together and embraced as though a lifetime had just passed. Our two cats refused to venture more than ten feet beyond the building boundaries. We were all numb.

My car, which I'd tucked tightly between other vehicles in a protected area below, was covered with debris, but was still intact and surprisingly dry, despite its soft convertible top. Strong wind had blown minute bits of debris into every seam in the car and sealed the inside from the heavy rains. Bob's car was still intact too, but given the unidentifiable utility lines draped behind it, we treated it as an "unmovable."

Soon the occasional vehicle passed slowly by, as drivers asked us if all was okay. The owners of Bob's company stopped by to see if we needed any help. (Bestech, like most companies on the island, was closed.) Chuck and his wife Diane were on their way to town to survey the damage. Without a telephone, I was cut off from work, though we had little time to ponder the problem; there was too much else to do.

So Bob and I began the tedious task of ringing out the numerous towels on the floors and mopping up the standing water remaining. We hung eighteen towels to dry from our porch railing, along with damp clothes that covered every surface. The outside of our building was plastered with a thin layer of debris that quickly dried in the hot sun and defied all attempts short of a pressure washer to remove it. Karen convinced us the wires draped behind Bob's car were just phone and cable TV wires; she'd lived through multiple hurricanes on St. John, she said, and she was sure that's all they were. This thrilled Bob, as he was anxious to be out on the road to check the island's shelters and offer assistance where needed.

While Bob went off to his joy ride, I tested our propane tanks and began removing furniture from the black hole that was our swimming pool. All of Cruz Bay was under generator power, Bob told me when he returned, and Marina Market and the St. John Ice Company were already open for business. The local dry cleaners where Jay worked was also open, and Jay was there already, though with nary a customer in sight except Bob. My husband had had the unusual foresight to put a load of laundry in the car before he left for town.

The huge blocks of ice Bob brought home arrived just in time to save lots of foodstuffs that would otherwise have required throwing out. I lined up our assortment of ice coolers and worked frantically to sort refrigerated items based on their perishability. Some blocks of ice had to be cracked into little chunks to fit the smallest coolers, but the effort was worth it, as our full freezer was thawing like crazy and leaving puddles on the kitchen floor. By the time the transfers of food were complete, we had very wet, very muddy floors. So again we mopped and wiped and wrang out towels. By the time we were finished, daylight was gone. A mandatory 8:00 PM curfew made the night eerily quiet, allowing us to fall into an exhausted sleep quickly.

The next morning, Moe brought up a generator that the two buildings could share. It saved most of our foodstuffs. The generator also gave us toilets again, to everyone's great relief, as we all strove to return to normal. Surprisingly, our television also worked off the generator, but without cable we could only get two English stations. The national news said the Virgin Islands had been devastated by the storm, but friends and neighbors—and even our own eyes—assured us it wasn't true. Many telephones on St. John had remained working throughout the storm, but no one could call long distance. There was no way to reassure relatives or friends outside of the Virgin Islands for two long days.

A day after the hurricane passed, Bob was back at work and extremely busy. I managed to unpack my notebook computer and put in a few hours of work using my battery pack and extra power from our generator running through a backup device. It quickly became obvious that I needed a telephone.

Diane, her home high up on the hill overlooking Rendezvous Bay, had a satellite telephone and a satellite system for her television. When she heard the Virgin Islands were decimated on a national news network, she decided to take action on behalf of all of us. She dialed the network, demanded they retract their story and accurately report on the facts. Her efforts made her a heroine to everyone I knew.

As soon as long distance service was restored, I put my work contingency plans into action. Chuck had kindly offered me the use of an empty classroom to work from at his Bestech offices in town. I spent hours making phone calls and catching up on my e-mail, but the small, windowless, air-conditioned room made me claustrophobic. The next day, I set up shop at Jay's house, since by that time everyone had gone to work or school for the day. This was perfect, since I was only a two-minute walk from all of my file folders and other work paraphernalia. Thanks to the kindness of these folks, I was able to function for the six long workdays before my own telephone was finally restored.

Without ceiling fans constantly moving the air, our apartment stayed rather stuffy, despite our leaving the doors and windows open whenever we could. Moe's small generator needed to rest at night, so even a small floor fan was out of the question. Bob and I were concerned about mosquitoes and other flying creatures of the night, but solved that problem by finally hoisting the mosquito net I'd gotten years ago over our bed. Even swimming in our pool wasn't an option for cooling down, and the beaches were still declared off-limits until lab tests were done to check the water quality.

Then came the mutant ninja mosquitoes. Instead of the occasional bug, as we'd had before the storm, we'd become inundated with these flying bloodsuckers, and no one on the island was immune. These large parasites were unaffected by, and even seemed to enjoy the taste of, most mosquito sprays. Using five cans in less than five days, we still had bites all over ourselves. Only when Bob and I were tucked under our mosquito net at night were we protected.

On a related note: It took only one night for our cats to figure out how to slide in between the mosquito net and the mattress. They too preferred sleeping away from the flying creatures. It was a great relief when we got power back five days after Georges passed by, but by then we had grown to like the idea of the mosquito net and the added protection it afforded us, especially when we lost power at night, as we did almost every week. The mosquito net became a normal part of our sleeping environment from that point forward.

Eight days after Hurricane Georges, our telephone lines were back up and working. I was in heaven. Even our swimming pool was starting to look like normal, though I wasn't quite ready to risk a swim, since the amount of chlorine we used to shock the pool back to safe levels would probably have bleached my body white. Finally, the beaches were declared safe. Two weeks after Georges, Bob and I spent a whole day at the beach, just floating on the water and ignoring reality. It would take another month before our cable TV access was back in order, though we didn't have to miss most prime-time shows since Diane taped shows religiously on her satellite TV to pass on to us less-fortunate souls. CNN also came to our rescue when they allowed our Public Broadcasting System to air a half-hour of national and world news four times a day. Since our own TV got mostly Spanish stations without our cable hook-up, after a few weeks Bob and I decided to take Spanish lessons.

Some St. Johnians missed Hurricane Georges and its immediate aftermath by being off-island for business or vacation when the storm hit. Our friend Jan was one of these. Unaware of the pending storm, she had gone to Chicago for a long-needed vacation only days before the hurricane hit. Jan was facing a crossroads in her life, trying to decide whether to make a long-term commitment to St. John or move on in search of some other Paradise. She hoped a little time off-island would help her decide what to do.

Right before we lost our telephone line in the hurricane, Jan called with offers to bring back any anticipated emergency supplies that we hadn't had time to buy ourselves. Bob took advantage of the situation by requesting a portable twelve-volt boat fan—for whatever purpose I could only guess. I thought he was nuts. He said he could rig it to run off a battery that he could recharge during the day from a generator. So much for my rugged adventurer—the one who needed no modern con- veniences. Bob was clearly a spoiled, material kind of guy.

When Jan returned ten days after Georges left, she had Bob's fan in tow. Our power was back on, but Bob was still happy to see a new toy. Jan had also had the foresight to bring a caseload of mosquito spray, enough for the entire neighborhood. The mutants were in full force by now, and we were all grateful. I told Jan she was lucky to have missed all the excitement, and I was surprised when she shook her head.

"I know my worries and concerns were like nothing you all went through, but it was just awful. The news said the islands had been devastated, and I couldn't get through on the telephone. For days I tried to get news and I worried about everyone and everything. Friends and family up north said at least I was home when the disaster struck, but that's when it hit me. Chicago isn't my home. St. John is my home now."

We'd all known Jan belonged on St. John even when she wasn't sure, and it was wonderful to know she'd finally figured it out herself. While I'd been anxious for friends in New England to know we were okay after the hurricane, I was more concerned about the people who'd become my own extended local family. Neither Bob nor I had any thoughts of leaving to avoid the cleanup or the mosquitoes or the aggravations of getting our lives back to normal. This was our home now too.

In the wake of Hurricane Georges, lots of iguanas lost their secluded nests, but they survived. On the short stretch of road to Cruz Bay, I saw no less than six huge iguanas crossing the roads one morning. All around us, recovery was taking place. The papaya tree in front of our house grew back its beautiful foliage fast, and many trees and bushes on the island were soon fooled into blossoming off-season. The hurricane had forced Bob and I to do an island version of spring-cleaning and got us all to reassess our priorities.

Some things may never be the same. The gutters that came off our upper roof proved to be a blessing in disguise. Before Georges, most rainstorms caused rain to rush down the upper gutters so fast that water gushed off the lower roof and onto the ground. Now the rain flowed more evenly into the lower gutters and into our cistern. The plywood fork in the road had lost a tine but had survived. In fact, it was now a more accurate depiction of the real fork in the road it described. The shiny white "FORK IN THE RD." sign was still intact, but it was now turned at an angle that was more accurate. Unfortunately, my favorite tree on the island, a beautiful pomegranate, was doomed because of windburn.

No one in our Adopt-A-Trail group seemed anxious to visit the Brown Bay Trail after Georges. Everyone told me that nature had probably undone all the hard work and effort that we'd put into it, and no one seemed to have the energy to start all over again. Eventually I went by myself, without any tools, just to survey the damage. Before I went, I'd convinced myself that the hurricane had probably helped to widen the trail. As I saw on my way to the trail, though, the normally dry East End of St. John was dense with new foliage, and by the time I reached the trailhead, my expectations were low.

Prior to the storm, the beginning of the trailhead had never been cleared wider than the modest width I'd insisted on to discourage the Ketch-an'-Keep plants from attaching themselves to me. Still, the trail was narrow enough to discourage tourists from wandering up the hill until the whole trail was up to par.

But now, as I started up the path, I found it was lined with a beautiful new array of short bushy flowers in all the colors of the rainbow. There was a strong woodsy smell in the air that reminded me of a deep, dark, decaying forest. As I started up the path, the woodsy scent gave way to a beautiful fragrance that became more exotic and rare with every step I took. Unknown flowering vines created a loose, shaded canopy overhead. Our hard work had not been in vain.

I was able to make it up the first third of the trail to the top of the ridge with only five fallen trees in the way. To be honest, two of these were mere branches, but without tools or gloves, I made no attempt to move them. Still, our path was clearly visible, and thanks to all our hard work, not one Ketch-an'-keep plant caught me in its grasp. In one short morning, I was sure our Brown Bay crew could bring the front of the trail back up to snuff, and the fragrance and beauty surrounding us would make the work utterly pleasant. If only I could convince them to try. On my way back to the car, I pondered the problem, finally deciding to let island time lull them all back to this special place.

* * *

Two short months later, our lives were to change dramatically again. Moe and Bev had decided to lease the apartment buildings many of us lived in to the Westin resort, as part of a plan to sell them the property. The Westin was desperate for apartments for their employees. Bob and I and our friends were all to become homeless at the start of tourist season. It was a disaster.

For every advertisement in *Connections,* there were at least twelve desperate people vying for the privilege of a new place to live. Apartments were so hard to find that Doug Franklin, owner of the only long-term rental agency on the island, changed his answering machine to ward off prospective clients.

The island grapevine was everyone's saving grace. As during the aftermath of a hurricane, everyone shared tips. Places not yet on the market, and even some apartments beneath private homes that were in the process of being built, yielded opportunities. Nothing was ever definite until deposits were paid and move dates had counted down to two weeks, so everyone had secret back-up possibilities in case their first choice didn't work out.

Bob and I were pushed into making a life decision. We knew we'd be living on St. John for the foreseeable future, and we had some cash reserves. So, along with apartments, we looked at homes and condos on the lower end of the market. In the process, we explored nooks and crannies on St. John that boggled the mind: A two room shack on top of a mountain with a gorgeous view, and a high-tech rental apartment with an electronic hurricane shutter for a front door were both considered options. We were pickier than most, and while the pickings were slim, we were persistent.

In seemingly no time at all, Bob and I had put a deposit on a place of our own. We settled on one of the few condos available that allowed year-round owner occupancy. (Most complexes were geared strictly for the short-term rental market, and year-round residents weren't allowed.) Cost of ownership was high everywhere, and we could only afford a one-bedroom condo. We weren't quite ready to own a house—not yet, anyway; besides, the smaller space meant less space to keep clean.

Yard sales and consolidation of possessions would again be necessary if we were to fit into the smaller space. Still, Bob somehow managed to make another of his pipe dreams come true: He would soon be part owner of a nice-sized swimming pool that would daily beckon to him just below our huge outside porch.

* * *

Last week, as we packed to move into the condo, a strong storm front passed by. This tropical wave brought lots of rain. A couple of days later, the termites swarmed outside on our porch. This time we were ready for the onslaught. Our cats enjoyed the show from inside our darkened apartment, while Bob turned porch lights on for their viewing enjoyment. In the dim glow of the outside bulbs, I planted tomato seeds in little pots, with renewed hope for a year of bounty at our new home.

Yesterday morning, Bob got e-mail from a kayaker friend up north. With it came an offer to sell Bob's drysuit—which was still stored in New England—to another boater. My husband got excited about the prospect and immediately replied that he wanted to sell it. While Bob was unloading his past, some things from my past were coming back to us, just in time for our move.

A neighbor had dropped off a copy of *The VI Daily News* at our place over breakfast, and while Bob played with the computer, I perused the news. Included in this edition was the newspapers' regular "Police Reports" column, with police logs from St. John. The first entry I read was a complaint from a man who'd seen someone wearing a pair of his boots in Cruz Bay. Those boots had purportedly been stolen from the man some time ago. A few entries further down in the column noted a pair of boots had been returned to their rightful owner. As I chuckled over this tidbit, someone knocked on our door.

"Are any of these yours?" asked a brawny man with his head buried behind a mountain of shoes. Was this man the boot burglar, trying to make restitution for his crimes? Stunned by the thought, I was caught between gaping and laughing at the crazy sight before me.

"Or, do you know who any of these belong to?" the man added despairingly.

A while back, I'd lost a pair of sneakers and some sandals when I'd left them outside our front door while cleaning. Sure enough, as the man twirled slowly in a half-circle, I spied my very own sneakers dangling by their ties from the man's right elbow. My discovery brought a frown to my face.

"Which ones are yours?" the relieved man asked, with sagging shoulders. "I'm not a thief," he added, as a way to begin explaining the whole story. It seems that the man's one-year-old dog had developed a shoe fetish, but had kept it hidden from his owner for quite some time. Judging from the quantity and variety of shoes the man carried, this dog had a real problem. The owner had discovered the huge cache of shoes by accident a couple of hours earlier. He was trying in vain to make everything right, but everyone he met thought he was the infamous "boot burglar" we'd all just been reading about. Watching him continue down the road two sneakers and three sandals lighter, I could only hope that he'd find the other owners soon.

* * *

Across the road and looking east, I can just see the vacation villa we rented with family and friends a couple of years ago. I remember how we'd all shared expenses to afford the luxurious three-bedroom villa, with its courtyard pool on a small private peninsula, during that last vacation to Paradise. Every day we'd played and spent time on our private beach; the word "work" was not part of our vocabulary that vacation. Every night we ate in fine restaurants. The villa itself was a fantasy retreat: the word "perfect" comes to mind.

Bob and I are unlikely to experience such luxury again on St. John, even for a week, but it doesn't matter. Now when I see the landmark roof of that vacation villa less than a mile away, there's no longing in my heart. Instead, I feel a soaring of the spirit, and I smile at the possibilities and the adventures life has to offer.

With a silly grin, I find myself saying "Good Afternoon" to the feral donkey grazing across the street. This tail-swishing island neighbor is a reminder that Bob and I have come a long way in the past year. A year ago today it was just another normal day in Paradise, and my naivete was evident. The scent of jasmine kissed the air, while hummingbirds fluttered nearby. St. Thomas formed a distant backdrop to our island panorama. Our covered porch was a perfect workplace for me, with mild trade winds mellowing the sun and wind chimes providing subtle background music. Down a short staircase, our inviting little swimming pool warmed among the splendor of our garden.

I had some paperwork to do, and could think of no better place to work. By break time, the pool would be ready to soothe. Moving my home office outdoors for the morning was a brilliant idea. My creative energy was strong and my work focus was singular. In a short time, I was completely engrossed in my work. And so the morning progressed, until an unpleasant smell wafted through my Paradise. Its presence was distracting. At first I thought it just a quirk of the breeze carrying, perhaps, the memory of a garbage truck passing down the hill. (This happens occasionally, even in Paradise.) But the smell got stronger. My focus on paperwork was lost to annoyance.

Just then I caught a movement out of the corner of my eye. Assuming a neighbor was heading for the pool, I turned to comment, with a complaint on my lips.

Now, there are neighbors and there are *neighbors*. And these were of he latter variety: three wild donkeys who'd come to visit. And what a visit! They were just yards away from me, drinking from our garden-side pool. As I watched, horrified, they proceeded to feed on all my downstairs neighbor Ricky's favorite potted plants. With a single bite, whole branches were defoliated. Their foul stench ebbed and flowed with every movement they made. I shouted and I screamed, my work long forgotten, but no amount of noise seemed to bother these hungry beasts. (Where were the neighborhood dogs when you needed them?)

Disgusted, I gave up trying to scare them away. The donkeys had won. By the time I'd reorganized my paperwork and retreated inside, the donkeys were gone, the garden devastation complete. Their stench, however, remained for hours.

Of course, since I got smarter and procured a 175-XXX double-barreled squirt gun for Christmas—one that can shoot water over fifty feet—the donkeys don't seem to like to come around much any more. Like this morning's visiting donkey across the road, they seem to keep their distance. Perhaps they've heard about Karin and Bob's donkey defense system through the island grapevine. If they ever do show up again at our new home, I'm well prepared. And in a ghoulish sort of way, I'm looking forward to it.

Walking past my car with the goat skull on its grate, I wonder what the next year will bring. Surely Bob and I will learn to be more in harmony with the seasons on St. John. We now have close friends scattered throughout the island, to visit and share adventures with. Maybe we'll finish bringing the Brown Bay Trail up to VINP specs and hike it for pure enjoyment, without any tools in hand. Or maybe we'll find some other place to make special.

To date we've only driven a small portion of the back roads on St. John; there are so many ruins and hiking trails still to explore. Bob and I have only been to thirty of the purported thirty-nine beaches on this island Paradise, and there are still dozens of Cays nearby that we haven't kayaked as yet.

Maybe our old neighborhood group will get it together and have its own float in next year's Carnival parade. We've been toying with the idea of a float dedicated to the snowbirds that visit each year, with a fake ski slope and a live snowman. There would be lots of soap-flake snow and Styrofoam snowballs we could throw at the crowd. Of course, this would all require planning and commitment and effort. Or maybe we'll just talk about it and convince someone else to do all the work— as a fundraiser, sure, and for some good cause. Then we can all get together on the sidelines, sit back under our umbrellas, enjoy the Carnival parade, and cheer them on. I mean, really cheer.

This afternoon, as I'm finishing up the book, the sun is shining bright and the trade winds are steady. Still, from my viewpoint overlooking Rendezvous Bay, the water looks smooth as glass. Bob and I are putting aside our weekend chores this afternoon and sneaking away to a little cove we know for some fun. The snow-floats are already loaded into the car. With the warm sun washing away our worries and the quiet waters slowly washing us along, we'll smile as tourists take our pictures from far-away overlooks, and if we get really energetic, Bob and I might even turn toward each other and, as we so often do, whisper spontaneously and in unison, "We LIVE here, now!"

Ah, Paradise!

A Special Note from the Author

The taxi drivers, shopkeepers, street vendors, government workers, National Park Service employees and in fact—all residents of the USVI—work hard to make sure our islands are a memorable Paradise for all our visitors.

Their caring and consistent desire to make visitors welcome is a big part of what makes this a Paradise. Pristine beaches and perfect weather are only the beginning.

I thank them for their continued efforts, and count myself blessed to be part of this fine community!

Island Car

*(Written and recorded by Michael Beason,
aka the 'ice cream dealer', and presented here
by his kind permission)*

Saw an ad in the paper, it said "Island Car,

Only eight hundred dollars, runs good so far"

So I went to see what kind of car they had,

And for eight hundred dollars it was not too bad

It was once a jeep but it's now half wood,

And the brakes are broken but the horn works good

The lights all work unless it rains,

And the windshield wipers do the same

(chorus)

It's an island car, it's an island car

In the USA it wouldn't get you far

But sweet St. John is only nine miles long

It's an island car, you can't go wrong

The bottom's rusted out and the spare tire's missin'

When it overheats you hear it hissin'

The seats fall over but the seat belts work,

And the clutch is so bad it'll never jerk

You can't fall in love nor even in lust

Because before too long it'll just be rust

An island car really sets you free

Cause in your heart you know it's temporary.

(chorus)

It's an island car, it's an island car

It won't go real fast, it won't get you far

But nothing here's far from anywhere

It's an island car, it'll get you there

It's got no fourth gear, you don't need it here

And the sticker's good 'til sometime next year

Uphill it's slow, but there's the radio

Downhill you can pass if they go too slow

It's painted purple so it looks real sharp

I made myself a top with a FEMA tarp

The hood is loose and it's got no trunk

And it can drive itself if you get too drunk

(chorus)

It's an island car, it's an island car.

In the USA, It wouldn't get you far,

But the motor runs, and the wheels ain't square

It's an island car, it'll get you there

Afterword

The FORK IN THE RD." remains a St. Johnian
landmark, but the piece of plywood that gave
the road it's name, has been replaced many
times. The intersection now boasts an an exact
replica of the original plywood fork, but this one
is made of concrete. Steve, the sign's architect
and a resident of the FORK IN THE RD., has
kept this icon alive.

Thank you, Steve, for making sure that this
island icon endures for a long time to come.